The future 100

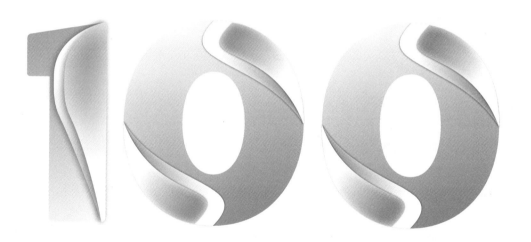

改變未來的100件事
2022年全球百大趨勢

WUNDERMAN THOMPSON

書　　名 / 改變未來的100件事-2022年全球百大趨勢
作　　者 / Wunderman Thompson Intelligence
總 編 輯 / Emma Chiu
編　　輯 / Emily Safian-Demers
撰 稿 人 / Marie Stafford, Elizabeth Cherian, Sarah Tilley, Carla Calandra, Jamie Shackleton, Safa Arshadullah
副 編 輯 / Hester Lacey, Katie Myers

設計總監 / Shazia Chaudhry

協作編輯 / 張玫 Jill Chang, 李慈琳 Ophelia Lee, 簡邑儒 Jessica Chien, 解善筑 Dora Hsieh, 蔡昆莛 Easy Tsai, 黃昱嘉 Chia Huang, 劉苡芊 Bona Liu, 陳嘉安 Ann Chen, 高邦旂 Cloud Kao, 黃靖凱 Kevin Huang, 羅雅菊 Joyce Lo, 劉昀欣 Vik Liu, 蕭曖 Ai Hsiao, 徐慧真 Pin Hsu

中文版團隊 / 香港商台灣偉門智威有限公司台灣分公司
翻譯 / 林庭如 Rye Lin

出版者 / 香港商台灣偉門智威有限公司台灣分公司
地址 / 台北市南港區市民大道7段8號13F之五
電話 / (02)3766-1000
傳真 / (02)2788-0260

總經銷 / 時報文化出版企業股份有限公司
電話 / (02)2306-6842
地址 / 桃園市龜山區萬壽路2段351號

書籍編碼 / Z000150
出版日期 / 2022年4月
定價 / NTD 500

ISBN / 9789869899222

WUNDERMAN
THOMPSON
A REPORT BY WUNDERMAN THOMPSON INTELLIGENCE

序言

和我們一起踏上旅程，了解未來一年的趨勢吧！本書涵蓋了元宇宙和地球再生的種種日常，並加入大量的健康管理資訊，最重要的是，這些趨勢都指向了一片燦爛的未來。現在就和我們一起探索《改變未來的 100 件事：2022 年全球百大趨勢》吧。

隨著這波全球疫情邁入第三年，世界衛生組織的秘書長譚德賽博士（Dr Tedros Adhanom Ghebreyesu）相信，只要所有人一同努力，新冠肺炎（Covid-19）疫情就能在 2022 年劃下終點。

2022 年迎來的是一股堅定的正向氛圍，鼓勵玩樂與創意，Pantone 甚至為此打造了一款全新色彩（詳見第 4 章〈無限樂觀〉）。品牌與行銷人員積極為大眾生活提供歡樂，他們設計出振奮人心的廣告（第 36 章）以搭上這波樂觀思潮。

身心健康在各行各業依然都扮演要角，從大幅增強免疫力的飲品（詳見第 42 章〈喝出免疫力〉），到世界各地專為需要充電的人所設計、讓人釋放情緒的空間（詳見第 90 章〈情緒健康〉）...... 過去兩年的身心健康債開啟了一波全面、敏感、縝密的身心健康照護潮流。

由於生活習慣和商業模式都朝向氣候友善的方向發展，因此僅僅做到永續並不足夠。品牌、政府、社群開始為了地球再生以及人類的未來共同努力，畢竟有高達 88% 的全球消費者相信企業和品牌有責任要照顧這顆星球與地球居民。

最後，隨著元宇宙從科幻故事躍入現實世界，新的數位時代也即將浮現。虛擬世界成為新的群聚空間，不管聚會、創作、買賣、社交、生活、工作都可以在上面進行（詳見第 34 章〈品牌的虛擬世界〉）。

舉凡升級版虛擬化身（第 15 章）、虛擬任意門（第 18 章）以及 NFT 市集（第 69 章），它們背後運用到的技術正大幅改變虛擬互動的方式。數位資產及數位所有權的崛起帶動了新的數位交付零售模式（第 61 章），元宇宙也改變了實體世界的運作規則，臨界空間（第 6 章）開始出現，擴增實境也成為廣告業者選用的媒介（詳見第 40 章〈擴增實境廣告〉）。

快翻開《改變未來的 100 件事：2022 年全球百大趨勢》，和我們一起發掘新的一年值得關注的百大趨勢吧。

Emma Chiu
偉門智威智庫全球總監
wundermanthompson.com/expertise/intelligence

序言

後疫情、元宇宙、通膨、俄烏戰爭、成就了很難預測的一年。「難預測」儼然已經成為我們的日常。

當大家已經慢慢學習與疫情共處、大家對於元宇宙的未來充滿期待，但伴隨而來卻是“通膨”帶來了經濟課題、俄烏戰爭帶來的全球危機，我們所面對的是一個有期待卻又充滿恐慌的未來。是否真有時空穿梭機可以帶我們到未來看看現在，讓我們更有信心可以大步向前？答案當然是沒有。

馬克吐溫曾說：「歷史不會重演，但會押韻。」“History does not repeat itself, but it rhymes.” 這正是我們出版「Future 100 改變未來的 100 件事」的目的所在。偉門智威透過全球的研究團隊整理出 100 件來自全世界正在發生的事，以作為未來趨勢的參考。

在這一次的趨勢報告中，我們看到因為疫情而大大改變了我們的生活與工作方式，也帶來許多反思。經過近兩年的社交隔離和人際疏離，人們對親密關係的有了的全新期待。隨著極限冒險與傳統旅遊變得難以實現，輕旅行、在地旅遊就成了相當火熱的替代方案。甚至數位科技成就了虛擬旅遊任意門，讓人們在舒適的家裡也能來場身歷其境的旅遊體驗。

因為疫情所帶來的恐慌，獲得快樂變成是一種奢侈！於是有了快樂處方箋。情緒充電站也開始出現在世界各地的公共空間中。隨著世界各地漸漸開放遠距工作，造就了數位遊牧民族。因應這種全新的工作方式。新的經濟型態正在崛起。

面對元宇宙的全新世界即將來臨，人們期待元宇宙有機會創造出一個兼容並蓄、合乎道德，且所有人都能理解的世界，元宇宙辦公模式，元美妝也因應而生。電競業者在遊戲中展示虛擬妝效與實體美妝產品，提高玩家的參與度。

因為在數位世界中，「人們不再是被動的消費者，而是更主動用虛擬身份去表達自我。」從 B2B、DTC 到 DTA（direct-to-avatar，DTA）—最新的商業模式是將數位商品直接發送至消費者的數位裝置上。數位世界裡更興起「無人帶頭品牌」（headless brand）的全新概念。

然而環保課題從未停歇，全球開始朝向淨零排放邁進，除碳科技的新風潮隨之而起。除了有碳中和網站，「少即是多」的概念開始出現在社交網路當中，實體世界也開始了微劑量保養守則。

「藍區」（Blue Zone）飲食概念的興起，還有純素飲食也以正式進到上流社會。繼人造肉和人造海鮮之後，咖啡將會是是下一個在實驗室中的產物。烈酒公司透過環保永續的新熟成方式，加速熟成以避免浪費。

環保倡議的，除了「農場到餐桌」（farm-to-table），甚至有了「農場到衣櫥」（farm-to-closet）的全新概念。企業持續正視 ESG 課題，於是有個高人氣的新職位，那就是影響長（Chief Impact Officer，CIO），其任務就是彰顯品牌的社會影響力。

在這波環保浪潮中，甚至廣告業也遭撻伐。所謂「Badvertising」的行動，便是將廣告業視為「污染大腦」的元兇。此外，我們也關注到數位貨幣將可能成為合法的日常支付選項之一。

世代更迭，全新世代崛起，比 Z 世代更年輕的 Alpha 世代（出生於 2010 至 2025 年的世代） 正帶起全新一波零售風潮。而對話式商務（Chat commerce）這種私人網域商務正廣泛出現在通訊平台上。品牌也開始嘗試在非同質化代幣（NFT）領域尋求新的獲利方式。

有趣的是，科技新創公司計畫以美甲機器人顛覆美甲生態，因為美甲機器人「不會出錯，不會變慢，更不會聊些有的沒的。」更有專家認為，未來十年內飛船將會引發飛航革命。

這是來自全世界 100 件正在發生的事，你看到了嗎？

鄧博文
台灣偉門智威 執行長

01

文化

10

11

科技 & 創新

20

21

旅遊 & 觀光

30

31

品牌 & 行銷

40

41

食品 & 飲品

50

美容

零售 & 商業

奢華

220

健康

工作

文化
10

01

元宇宙競賽

各品牌搶進元宇宙，品牌之爭正式拉開序幕。

2021 下半年，元宇宙一詞搶佔報紙頭條、各大螢幕及各大公司董事會，現在品牌與企業也開始加速規劃，為即將到來的數位之爭。

科技巨頭開始聚焦元宇宙的發展。臉書（Facebook）在 2021 年 10 月更名為 Meta，同時公布了品牌重要發展方針；馬克・祖克柏（Mark Zuckerberg）先前也已大張旗鼓地宣告，將轉型為元宇宙企業，形塑該品牌的未來發展。微軟總裁薩蒂亞·納德拉（Satya Nadella）在 8 月時表示，微軟正在打造「企業元宇宙」。

2021 年間，遊戲公司亦開始正視為平台上打造元宇宙的必要性。Epic Games 在 4 月時獲得 10 億美元的融資，該筆資金將用來支持「元宇宙的長期願景」。寶可夢遊戲的開發者 Niantic 在 11 月募集了 3 億美元，意圖打造「真實世界的元宇宙」。輝達（Nvidia）計畫要創立「工程師的元宇宙」，旗下 Omniverse 平台於 8 月公開；據其表示，該平台在 12 月會推出 beta 測試版，結合「工程師、設計師甚至自動化機台，一起打造數位孿生工廠與工業元宇宙。」

就連和元宇宙誕生無直接相關的產業（例如法律、財富管理業），於 2021 年都開始期待元宇宙帶來的成長。2021 年 3 月，Metaverse Group 宣布會發表全球首款虛擬資產專用的房地產

投資信託 Metaverse REIT。法律事務所 Reed Smith 認為元宇宙是「史上最大的工業革命」，因此於 2021 年 5 月發布了元宇宙法務指南，議題涵蓋智慧財產權、隱私、競爭等，囊括各層面的法律議題。同年 6 月，投資公司 Roundhill Investments 和資深投資顧問 Mattew Ball 共同發表了名為 Roundhill Ball Metaverse 的基金，裡面精選了輝達、騰訊、Roblox 等公司的股票。

値得關注的原因：

元宇宙的創立、定義和所有權，都已變得炙手可熱。數位藝術家 Krista Kim（同時也是全球首間 NFT 企業 Mars House 的創辦人）對偉門智威智庫表示：「以前 60 年代有太空競賽，現在 2021 年變成元宇宙競賽。大家都在爭相創立新的元宇宙。」

Left: Horizon Worlds. Image courtesy of Meta
Right: Nvidia Omniverse for AEC, showing Leeza Soho by Zaha Hadid Architects

02

城市新森活

迷你森林在都市中如雨後春筍般出現，
為居民提供新型公共空間。

Heritage Forest. Image courtesy of Sugi

城市中的生物多樣性日漸受到關注，全球各地的社群都開始在公共空間種起原生植被，希望集結大眾之力保護地球，重新野化都市，也為居民提供新的互動場所。

2021 年 10 月，微型森林在洛杉磯的都會公園冒出，這是洛杉磯公園基金會（Los Angeles Parks Foundation）發起的森林公園提案之一。提議挑選蒂普阿納和藍花楹等大型樹種，來為都市社區提供遮蔭，栽種地點包括以下公園與遊樂區：Lemon Grove Park、Mar Vista Recreation Center、Robert Burns Park、Ross Snyder Recreation Area。

英國一座面積 240 平方公尺的森林「遺跡」，經過重新移植後，現坐落於倫敦雀兒喜（Chelsea）社區，希望為當地恢復生態多樣性，並重新搭建當地居民與自然的連結。在重新野化公司 Sugi、時尚品牌路易威登（Louis Vuitton）、資產管理公司 Cadogan 的共同努力之下，該計劃共栽種了 630 種原生樹木與灌木。Sugi 的創辦人 Elise Van Middelem 對《Time Out》表示：「這片森林會成為當地居民的綠地，為他們提供片刻的靜謐，讓他們能在繁華又緊湊的都市生活中享受自然。」

同樣在倫敦，伊斯靈頓議會（Islington council）宣布要在 2021 年 10 月前，為每個住宅區指派樹木專家，為當地另一綠地計劃 Islington Together 補足缺口。此計畫涵蓋了園藝農場和公園。

2021 年 1 月，另一微型森林倡議 Nelson Whakatu Microforest Initiative 的成員，在紐西蘭 Enner Glynn 山坡地找到了一塊 100 平方英尺的土地，並計劃在此打造微型森林。這項社區倡議希望讓動植物重新回到都市，藉此對抗氣候變遷。

> 城市正為微型森林騰出空間，
> 重建都市居民與自然
> 和野生生物之間的連結。

印度公司 Afforestt 利用 Miyawaki 生態造林法，在停車場和後院打造了密集的微型公園，做法包含將原生樹種緊密地栽種在一塊，這樣植物生長的速度就可以比平常快上 10 倍。

值得關注的原因：

城市正為微型森林騰出空間，透過培育綠色走廊，重建都市居民與自然和野生生物之間的連結。

SUGi Heritage Forest

03

天韓地動

韓國文化在全球的影響力與日俱增，並擴大至各個層面，
從電影、時尚到食品、追星，一應俱全。

2021 年 10 月，Billboard 告示牌公告熱門歌曲排行榜，以歌曲在推特（Twitter）上的討論熱度加以排名；新歌排行的前 20 大歌曲中，居然有高達 14 首歌來自韓國娛樂圈，演唱者包含男團 BTS、他們的勁敵 Enhypen、Blackpink 饒舌歌手 Lisa 等。韓流偶像培養出一眾忠誠粉絲，相關粉絲文化也成為全球社群媒體上的重要文化驅力（詳見《改變未來的 100 件事：2021 年全球百大趨勢》〈狂粉總動員〉）。韓流（Hallyu）以旋風之姿席捲全球。

韓星隨之晉升 A 咖名單，贏得許多品牌青睞。Exo 成員 Kai 和 Gucci 合作；Blackpink 的成員也連續拿下許多品牌合作機會，合作對象包含 Chanel、Celine、Dior、Tiffany 等；Burberry 和女團 Itzy 簽約；Blackpink 的主唱 Rosé 和饒舌歌手 CL 也在 2021 年間，成為獲邀出席紐約大都會藝術博物館慈善晚宴（Met Gala）的首組韓國女藝人。

韓國文化大量輸出，韓流只是其中一環，還有許多其他的文化內容在全球各地發光發熱。韓國飲食和美妝品牌的熱門程度登上高峰，據南韓政府的官方統計，韓國美妝品在 2020 年的產值超過 60 億美元。連英文字典都出現了韓流現象，牛津英語詞典

（Oxford English Dictionary）為 2022 年新增了 20 個以上的韓國詞彙，包含韓國烤肉（bulgogi）、吃播（mukbang）等等。

最讓人訝異的應該是韓國娛樂產業（或說韓國影視作品）猛然竄起，從 2020 年獲得奧斯卡的《寄生上流》，到 Netflix 紅遍全球的《魷魚遊戲》和《地獄公使》，都是最佳例證。《地獄公使》於 2021 年 11 月開播後，在短短 24 小時內就登上全球 80 個國家的收視冠軍，成為 Netflix 上最受歡迎的原創影集，甚至贏過《魷魚遊戲》。《魷魚遊戲》的女主角鄭浩妍（Jung Ho-yeon）被路易威登（Louis Vuitton）相中，和韓流巨星男團 BTS 並列全球品牌常任大使。Netflix 對韓流極具信心，在 2021 年投資了 5 億美元製播韓劇，其中包含 12 月推出的《不可殺：永生之靈》。

韓國的新秀看似異軍突起，但在近期《BBC》文化系列報導中，就揭露了韓流的成功其實是韓國政府長期投入資金培育的成果，他們希望培植該國的「軟實力」。韓國文化的竄起，現在也有展覽加以呈現，從 2022 年 9 月至 2023 年 6 月，倫敦的 V&A 博物館（Victoria and Albert Museum）舉辦了韓國文化影響力特展《韓流！》，這是首檔展現韓國流行文化的特展，韓國文化體育觀光部亦有贊助。

值得關注的原因：

韓國流行文化的廣泛流傳與創新，使它們躍上世界舞台，讓韓國成為音樂、時尚、娛樂等不同文化的輸出大國。品牌可以多加利用韓流風潮，從有跨國影響力的韓流巨星身上尋求商機。

Top: Noh Juhan, creator of Netflix's Squid Game, with cast and crew
Bottom: Blackpink. Image courtesy of Spotify

Left: Korean musical artist Psy on Today 2012, New York. Courtesy of Jason Decrow, Invision, AP, Shutterstock Right: Tchai Kim Young-Jin Hanbok Collection, 2015, modeled by Bae Yoon Young. Courtesy of YG Kplus

04

解 FUN 2022

各品牌對2022年的展望都很樂觀正向，鼓勵玩樂與創意。

Pantone 為 2022 年特製了全新的「長春花藍」（Very Peri）做為其年度色，該色受到創造力啟發，也希望鼓舞更多的創意人才。長春花藍的代碼為 AKA17-3938，是「一種充滿活力的紫藍色，並帶有活潑的紫紅色基調。」該品牌表示，他們希望「展現朝氣、愉悅、活力，藉此鼓勵大膽創作、盡情發揮」。

英籍奈及利亞裔藝術家兼設計師 Yinka Ilori 和樂高公司（Lego）共同打造一座彩色裝置，慶祝玩樂與社群生活。這座名為《夢境自助洗衣店》（Launderette of Dreams）的互動裝置位於東倫敦，希望鼓勵孩童創作、玩耍、分享點子。

奧多比圖庫（Adobe Stock）的 2022 年創意趨勢（Creative Trends）涵蓋了「用力玩耍」這樣的主題。奧多比的消費者與創意總監 Brenda Milis 對偉門智威智庫提到：「玩樂是我們的原始需

2022年要傳遞的是象徵成長和自由的創意玩樂。

求。一年前，大家一直聽到『恢復力』這個詞，但疫情持續這麼久，一切都不確定，要怎麼持續保有恢復力？」

對於來年，Milis 表示「品牌開始以玩樂和樂觀的態度出發，因為消費者很願意為此買單，從這個角度切入的話潛能無限，一切都會環繞著崇敬、美好、啟發、創意等等感受。以玩樂為主軸是因為消費者長期以來已經筋疲力竭，需要喘一口氣，也需要一些娛樂。」

得利塗料（Dulux）宣布 2022 的年度色彩為「明亮天空」（Bright Skies），這款充滿空氣感、煥然一新的顏色「完美詮釋了樂觀和對『新的開始』的想望，很適合此刻的狀態」。

值得關注的原因：

度過難以預料的兩個年頭後，2022 年要傳遞的是象徵成長和自由的創意玩樂，這股活力會成為配色和設計的主軸，廣告和行銷活動當然也會一脈相承。

Powerfully Playful image by Stocksy. Adobe Stock

Yinka Ilori and Lego's "Launderette of Dreams."

05

虛擬 真 網紅

新型態的網紅正在崛起。

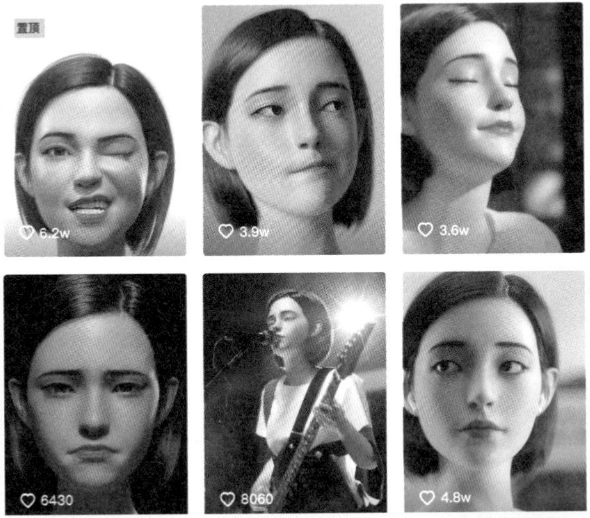

Douyin's virtual influencer Angie, created by Jesse Zhang

來認識一下生活型網紅（geniunfluencer）吧！這是潮流預測公司 WGSN 創造的新術語，這些網紅不為粉絲帶來靈感或啟發，而是透過讓人有共鳴的生活方式來獲得追蹤。

由Jesse Zhang創造的抖音虛擬網紅阿喜（Angie），以「不完美」的形象在中國樹立了新的美妝標準。其他的虛擬網紅皮膚透亮無暇，五官完美對稱，但阿喜的皮膚有時會乾燥或泛紅，會長痘痘，會有痘疤，她的眼摺和牙齒也沒有非常整齊對稱。她沒有穿著名牌服飾來擺拍，而是穿著簡單的白色 T 恤和運動短褲。「我喜歡

Douyin's virtual influencer Angie, created by Jesse Zhang

阿喜，因為她比很多真人還更真實」，千禧世代的小琪（來自中國西南部城市重慶）對《CNN》如此表示。截至 2021 年 12 月，阿喜已經累積了 30 萬名粉絲，小琪是其中之一。

Yoox 是 Yoox Net-a-Porter Group 集團旗下的線上奢侈品賣場，他們於 2018 年首次展示虛擬網紅 Daisy，其經營策略也正在轉變。Yoox 品牌和傳播總監 Manuela Strippoli 告訴《Vogue》，2021 年 Yoox 的首要任務是提升 Daisy 的親和力。「我們讓她和最初設定的形象漸行漸遠。以前她無時無刻都完美無瑕，現在我們讓她開始展現好惡和缺點，讓她更加人性化。」這也包括讓她能夠發聲，能夠參與更多社會議題。「不管是時尚還是社會議題，她都有自己的觀點，而且重要的是，她不會只保持中立。」Strippol 補充說明。

Z 世代對品牌的態度可能是這種造成轉變的重要因素，因為多數人更喜歡會讓他們產生共鳴、和他們共享價值觀的品牌。偉門智威數據 2020 年 10 月的調查結果顯示，美國 73% 的 Z 世代支持能夠理解他們想法的品牌，76% 則追求可以接受各種身份和人生經驗的品牌。

值得關注的原因：

影響力正在產生改變。《衛報》（The Guardian）在 2021 年 8 月報導，「現在太過有抱負會讓人討厭。」這種觀念也開始滲透到虛擬世界，品牌現在有機會從他們的核心價值觀和親和力出發，重新塑造旗下的虛擬網紅。

06

臨界空間

虛擬空間和實體場地開始整合，新的活動場所因之而生。

WUNDERMAN THOMPSON

Holiday Space augmented reality artwork by Kaws, 2020
Image courtesy Kaws and Acute Art

隨著全數位的虛擬空間興起，延展實境開始融入實體空間，將活動互動與體驗不再受任何限制。

獨立主機 Surreal 於 2021 年 3 月發布混合式活動平台，在實體空間中提供虛擬體驗。該平台採用 Epic Games 的虛幻引擎（Unreal Engine）來建構，可實現無限多種可能。作為實體環境的「數位孿生」平台，Surreal 整合臨界互動模式，為主持人和觀眾提供全新體驗，同時也與 DNABlock 合作，為平台加入超現實的 3D 人物角色。

在紐約市，High Line Art 和位於西區的文化機構 The Shed 合作，打造了《The Looking Glass》這件作品，這是一個以虛擬雕塑為基礎的擴增實境裝置，於 2021 年 7 至 8 月間在 High Line 公園展出。參觀者可以使用應用程式 Acute Art 來觀看隱藏的互動藝術作品。

TeamLab 在東京舉辦的展覽《Borderless》讓當地民眾和國際

觀光客都趨之若鶩，該展於 2021 年 7 月創下金氏世界紀錄，成為展出單一藝術家作品的博物館中，坐擁全球最高參觀人次的展覽。據《華爾街日報》報導，《Borderless》也在舊金山展出，並以音樂和鏡牆為特色，讓人聯想到萬花筒，「相對於藝術活動而言，這個展覽其實更偏向娛樂活動」。

數位平台《Dezeen》在 2021 年 4 月開設虛擬社交俱樂部，專為希望融入現實的社交名流而打造，讓創作者可以在虛擬的屋頂酒吧碰面，進行以元宇宙和設計為主題的座談。

皇家莎士比亞劇團（The Royal Shakespeare Company）使用虛幻引擎來演出《Dream》一劇，這是一場互動型的表演，由現場演員帶領觀眾一起演出，讓觀眾獲得近乎遊戲般的體驗。

值得關注的原因：

臨界空間融合了虛擬和實體體驗，讓品牌有機會重塑現場體驗和實體空間的未來樣貌。

Left: Surreal conference. Image courtesy of Meta
Right: Dream by the Royal Shakespeare Company

07

無性別運動服

女性運動員開始根除過時的聯盟規則，挑戰體壇常規。

2021 年間，眾多女性運動員站出來反對一直以來的性別歧視，拒絕再穿著過往那般暴露的服裝出賽。

英國撐竿跳選手 Holly Bradshaw 對她參加 2020 東京奧運的選手服（短版上衣加比基尼泳褲）十分失望，她希望可以改穿修改過的愛迪達划船用連身服參賽。德國體操選手 Sarah Voss 也在歐洲體操錦標賽中，以長袖連身衣取代綁帶的緊身體操選手服。她的兩位德國隊友 Kim Bui 和 Elisabeth Seitz 也隨後跟進，穿上長袖連身衣出賽，共同對抗體操界的性別歧視。

許多女性運動員會受到粉絲、賽評、甚至教練的物化。那些帶有歧視意味的著裝規定，要求女性穿上毫無必要的暴露服裝，現在，這類規定在全球引發眾怒。2021 年 7 月，美國創作歌手 Pink 在推特上推文表示，她願意為挪威女子手球隊支付「服裝不合規定」的罰款，該球隊未穿上比基尼泳褲，改穿和男性球員一樣的短褲上陣，卻因此遭罰 1,500 歐元。隨後在同年 11 月，國際手球總會從善如流，更改了女性球員的服裝規範。

值得關注的原因：

性別差異仍在體育競賽中壁壘分明，但女性選手開始起身對抗不平等。品牌可以挺身支持這些女性運動員，與她們共同對抗差別待遇，抓緊機會重新定義文化常規，這麼一來，女性參與體育活動的比例也會提升。

08

社群化娛樂圈

完全根據個人檔案發展的情節，在平台中超展開的劇情，和關注者聊天的虛構人物......這會是翻轉娛樂產業的重要關鍵嗎？

據《Fast Company》報導，FourFront 正「透過 TikTok 來徹底改變電視文化」。FourFront 於 2021 年 10 月獲得了 150 萬美元的種子資金，是一間新型態的內容工作室。它在社交媒體上貼出敘事型的貼文，內容和一般的帳號類似，其中的虛擬人物有自己的故事、社群媒體版面，也積極地和關注者互動。據報導，截至 2021 年 10 月，FourFront 的虛擬角色群，在 TikTok 上獲得的關注總數高達 190 萬人，並獲得 2.81 億次的總觀看數。「我們要模糊現實和故事之間的界限」，FourFront 共同創辦人兼執行長 Ilan Benjamin 對《Fast Company》如此表示。

這可能會帶起一股以社群媒體為基礎的新型互動娛樂風潮。Benjamin 表示：「我們在 TikTok 上創造的不只是虛擬人物宇宙，還創造了一種新的互動模式。以電影為開端，娛樂圈正在進化，但看電影時，觀眾無法和我們所謂『活生生的情節和活生生的人物』有所互動；相反地，我們創作的人物就存在在我們的世界裡，生活在社群媒體上，而且會及時和觀眾互動。媒體和大眾的第四面牆已經完全被打破了。」

Invisible Universe 是另一家專為社群媒體編寫娛樂腳本的新創公司，執行長 Tricia Biggio 曾出任米高梅（MGM）無腳本節目部門的資深副總，他宣稱 Invisible Universe 是「網路版的皮克斯動畫（Pixar）」。為了創造該公司所謂的「下一個百年動畫事業」，它們與知名度高的名人、網紅和品牌合作，在社群媒體上開發原創動畫角色。Invisible Universe 由 Snap 前高層 John Brennan 於 2021 年 8 月創立，並從 800 萬美元的資本出發，與珍妮佛安妮斯頓（Jennifer Aniston）和小威廉絲（Serena Williams）攜手發布新角色。

值得關注的原因：

說故事的方式正在轉變，現在也多了專為社群平台設計的新興模式。電影院面對的票房難關和電視頻道下降的收視率，讓娛樂產業重新思考觸及和服務觀眾的方式。

Above: FourFront, courtesy of TikTok
Right: Invisible Universe

09

親密關係再進化

經過近兩年的社交隔離和人際疏離，大眾對親密關係的全新期待正在撼動現有約會文化。

根據《Match》的說法，認真看待約會的人越來越多，在其 2021 年 11 月的美國單身人士研究（Singles in America）中，有 62% 的美國單身人士表示他們想尋求認真、忠誠的感情，只有 11% 的人想「隨性約會」。金賽研究所（Kinsey Institute for Research in Sex, Gender, and Reproduction）2021 年 4 月的報告指出，有 44% 的美國人表示，在疫情之後，承諾對他們來說變得更為重要。《Match》的調查結果顯示，連年輕用戶也在尋找忠誠的關係，81% 的 Z 世代希望明年可以找到認真交往的對象。

新的應用程式和平台也希望為大眾媒合更深度的親密關係。Elate 於 2020 年底推出，是一款「防人間蒸發」的應用程式，旨在鼓勵「慢約會」以及建立更強的情感連結。與其讓用戶毫無止盡的左滑右滑，Elate 選擇每天為用戶推薦 10 個人選，而且一次最多只能和三個人聊天。

Raspberry Dream Labs

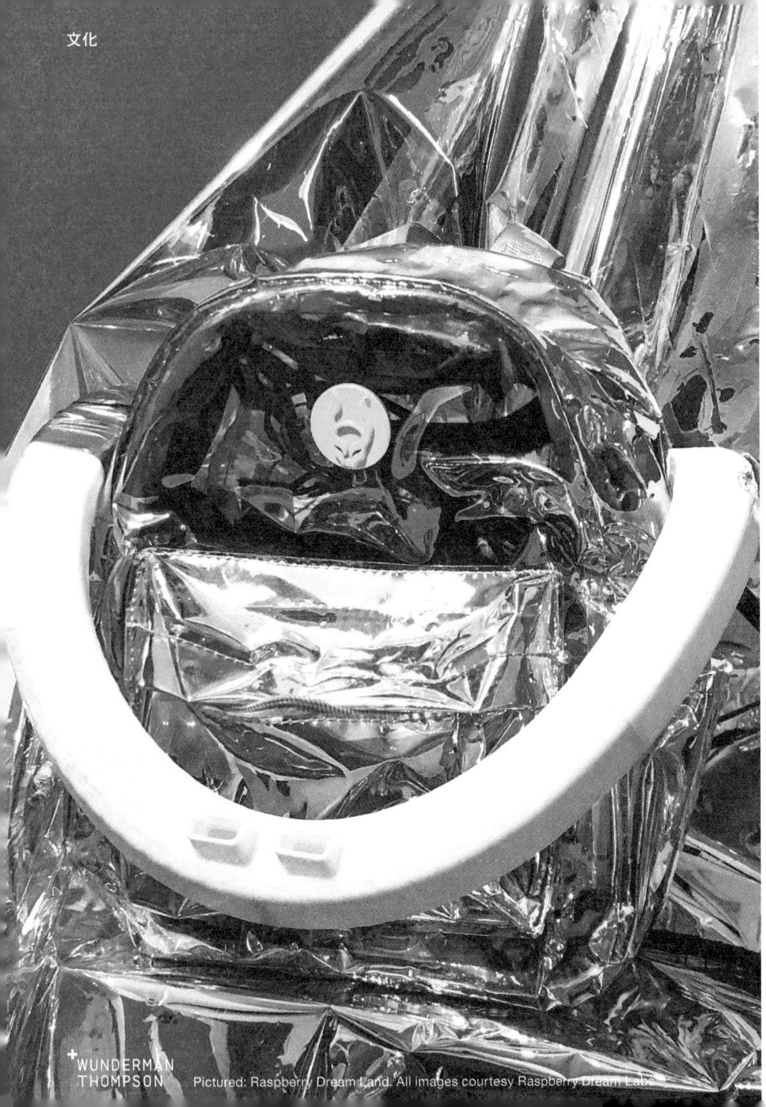

Pictured: Raspberry Dream Land. All images courtesy Raspberry Dream Labs

Raspberry Dream Labs 想打造新的網愛體驗，藉此建立人與人之間的真實連結。第一個企劃 Sensory Seduction 使用延展實境技術（XR），讓用戶得以感受自己身上的觸覺脈衝，模仿被觸摸的感受。這種體驗模式讓用戶能有機會「透過感官刺激來探索性慾，並開發自己的敏感帶。」該公司先前已發布 Raspberry Dream Land 的測試版，那是一個 XR 社交活動平台，為「激進的自我表達、革新的藝術和娛樂、社交互動和虛擬關係」提供虛擬的活動空間。

值得關注的原因：

「我們正在見證約會態度和行為的巨大轉變。」金賽研究所執行董事兼《Match》 科學顧問 Justin Garcia 為《華爾街日報》撰文，並在 2021 年 12 月發布的文章中寫道。「過去一年間，我們尋求和維持親密關係的方式有了轉變⋯⋯現在，單身人士追尋的是成熟的伴侶，也很努力培養長期的親密關係」，他認為這種轉變是「對現代約會文化的重置」。

10

元社會

可以反映實體世界當前的價值觀和標準，甚至實現更高品質的生活……這樣的數位世界正在成形。

元宇宙有機會創造出一個兼容並蓄、合乎道德，且大眾都能理解的世界。「可以想成要創造一個新的網路世界，但從第一天開始，一切就都得做好。」Together Labs 執行長 Daren Tsui 如此告訴偉門智威智庫。這是他對該公司旗下產品 IMVU 的描述，這個基於 3D 數位化身所打造的社群交友平台，旨在促進社會臨場感（social presence）並提供真實的人際連結。

科技的發展為元宇宙指出了樂觀的前程：根據偉門智威數據 2021 年 7 月的調查，全球 88% 的消費者認為科技可以讓世界變得更美好，78% 的人同意科技可以促成一個更平等的社會。該項研究發表於〈進入元宇宙〉（Into the Metaverse）報告中。

IMVU. Image courtesy of Together Labs

Top: Nowhere's Networking at Crane Gallery; exhibit by The Most Famous Artist
Bottom: Microsoft Mesh
Right: Meta's Horizon Worlds

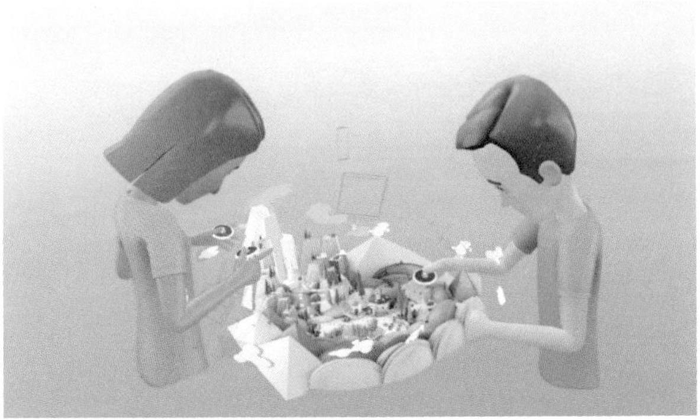

各公司爭相創造能促進連結、增加合作、鼓勵探索的虛擬世界，這樣的競賽正如火如荼地開展。Nowhere 是一個新的社交網路平台，讓用戶可以身處 3D 環境中，活動範圍一路從森林橫跨到空中島嶼上。Nowhere 的執行長 Jon Morris 對該平台的描述是「第一個可以身歷其境的線上活動空間，可以感受到虛擬演出原汁原味的能量，也可以和剛好偶遇的陌生人互動交流。」

Meta 的 Horizon Worlds 希望實現「虛擬實境（VR）社交體驗」，讓探索者可以一起玩樂、創作、建構世界。Microsoft Mesh 使用混合實境（MR）來打造相互連結的世界，讓身處不同地區的用戶可以即時透過全息投影相聚一堂。

值得關注的原因：

元宇宙的發展仍處於起步階段，從頭開始建構虛擬世界和社會的機會之窗，也隨之敞開。

11

科技&創新

20

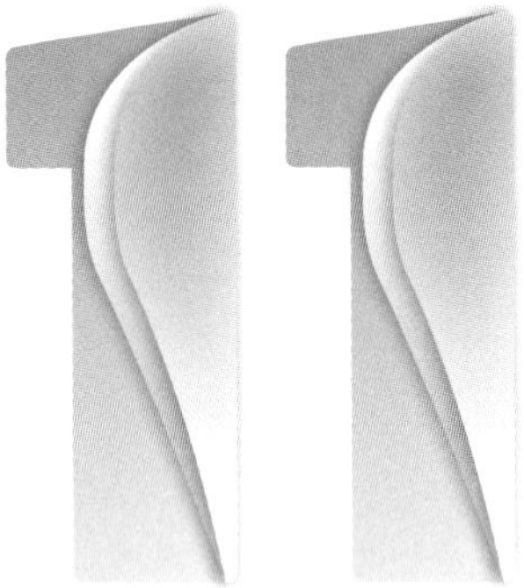

3D 空間音訊

沉浸式聆聽開啟了新一代聽覺體驗。

蘋果（Apple）在旗下產品中加入新的立體空間音訊功能，可以模擬環繞音效帶來的沉浸式、多維度音響體驗。在 2021 年 10 月的 Unleashed 發表會中，蘋果宣布旗下全新的 AirPods 3 耳機和 MacBook Pro 筆腦，將會配備空間音訊功能。該功能由杜比全景聲（Dolby Atmos）提供技術支援，且早在 2021 年 6 月，蘋果就已宣布會將這項技術運用到 Apple Music 當中。「這是 Apple Music 有史以來最有感的音質進化。」，Apple Music 與 Beats 部門副總 Oliver Schusser 如此表示。

索尼（Sony）在 2021 年推出兩款新的家用音響系統，採用 360 度空間音效技術，提供身臨其境的聆聽體驗。

Apple AirPods: third-generation spatial audio

音效公司 Spatial 於 2021 年 3 月推出第一套產品。這家新創公司為公共空間打造了身歷其境的互動聲景，其中包括大廳、零售商店、辦公室，甚至還有醫院。專為不同地點打造的聲景，是希望為聽眾帶來特定的情緒，例如鼓勵他們放鬆、專注，或者達到舒壓效果。Spatial 共同創辦人兼執行長 Calin Pacurariu 告訴《Fast Company》，各企業「開始從根本上重新思考，在虛實整合的環境中，未來的工作會是什麼樣貌，而他們也紛紛將聲音視為一項競爭優勢。」

2021 年 11 月，卡地亞（Cartier）打造的音效特展《The Great Animal Orchestra》在北美首次亮相，從巴黎移師麻州沙倫的

皮博迪埃塞克斯博物館（Peabody Essex Museum），展出讓人身臨其境的音效體驗。該展覽於 2016 年在巴黎首先推出，以聲音地景展示了北美洲、拉丁美洲、肯亞、盧安達、辛巴威等地的生物多樣性。這些聲音由聲景生態學家 Bernie Krause 錄製而成，《Elle》認為此檔展覽是「對聲音的探索，看看我們如何理解聲音，而動物又是如何發聲。」

值得關注的原因：

在過去十年中，Instagram 等社交媒體平台催生了以視覺為導向的社群文化。現在隨著數位平台漸趨成熟，互動方式也有了轉變後，焦點開始轉向多重感官元素，來實現真正的沈浸式體驗，而聽覺在其中也扮演至為重要的一角。

Left: The Spatial experience
Right: The Spatial concept

12

超級 APP 崛起

中國向周遭引頸企盼的國家，傳授
超級應用程式（super apps）的成功方程式。

WUNDERMAN THOMPSON

Top: GrabPay's QR-scan service
Bottom: GrabTaxi

即使中國的超級應用程式受到中國政府反壟斷政策打壓，其「海外後裔」卻不斷壯大。超級應用程式可在單一平台提供多項功能，用戶可以無痛切換，從通訊到電商，再到叫車、支付、金融服務，一應俱全。

印尼的 Gojek 最初是以機車載客服務起家，希望能改善大眾在雅加達的交通體驗；現在，進一步提供各式各樣的外送服務，從食物、藥品到按摩服務應有盡有。2021 年，Gojek 宣布與該國最大的網購平台 Tokopedia 合併，除網購外，該平台也提供金融科技和物流服務。這起併購的金額高達 180 億美元，合併後他們巧妙地將公司命名為 GoTo，並坐擁超過 1 億名活躍用戶、1100 萬個商家、200 萬名司機，獲利佔印尼 1 兆美元經濟規模的 2%。

GoTo 不是東南亞地區唯一的超級應用程式。總部位於新加坡的 Grab 自稱是「全能日常應用程式」，從東南亞的叫車服務開始，迅速加入了快遞、支付與金融服務，並於 2020 年與新加坡電信（SingTel）合作，獲得數位銀行牌照。在特殊目的收購公司（SPAC）的上市案例中，Grab 的交易金額全球最高，2021 年底在納斯達克上市時，募集到 45 億美元的資金。

GoTo 和 Grab 擁有眾多投資者，包括中國科技巨頭阿里巴巴、騰訊、美團和滴滴出行，以及臉書（Facebook）、谷歌（Google）、紅杉（Sequoia）、軟銀（SoftBank）和新加坡政府基金淡馬錫（Temasek）等。

根據 Forrester 的數據顯示，2020 年，東南亞網拍業務的成長速度居全球之冠。當地的線上銷售額增加了 53%，來到 500 億美元，其中，食品雜貨的銷量更引領群雄，漲幅高達 97%。該地區的線上銷售總額預計會以每年兩位數的速度持續成長，到 2025 年將達到 1,430 億美元。

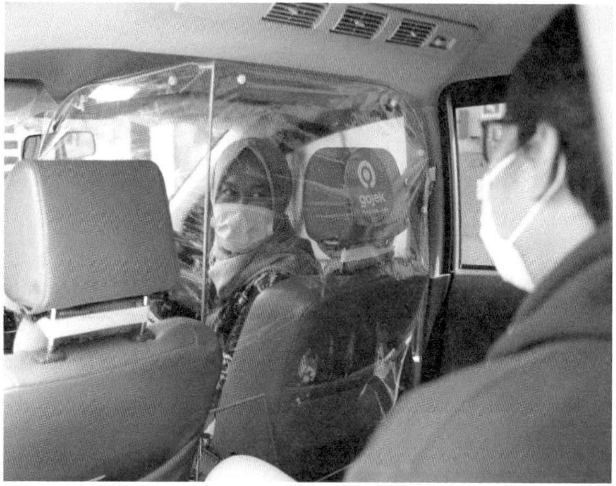

Gojek and Tokopedia's GoTo GoCar

值得關注的原因：

中國科技巨頭很早就開始投資東南亞線上平台，並將許多中國超級應用程式首創的概念輸出到這些地區。隨著中國科技公司在國內面臨越來越多的監管，此刻他們可能會比過去更加關注海外市場能帶來的成長機會。

東南亞國家的許多消費者，確實比其他地區的民眾更熱愛這類整合大量服務的超級應用程式。根據偉門智威 2021 年的《未來購物者調查》（Future Shopper Survey），泰國和印尼每 10 名消費者中，就有 8 位同意以下的觀點：「我希望品牌能透過不同管道來和我無縫接軌地溝通」。

13

碳中和網站

品牌開始改造線上平台，來減少對環境的衝擊。

2021 年 2 月，Cleanfox 在關於電子郵件污染的報告中提到，「如果網路是一個國家，那它會成為世界上第六大的碳排來源國。」該報告還指出，促銷型電子郵件每年在英國造成 200 萬噸的碳排放量。

因此，品牌開始大幅更新官網來回應此議題，希望降低線上活動的碳足跡。

總部位於阿姆斯特丹的設計工作室 Formafantasma 於 2021 年 2 月為工作室網站進行改版，以求提高能源使用效率，他們使用小圖和基本字型，並改以標準 Unicode 字符來創造 logo。簡單的視覺效果可以降低載入頁面的耗能，進而減少碳排量。

福斯汽車（Volkswagen）於 2021 年 2 月重新改造品牌的加拿大官網，以追求更永續的瀏覽方式。這項碳中和改版計畫剔除了網頁內的所有色彩，並替換原本的照片，改以數據傳輸量低的文字符號來設計馬賽克圖案，藉此縮小品牌的數位碳足跡。此計畫顯著地降低了瀏覽網頁所產生的碳排，根據數位碳排計算器 Website Carbon 評估，瀏覽網站時，載入每個網頁平均只會產生 0.022 公克的碳排，而瀏覽其他網站的網頁，每頁的平均碳排量則有 1.76 公克。

值得關注的原因：

去年，我們發現數位生活習慣的成長，讓大眾更加意識到數據永續的重要。從那時起，品牌已對數位平台展開新的規劃，來符合消費者的價值觀。此刻，虛擬世界的永續實踐，在元宇宙出現以後，重要度也將更甚以往。

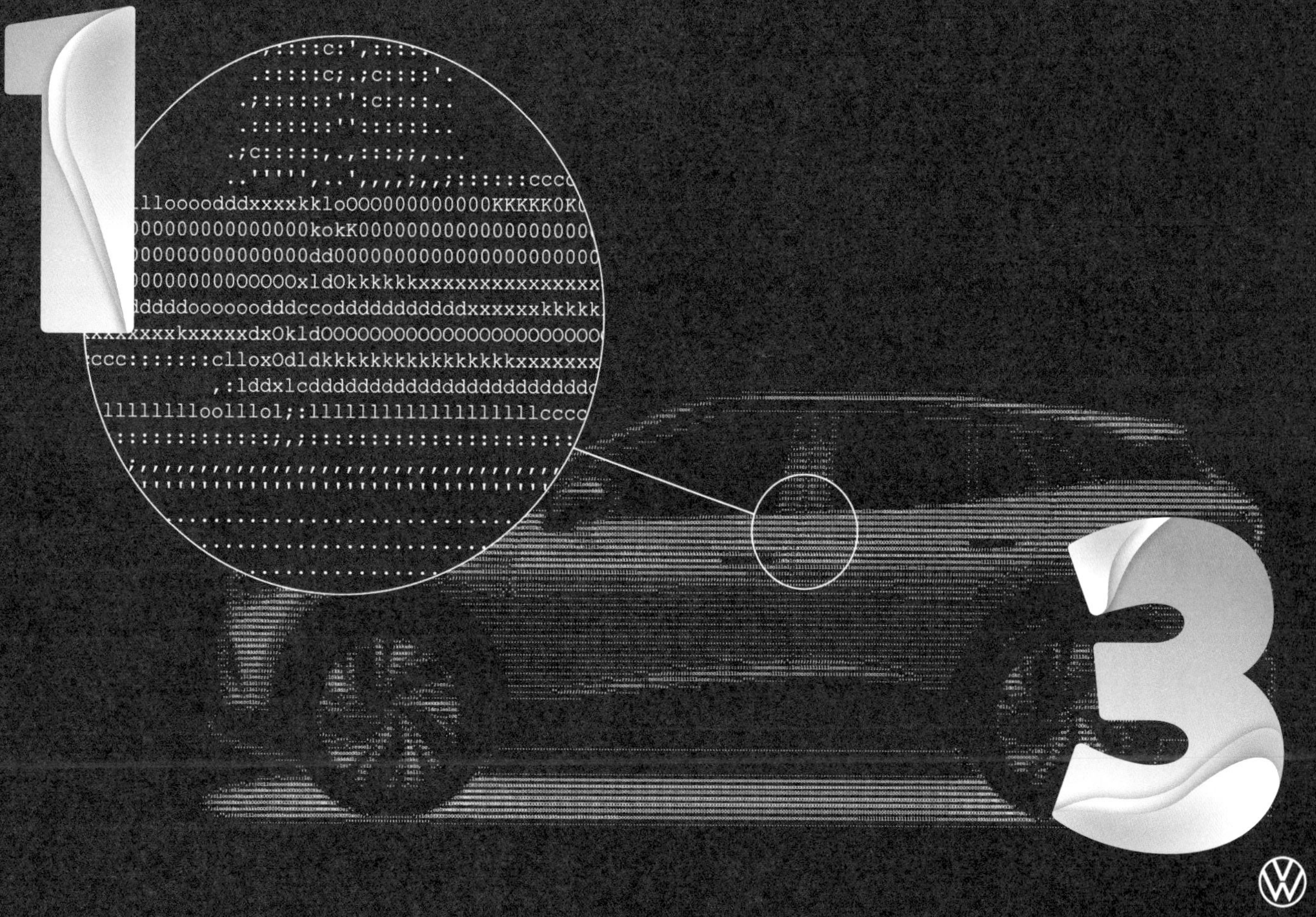

WUNDERMAN THOMPSON

Volkswagen Canada's Carbon-Neutral Net online redesign

14

有限社交網路

「少即是多」的概念開始出現在社交網路當中。

社交媒體的不良名聲其來有自，從讓人成癮、剝奪睡眠時間，到引發焦慮、憂鬱等狀況都是箇中原因。然而在 2021 年，臉書（Facebook）和 Instagram 上的全球每月活躍用戶高達數十億人，Twitter 上的每月活躍用戶超過 3 億，TikTok 9 月份的報告亦顯示，該軟體的每月活躍用戶達到 10 億之多。

許多應用程式希望透過限制用量來降低社群媒體的使用時間，例如 Social Fever、Offtime、Freedom 等等；但如果能夠減少社群媒體上的貼文數量，並以精選過的貼文取而代之呢？Minus 就提供了這樣的服務。該平台由 Ben Grosser 創立，旨在挑戰現有的社群交流模式。Minus 限制用戶終生只能張貼 100 則貼文，並自稱為「有限社交網路」，希望透過數量限制來提升內容的品質。

交友軟體 Thursday 也有類似的運作邏輯，用戶每週只能上線一天。該軟體發布於 2021 年 5 月，目的是要對抗網路約會帶來的焦慮。透過限制用戶每週上線天數（一週一天），藉以增加配對、聊天、約會的機會。而早在正式發布之前，已有逾十萬名單身人士出於好奇而註冊帳號。

值得關注的原因：

各公司開始以限制用量的方式來推動新的行為模式，希望降低干擾、減少永無止盡的線上內容，而這也為未來的社交網路注入一股更健康、更正向的使用風潮。

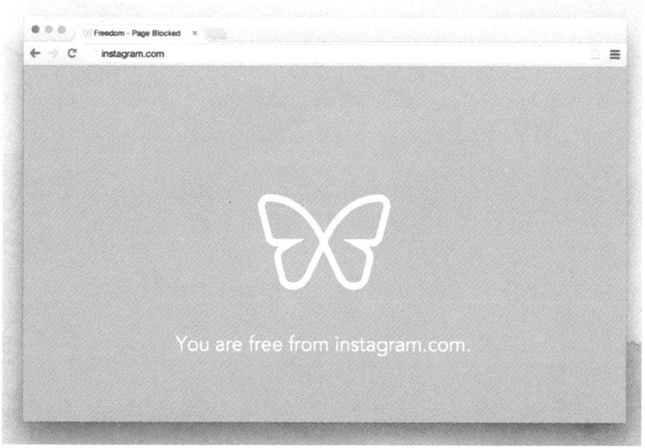

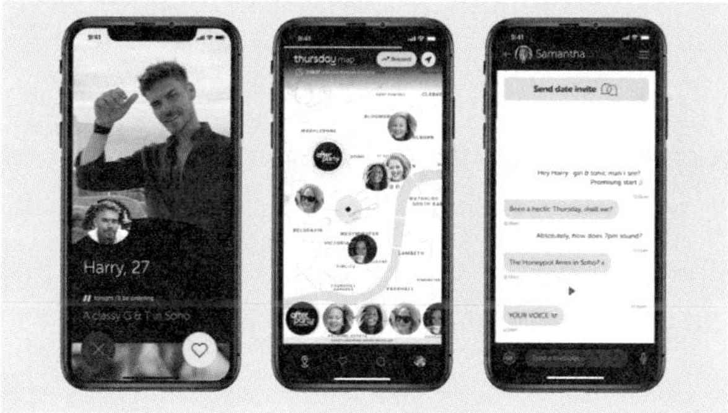

> 各公司開始以
> 限制用量的方式
> 來推動新的行爲模式，
> 希望降低干擾、減少
> 永無止盡的線上內容。

Top: Freedom app blocked site screen
Bottom: Thursday dating app

15

虛擬化再升級

超擬真的數位人形開始從我們的螢幕轉移到真實世界之中，
為下一代的虛擬化身開啟康莊大道。

MetaHuman Creator by Unreal Engine. Image courtesy of Epic Games

輝達（Nvidia）開始提前部署，以便讓具備 AI 會話能力的 3D 虛擬化身能在虛擬和實體世界中並存。在 2021 年 11 月的展示會中，該公司發表 Omniverse Avatar 平台，「智慧虛擬助理的發展已嶄露曙光。」輝達創辦人兼執行長黃仁勳表示。「Omniverse Avatar 結合輝達的基礎繪圖、模擬及 AI 技術，創造出一些史上最複雜的即時應用程式。」

Epic Games 旗下的虛幻引擎（Unreal Engine）相信「數位人類是未來的方向」。2021 年 4 月，虛幻引擎提前開放公測，只要幾分鐘便能以 MetaHuman Creator 即時生成超擬真的虛擬化身。這款雲端應用程式可以複製人類身上的精密細節，從膚色、皺紋、破裂的微血管再到疤痕，全都涵蓋其中。

總部位於加州的新創公司 DNABlock 專門製作虛擬化身，在

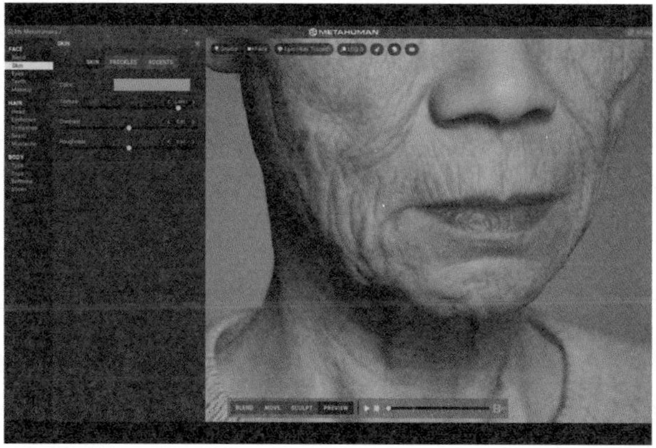

2021 年 9 月，他們募集了 120 萬美元的種子資金，要讓元宇宙更加多元與包容。「元宇宙需要為所有人而設計，」DNABlock 的共同創辦人暨執行長 Anthony Kelani 告訴《Protocol》。「必須能展現全世界的樣貌，在化身的領域尤其如此，要能生成和你或者其他有色人種容貌相似的化身。」

值得關注的原因：

拋開 2009 年阿凡達（Avatar）電影中的角色形象，在 2022 年，新世代的虛擬化身（avatar）看起來不僅非常現實，同時還能反映世界的多元樣貌。

Left: MetaHuman Creator by Unreal Engine. Image courtesy of Epic Games
Right: Omniverse Avatar by Nvidia

16

中國式數位整肅

中國對科技業的打壓正在重塑其社經風貌。

自 2020 年末以來，中國對國內科技大廠之附屬企業進行壟斷行為調查與罰款，阿里巴巴、騰訊、京東、美團、滴滴出行，都在名單之列。阿里巴巴旗下事業螞蟻金服的大型 IPO 案，在最後一刻被迫喊停；2021 年 4 月，阿里巴巴因對平台商家實施強制排他規則而遭罰 28 億美元，罰款金額創下歷史新高。

由於中國是世界上數位化程度最高的國家，因此這樣的制裁規模並不令人意外。中國的科技公司幾乎滲透到民眾生活的各個層面中，也因此收集到大量的用戶數據。

截至 2020 年底，中國使用網路的人口約達七成（9.89 億人），且幾乎都是透過手機上網。中國互聯網信息中心（中国互网信息中心）的數據顯示，有近八成的用戶會使用網購服務，86% 的用戶採用行動支付，94% 用戶會觀看網路影片。

中國政府的監管最初只集中於反壟斷、數據安全、資安問題，但現在也延燒到社會上的其他層面，例如兒童作業過多（所以禁止線上家教）、遊戲玩太久（所以管制未成年人的使用時間）、粉絲行為過於狂熱等。

「我認為中國監管機構試圖解決的問題，顯然不是中國獨有」，新加坡瑞聯銀行（Union Bancaire Privée）董事總經理暨中國網路經濟專家 Vey-Sern Ling 對偉門智威智庫如此表示。「中國更為集權，所以花在討論或協商上的時間會比別人少很多，執法也非常嚴厲。」

美國政府與歐盟同樣試圖限縮大型科技公司的影響力，針對反壟斷議題起訴臉書（Facebook）、亞馬遜（Amazon）、谷歌

（Google）等公司，不過這些措施都需要等待較長時間才能完成法院審理。

値得關注的原因：

對中國消費者以及面向此一客群的品牌來說，這些變化可能意味著更多的選擇機會，因為原先互相競爭的科技業者會被迫彼此合作。例如，使用阿里巴巴購物平台的買家原本無法使用微信支付（隸屬阿里巴巴的競爭對手騰訊）來付款，京東和拼多多（騰訊擁有部分股權）上的用戶過去也無法使用阿里巴巴的支付寶來消費，但現在這些互斥的科技高牆正在逐一瓦解。

Left: JD.com services
Right: Alibaba's ecommerce platforms

17

除碳未來商機

全球開始朝向淨零排放邁進，除碳科技的新風潮隨之而起。

Climeworks Orca facility in Iceland

在邁向淨零排放的轉型期間，全球對減碳策略有非常迫切的需求。隨著碳採集技術的創新成本開始降低，新一波的除碳科技似乎指日可待。

技術是解決碳排問題的關鍵。誠如瑞士碳採集公司 Climeworks 的創辦人 Jan Wurzbacher，在 2021 年 10 月對《Wired》發表的想法一樣：「我們必須緩解氣候問題，但這樣還不夠，就算以後出現生物科技解決方案，也還是不夠。我們需要的是技術型的解決方案。」

2021 年 9 月，Climeworks 在冰島開設了迄今為止最大的工廠，使用模組化的二氧化碳收集配備來過濾空氣中的碳，並將收集來的碳轉化為液體。他們還與另一家冰島公司 Carbfix 合作，將該液體灌入地底與冰島的原生岩石發生反應，把二氧化碳轉化為石頭。儘管它們目前從空氣中捕集的碳量佔比還很低，但模組化的設計代表該計畫很容易複製與擴展。

接著抬頭看看天空。以色列新創公司 High Hopes Labs 選擇以大型氣球來讓二氧化碳滯留於大氣層高處，讓氣體結凍至近乎固體的狀態以方便收集。在使用小氣球測試過低溫蒸餾的做法後，該公司希望未來兩年能擴大經營規模，且相較於許多「平地版」的減碳方案，他們能以更低的成本捕集等量的二氧化碳。

碳採集完成以後，會有其他品牌接手，運用在旗下產品當中，讓廢物變成寶貴的資源。總部位於芝加哥的 Aether 使用二氧化碳製造鑽石；而加拿大運動服飾 Lululemon 於 2021 年 7 月與生物科技公司 LanzaTech 合作，製造出以廢棄二氧化碳為原料的布料。

> 隨著碳捕集技術的創新成本開始降低，新一波的除碳科技似乎指日可待。

值得關注的原因：

雖然大規模的碳採集技術價格仍屬高昂，但新興計畫也證實了降低成本的可能，利用碳排廢氣來獲利的新興經濟模式也正開始興起。「除碳科技革命已經開始了嗎？」2021 年 6 月，《紐約時報》(The New York Times）如此下標。隨著淨零排放成為新常態，對於這些解決方案的需求，還會繼續成長。

18

任意門的可能性

科研人員正在開啟數位大門，虛擬任意門將有可能成真。

改變溝通和合作方式是頭戴式裝置 Varjo Teleport VR 的產品核心。這款 VR 眼鏡由赫爾辛基科技廠 Varjo 於 2021 年 10 月推出，使用旗下 Varjo Reality Cloud 平台，來達成超擬真的虛擬傳送。

Meta 也非常看好虛擬實境（VR），「我們計畫在 2030 年以前，推出新一代的 Oculus，讓用戶坐在沙發上就能從一個地點移動到另一個地點，」馬克・祖克柏（Mark Zuckerberg）對《The Information》旗下的 Podcast 節目《411》如此表示。

Microsoft Mesh 使用混合實境技術（MR）來連結實體和虛擬世界。微軟（Microsoft）此一新平台的賣點是讓身處不同位置的人能夠透過全息投影技術，即時使用各家廠牌的設備來合作同一專案。微軟技術人員 Alex Kipman 說：「讓你感覺自己跟其他合作者好像身處在同一個環境之中；或者你可以利用不同的混合實境設備，來把自己傳送到其它人所在的地點。」

倫敦設計工作室 Space Popular 提出一個更有企圖心的概念：一個能實現虛擬傳送的公共設施。他們在 2021 年 11 月的「第 15 屆 Dezeen 線上音樂節」發表此一構想，兩位創辦人設想「將這些虛擬的螺紋布料織在一塊，形成一個網路，讓我們的虛擬化身可以在裡面自由移動。」

值得關注的原因：

距離造成的阻礙已日漸減少。由於大眾現在花在線上工作、社交、合作的時間越來越長，新科技的出現為虛擬傳送打下基礎，更緊密、更貼近現實的互動體驗將有可能成真。

Left: Alex Kipman and John Hanke. Images courtesy of Microsoft Mesh
Right: Varjo Teleport VR

19

加密經濟學

加密貨幣終於要踏上合法化之路了嗎？

加密貨幣起起落落，而近期某些重要金融機構和政府機關所採取的行動，有可能讓數位貨幣成為合法的日常支付選項之一。

PayPal 於 2021 年 8 月在英國推出加密貨幣金融服務，讓英國用戶可以在這款熱門的電子支付平台上購買、持有、出售數位貨幣。這是 PayPal 加密貨幣自 2020 年底在美國推出以來，首次進軍國際市場。「虛擬代幣和加密貨幣都已經存在一段時間了，但過去入門門檻會比較高。」PayPal 區塊鏈、加密與數位貨幣部總經理 Jose Fernandez da Ponte 對《美國全國廣播公司商業頻道》（CNBC）如此說道，「如果在我們的平台上持有代幣，相對而言會是很好的切入點。」

紐約新科市長亞當斯（Eric Adams）於 2021 年 11 月公開表示，他希望他的薪資能以比特幣來支付。亞當斯以社交媒體為管道，對外表示他打算讓紐約成為「加密貨幣產業中心」，他也在上任後前三個月領數位貨幣為薪水。

有些國家則嘗試發行法定數位貨幣。中國目前正在試行數位人民幣（数字人民币），最終目標是要推出可供大眾使用的電子貨幣。據《CNBC》報導，在過去一年內，中國人民銀行透過特定應用程式，陸續發行價值達數百萬美元的數位人民幣，該程式可綁定中國六大國有銀行帳戶。北京、成都和深圳等主要城市也在近幾個月成為試驗，騰訊旗下的微眾銀行和阿里巴巴螞蟻集團的網商銀行也加入試行的行列。《CNBC》還於 2021 年 4 月透露，中國甚至有可能會在 2022 年的北京冬奧中，讓外國遊客一起加入測試。

2021 年 4 月，日本銀行（Bank of Japan）啟動了第一階段的數位貨幣實證試驗，初步探索期會一直延續到 2022 年 3 月。日銀將聚焦於技術試驗，測試發行、發送、贖回央行數位貨幣的各種方案。

同樣在 2021 年 4 月，英國財政部長 Rishi Sunak 也在金融科技產業會議上表示，英國財政部和英格蘭銀行（Bank of England）已成立聯合工作小組「來處理與央行數位貨幣有關的潛在探勘工作」。

值得關注的原因：

加密貨幣開疆闢土的計畫開始慢慢受到監管也緩步邁向合法化，為數位經濟的未來打開了一扇大門。

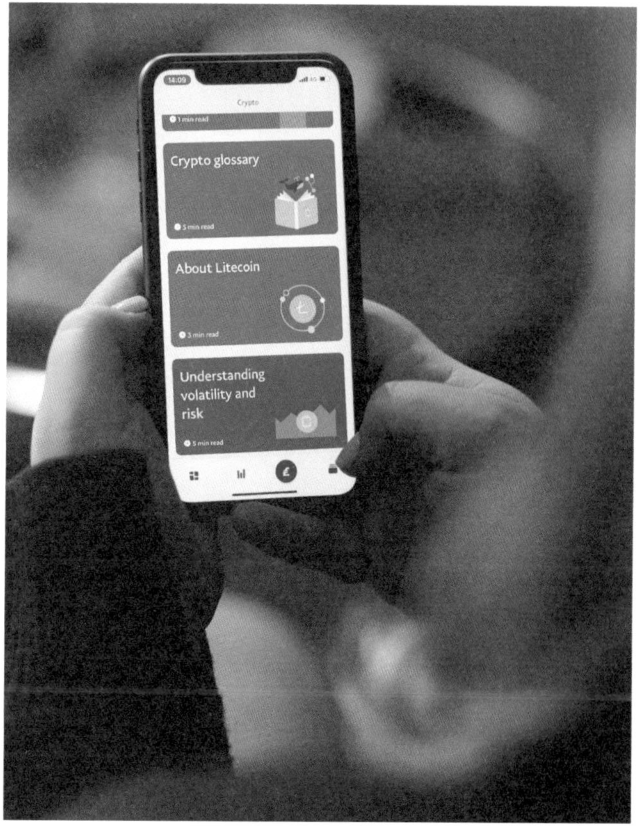

PayPal cryptocurrency service in the UK

20

科技拯救空氣

創新淨化科技正與公共場所中的溫室氣體一決勝負。

AirBubble, presented at the COP26 United Nations Climate Change Conference in 2021. Image by Naaro

AirBubble playground by EcoLogicStudio. Photography by Maja Wirkus

新一波的技術創新利用生物科技來淨化空氣，隨著此一技術的開發，公共場所開始對其進行功能測試，希望減緩氣候變遷帶來的影響。

建築創新公司 EcoLogicStudio 發表能去除空氣污染物的產品，這款 AirBubble 空氣淨化生態機目前已運用於波蘭華沙的一座兒童遊樂館中，它以光合作用的原理出發，利用太陽能生物反應器和藻類來去除空氣中的污染物和二氧化碳。遊樂場周圍的生物反應器，成功地讓空污指數維持在世界衛生組織建議的範圍之內。EcoLogicStudio 也在格拉斯哥的 COP26 聯合國氣候變化大會（United Nations Climate Change Conference）展示 AirBubble 的功能。

由西班牙 External Reference 和 Onionlab 兩家工作室合力打造的 3D 列印「智慧森林」，在 2020 年杜拜世界博覽會上首次亮相。這座人造森林由永續材料製成的生質塑膠樹木所構成，原料則是糖和能採集、分解溫室氣體的礦物材料 pure.tech。專為此檔展覽設計的微型藻類利用光合作用製造氧氣，提高含氧量之餘也降低周圍的溫室氣體量，最終目標是要減緩全球暖化帶來的影響。這座人造森林生產出來的氧氣量會比原生植物還來得高，同時還能生產生質燃料和富含蛋白質的食物。

值得關注的原因：

對空氣品質的高度關注，為新型技術與裝置開了一道門，公共場所的空氣也因此能長保清新。

Left: AirBubble playground by EcoLogicStudio. Photography by Maja Wirkus
Right: AirBubble presented at COP26. Image by Naaro

21

旅遊&觀光

30

21

輕旅行

旅遊愛好者發現，在地旅行也能提供滿意的解方。

如今旅客們透過小而美的短程旅遊，尋找與在地自然環境接觸的獨特方式。研究顯示，輕旅行對於心理與情緒健康的影響就和傳統的度假出遊一樣重要。

根據加州大學柏克萊分校與舊金山分校的至善科學中心（The Greater Good Science Center）研究，每週步行 15 分鐘的受試者會「感到更快樂」，甚至比對照組中的受試者更常微笑。這項結果為大型研究的一部分，指出不只有長途旅行才能讓我們感到驚嘆不已，簡單的遠足也能為我們的心理健康帶來正面的影響。

法國旅遊品牌 Chilowé 專門提供輕旅行規畫，鼓勵旅客以小型旅行團的方式在當地旅遊。該公司的經營理念著重法國本地人的在地旅遊，提供旅客永續且較於平價的旅遊行程。

英國的旅遊業者在偏遠地區提供兩天一夜的迷你探險行程：Much Better Adventures 旅遊品牌為生活忙碌、渴望冒險的客戶設計週末的短旅行。貝斯特韋斯特酒店集團（Best Western）則是在英國推廣輕旅行，標榜最長 48 小時的特殊度假行程。

要踏上冒險之旅，就必須有探險者的裝備。美國服飾品牌 M22 從生活服飾跨足到旅遊業，為密西根湖周遭的在地探險家打造新的冒險體驗。該品牌設計的輕旅行是為了幫助旅客脫離平凡的日常生活，並量身打造各種旅遊情境。在接受《Travel and Leisure》採訪時，營運長 Nick Madrick 表示，他希望透過衝浪、划獨木舟、健行、踏青等活動，打造在地的冒險行程，「讓人們走出家門，重新建立與大自然的連結，並體驗當地社區。」

值得關注的原因：

隨著極限冒險與傳統旅遊變得難以實現，輕旅行就成了相當熱門且令人滿意的替代方案。各大品牌正在尋找各種方法向現有的消費者推廣輕旅行，並利用新的旅遊行程來吸引新的顧客。

Left: M22. Image by Andy Noel
Right: Much Better Adventures

22

虛擬旅遊任意門

數位世界讓人們在舒適的家裡也能沈浸在
身歷其境的旅遊體驗中。

Microsoft Flight Simulator.
Images courtesy of Xbox

> 這種身歷其境的科技能夠降低預算帶來的旅遊限制，讓旅遊變得更平易近人、更富想像力。

任意門或許是科幻小說中才有的奇景，但虛擬旅遊任意門所帶來的感官體驗，讓旅客不必出門，就能沈浸在各大景點之中。

日本的航空集團全日空控股（ANA Holdings）和遊戲公司 JP Games 在 2021 年 5 月共同推出「Sky Whale」數位平台。該平台結合各種數位世界，讓消費者能與親朋好友共同暢遊其中，一起旅行與購物，並提供互動式的文化旅遊體驗。此外，該平台設有「Sky Park」、「Sky Village」、「Sky Mall」三項服務，並與澳洲、奧地利、加拿大、夏威夷、菲律賓和新加坡等地的公司合作，將世界各國的用戶連結起來。

微軟《模擬飛行》（Microsoft Flight Simulator）系統可與 Xbox X Series 和 S Series 相容，現在更推出波音版的飛行搖桿 TCA Yoke Boeing Edition，提供玩家絕佳的模擬飛行體驗。透過這款一比一的波音 787 飛行搖桿，玩家可以控制飛機的俯仰變化，還有額外的 Xbox 按鈕以及音源插孔，能夠與新的主機完美結合。這項產品自 2021 年 11 月開始接受預購，預計在次月就能讓消費者收到這款全新的不銹鋼搖桿。

值得關注的原因：

這種身歷其境的科技能夠降低預算帶來的旅遊限制，讓旅遊變得更平易近人、更富想像力。

Microsoft Flight Simulator. Images courtesy of Xbox

23

迷幻療養旅程

全包式度假村如今多了令人意想不到的誘因：
由專人引導的迷幻之旅。

在哥斯大黎加的全包式度假村「索塔拉治療中心」(Soltara Healing Center)，旅客會在當地希皮博族(Shipibo)治療師的引導下服用一款精神活性茶—死藤水。在牙買加 Silo Wellness 養生中心會替個人或團體量身打造專屬的迷幻蘑菇治療儀式。在迷幻蘑菇療養會所 MycoMeditations，客戶能享受為期一週的奢華之旅，並可加購由專人引導的迷幻儀式，費用 10,500 美元；MycoMeditations 在 2021 年 6 月更擴大服務範圍，為親友團設計「夥伴療養」(Companions Retreats)的行程，希望「以團體的形式，促進他們的精神、情緒與心靈健康。」MycoMeditation 的執行長兼主持人 Justin Townsend 表示。

這項療法也漸漸成為主流大眾文化的一部分。其中著名的例子是葛妮絲・派特洛(Gwyneth Paltrow)在 Netflix 節目《葛妮絲・派特洛：goop 好生活》(The Goop Lab)的第一集中就參與了迷幻療程。近期，迷幻療養也是 Hulu 影集《九位完美陌生人》(Nine Perfect Strangers)的劇情根據。

Silo Wellness 的執行長 Douglas Gordon 告訴彭博社(Bloomberg)，該公司的療程反映出人們對於「奢侈」的概念已經有了變化。「真正的奢侈是能夠穿著夾腳拖盡情享用晚餐，不一定要穿著正式服裝，你懂嗎？重點在於真實的體驗。這就是我們想要吸引的顧客類型，也就是認為體驗有其價值的人。」

值得關注的原因：

養生旅遊與奢華旅行持續結合，注重奢華享受的遊客除了想脫離日常生活、追求物質享受之外，更尋求深層的精神與心靈淨化。

Soltara Healing Center

24

綠色生活地圖

具環保意識的消費者在規畫短途與長途旅行時新增了節能考量。

2021 年 10 月，谷歌（Google）宣佈在 Google 地圖推出三項環境友善的新功能。環保路線能讓駕駛選擇最省油的路徑，而非只有以往的最快路徑。精簡導航（lite navigation）的功能則提供單車族簡單的指示，讓用戶能夠專心騎乘。此外，谷歌的第三項功能將單車與機車共享資訊推廣到全球超過 300 座城市，幫助民眾更容易找到可供租借的輕型交通工具。除了 Google 地圖以外，谷歌在 2021 年推出各式各樣的永續旅遊資訊。例如，在搜尋全球航班資訊時會出現預估的碳排放量，飯店也增列企業永續證書以及環保認證標章的欄位。

針對高消費族群，美國旅遊業者在 2021 年秋季推出沉浸式野外旅遊行程 Wild Nectar Immersive Travel Collection，希望提供遊客兼具環保與奢華的旅遊體驗。同時，透過獨特的節能評分機制 Eco Score，消費者也能依據環境保育、碳排放量與改善當地社區等因素來決定旅行的目的地。

全球奢華精品酒店（Small Luxury Hotels of the World）與全球永續旅遊委員會（Global Sustainable Tourism Council）合作，在 2021 年 10 月推出新的「深思精選酒店」（Considerate Collection），嚴選一系列致力於永續發展的飯店，積極實現促進當地生物多樣性、提升社區福祉等目標。

根據國際能源署的 2020 年運輸報告《Tracking Transport 2020》顯示，燃燒二氧化碳所造成的直接碳排量中，交通運輸就占了 24%。儘管 2020 和 2021 年的封城措施使得碳排量下降，但回升的幅度極大，國際運輸論壇（International Energy Agency）甚至在 2021 年預測，2050 年在交通運輸項目的碳排放量將比 2015 年高出 16%。人們逐漸意識到碳排放量增加所帶來的衝擊，促使交通應用程式的開發者和旅遊公司重新設計他們的產品，提供旅客們更環境友善的選項。

值得關注的原因：

消費者不想就此放棄旅行，他們期待各大品牌打造更多永續旅遊計畫。這類服務不僅能成功吸引價值取向的消費者，還有助於降低選擇太多所帶來的疲乏感。根據偉門智威數據指出，全球 79% 的消費者對於品牌所提供的永續生活提示和建議表示感興趣。

Bhutan Spirit Sanctuary in Shaba, Bhutan, one of the Small Luxury Hotels of the World's Considerate Collection destinations

WUNDERMAN THOMPSON

Arctic Bath in Harads, Sweden, one of the Small Luxury Hotels of the World's Considerate Collection destinations

25

全球三大熱門景點

2022 年最熱門的三大景點展現適合所有人的旅遊特色：
永續觀光、疫情下的安心長住保證以及生態奇觀。

Ljubljana, Slovenia. Photography by Martino Pietropoli, courtesy of Unsplash

斯洛維尼亞的盧比安納

對於具環保意識的旅客來說，斯洛維尼亞的首都是個好去處，因為盧比安納是歐洲最佳旅遊地（European Best Destinations）評選的 2022 年歐洲最佳綠色城市。這座城市擁有人均面積超過 542 平方公尺的公有綠地以及超過 200 公里的自行車道，由於免費的單車共享計畫，無論當地人或遊客都能善用這項公共設施。斯洛維尼亞的永續觀光產業獲得全世界的肯定，也是歐盟執委會認定最佳的永續旅遊城市。

馬爾他的瓦勒他

在新冠肺炎（COVID-19）蔓延之際，旅客仍可在馬爾他的首都瓦勒他安心旅遊。該國的疫苗接種率是全球數一數二，甚至是歐洲最高，根據《BBC》在 2021 年 11 月的報導，當地 81% 的居民已完全接種疫苗。2021 年 5 月，路透社（Reuters）更報導馬爾他已達群體免疫。

此外，在 2021 年 6 月推出的「游牧居留許可」（The Nomad Residence Permit），讓馬爾他成為長期居留的絕佳地點。這項許可讓遠距工作者能在馬爾他居住和工作長達一年，並可選擇是否續簽。

Left: Ljubljana, Slovenia. Photography by Greenvalley Pictures, courtesy of Unsplash
Right: Valletta, Malta. Photography by Mike Nahlii, courtesy of Unsplash

西雙版納擁有
中國最完整未受
破壞的熱帶生態系統，
具有茂密的熱帶雨林
和壯闊的瀑布，
其動物種類占
全中國的四分之一。

中國的西雙版納

西雙版納位於中國西南部的雲南省，獲《孤獨星球》（Lonely Planet）評選為 2022 年前三名值得造訪的地區。《孤獨星球》表示，這些旅遊地上榜的原因在於其「話題性、獨特體驗、精彩亮點以及對永續觀光的長期承諾」。西雙版納獨特的環境與亮點著重在植物與生態的多樣性。西雙版納擁有中國最完整未受破壞的熱帶生態系統，具有茂密的熱帶雨林和壯闊的瀑布，其動物種類占全中國的四分之一，植物種類則占了六分之一。

Xishuangbanna, China. Image courtesy of Unsplash

26

冥想旅行

冥想與旅行的結合，讓每趟旅程都是心靈覺察之旅。

旅遊和導航品牌紛紛推出冥想練習的應用程式，以撫慰旅客的心靈。

Waze 導航公司和 Headspace 冥想推廣公司合作，希望降低駕駛在通勤時的壓力。他們在 2021 年 10 月推出 Drive with Headspace 服務，將冥想、放鬆的 Headspace 體驗與導航應用程式結合，並提供五種心情模式可供選擇：覺察、明亮、愉悅、希望、開放。使用者可以根據他們的心情自由切換應用程式內的圖示與汽車圖像，將原先的導航語音助理切換成 Headspace 冥想專家伊芙・路易斯・普列托（Eve Lewis Prieto）的聲音，並收聽 Headspace 精選的 Spotify 冥想歌單。Waze 表示，這項服務具備四種語言版本，希望能幫助駕駛「找到在旅途中的愉悅和意義」。

英國的火車公司 Avanti West Coast 將為乘客推出催眠療法應用程式，幫助他們度過情緒低潮與疲勞。該公司在 2021 年 10 月宣布，其 20 分鐘的療程能提供聽眾小憩充電的訣竅、提升生產力的妙招以及建立自信的方法。這款催眠應用程式 Clementine 將免費提供給搭乘西海岸幹線（West Coast Main Line）的乘客使用，因為「旅途中的體驗和目的地本身一樣重要。」Avanti West Coast 的公司如此表示。

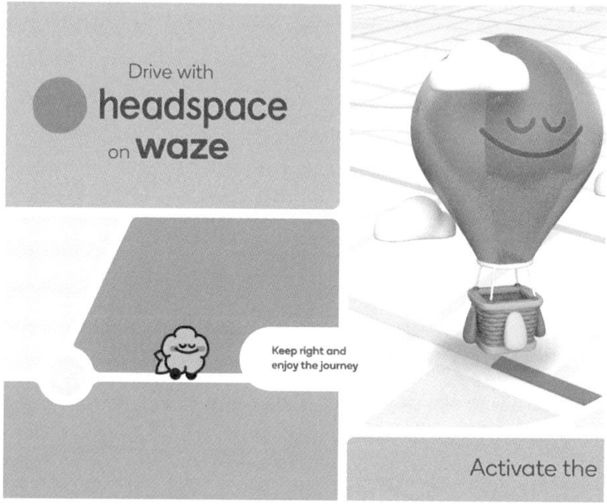

達美航空（Delta Airlines）也將在飛機上提供客製化的派樂騰（Peloton）放鬆、冥想及伸展課程，讓乘客可以在座椅後方的螢幕收看。此合作項目在 2021 年 11 月發布，希望幫助乘客在飛行時好好放鬆，課程時間從 5 到 20 分鐘不等，並由人氣健身教練進行指導。

值得關注的原因：

追求養生的冥想應用程式逐漸出現在旅遊領域，讓焦慮不安的旅客能沉浸在不同的療程，在路途中便能放鬆身心。

Left: Waze and Headspace
Right: Clementine and Avanti West Coast

27

知性之旅

美國太空總署的科學家和文化專家正帶領求知心切的旅客
踏上與眾不同的旅途。

Adero Scottsdale's Dark Sky Zone at the SkyTop Lounge

WUNDERMAN THOMPSON　Adero Scottsdale's Dark Sky Zone at the SkyTop Lounge

近年來，許多飯店與資訊公司開始打造由專家帶領的旅遊行程，為顧客提供獨一無二的旅遊體驗。

2021 年 8 月，《美國國家公共廣播電台》（NPR）推出旅遊服務，為電台粉絲和歷史、音樂與天文學的愛好者提供深度的知性之旅。自 2022 年開始，專家將帶領旅行團前往各地的景點，範圍一路從冰島到南美洲，每次僅接待最多 24 名旅客，還附上電台記者精心策畫的書單、曲目以及推薦景點。「這些導覽行程是個契機，能夠將喜愛旅遊和 NPR 電台的人聚集在一起。」消費產品總監 Jane Scott 表示。

Adero Scottsdale 飯店的旅客可以在 SkyTop 酒廊一邊啜飲著雞尾酒，一邊觀賞滿天星斗。飯店的「暗空專家」（又稱為「星際使者」）會透過雙筒望遠鏡和高倍望遠鏡帶領住客觀看星座，同時讓住客盡情享用「太空雞尾酒」。飯店也在房內提供望遠鏡，讓客人能在自己的房間內觀星。

2021 年，茂宜島凱悅度假村及水療中心（Hyatt Regency Maui Resort and Spa）的旅客有機會在美國太空總署大使 Edward Mahoney 的帶領下，深入探索從飯店可見的 80 個星座。美國太空總署參與飯店業者推出的「住宿、學習、娛樂」全包式行程，進駐專屬的教育空間，此合作實為無人能及的特殊體驗。

值得關注的原因：

隨著旅客持續追求旅途中的獨特學習體驗，飯店業者順勢推出更多的知性之旅，並尋求科學與文化專家協助策畫精英的獨特冒險。

28

奢華飛行享受

航空旅行提供水療般的舒適體驗，讓旅客養精蓄銳。

航空公司將機上設備升級，為旅客創造舒適與恢復精力的空間，讓他們在旅途中也能好好享受。

新加坡航空（Singapore Airlines）宣布與水療飯店 Golden Door 合作，將頂級的水療養生體驗帶到雲端之間。從 2022 年 1 月開始，搭乘洛杉磯至新加坡航線的旅客可以在 17 小時的直航航班上，觀賞放鬆身心的冥想影片，參加運動課程，享受新的美食菜單，甚至參與睡眠教育課程。Golden Door 的營運長 Kathy Van Ness 表示，Golden Door 的目標在於「為飛機上的每位乘客帶來正向的影響」。

Singapore Airlines and Golden Door

豪華商務艙的迷你套房設有房門可以保護隱私，也有舒適的躺椅，正漸漸取代傳統的頭等艙。卡達航空（Qatar Airways）從 2017 年開始提供私人的 Qsuites 機上套房，如今達美航空（Delta）、中國東方航空、捷藍航空（JetBlue）、英國航空（British Airways）、上海航空以及中國國際航空也紛紛提供類似的設備。

值得關注的原因：

旅程本身和目的地一樣重要，航空公司看準旅客對於舒適旅程的渴望，推出了創新的奢華飛行體驗。

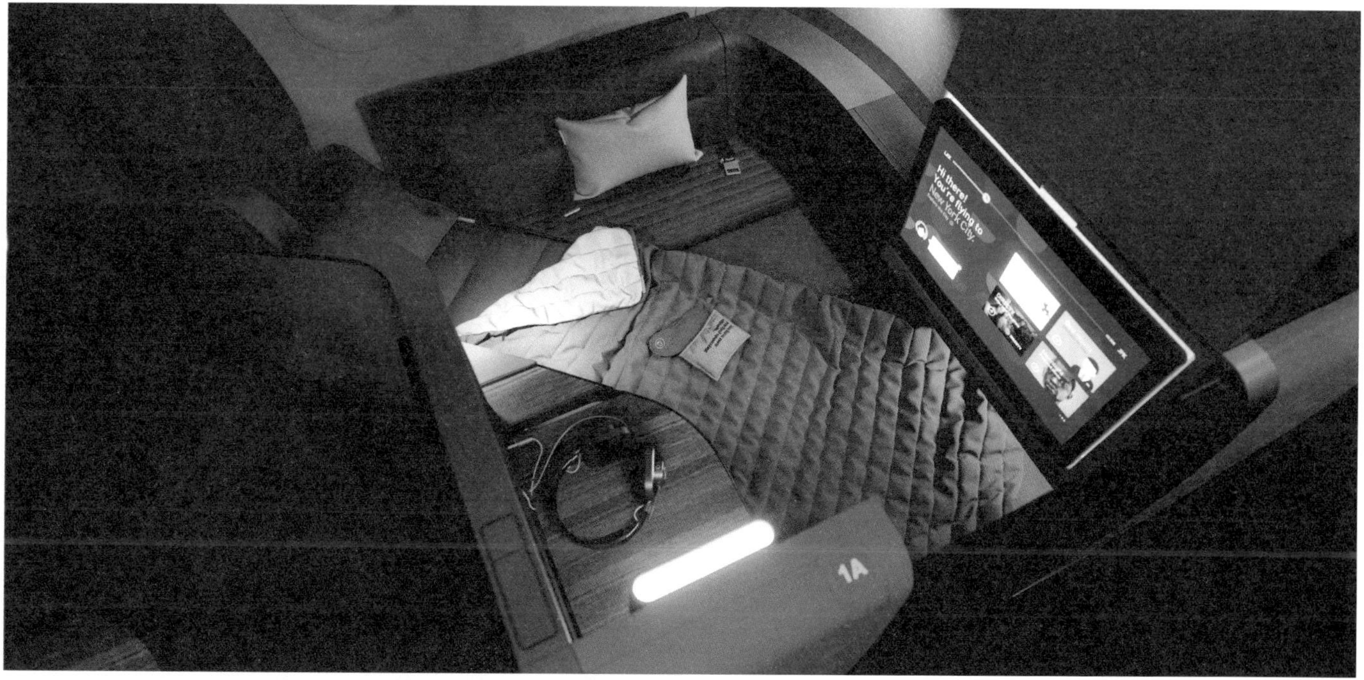

JetBlue Mint suite

29

推升中國的旅遊經濟

中國旅遊業透過新的大型機場、主題樂園，以及拓展免稅購物城，為後疫情時代做好準備。

中國的出國旅遊市場曾為世界第一，在 2019 年達 1.69 億旅遊人次的高峰。中國觀光客無所不在，夏威夷的飯店甚至雇用會說中文的員工，倫敦的馬里波恩車站也首度推出中文廣播服務。然而就在此刻，新冠肺炎（COVID-19）突然爆發，各國國界紛紛關閉。此時中國的旅遊經濟並非全然停滯，只是暫時轉向國內市場。

中國的文化和旅遊部指出，儘管面臨定期的防疫封鎖，2021 年 1 月至 9 月的國內旅行人數仍比去年同期增加了 39%，達到 26.9 億人次。

中國正透過三項措施來推動旅遊經濟：

一、機場升級

星芒狀外觀的北京大興國際機場是中國首都的第二大國際航班樞紐，於 2019 年 9 月正式啟用。該機場由札哈・哈蒂建築事務所（Zaha Hadid Architects）設計，斥資超過 110 億美元，設有以傳統中國建築為靈感的中央庭園以及引導旅客動線的天窗，預計每年將為 1 億名旅客服務，與世界最繁忙的亞特蘭大國際機場（Hartsfield-Atlanta International Airport）並駕齊驅。

在中國的西南地區，成都天府國際機場於 2021 年 6 月啟用，每年可容納 6000 萬名旅客，為四川省的第二個對外門戶。四川省以大熊貓以及辛辣美食吸引世界各地旅客。

二、推動免稅購物

由於無法飛往巴黎、紐約或米蘭購買最新的名牌包，喜愛奢侈品的旅客轉而飛往海南島的免稅區（又稱為「中國的夏威夷」）。

2020 年 7 月，中國將海南島的免稅購物額度提高了三倍，並擴大免稅商品的種類。根據海南島海關的數據，此後一年的免稅品銷售額暴增 226%，達到 72 億美元。

LVMH 集團、開雲集團（Kering）、資生堂（Shiseido）、萊雅集團（L'Oréal）等國際品牌皆在此設立店面，海南島也成為結合實體店面與社群商務、直播帶貨的實驗場。

海南島滿足了遊客對於國外奢侈品牌的報復性需求，其成功案例吸引北京、上海、廣州、天津和重慶五座大城市加入戰局，紛紛發展免稅購物區以建立「國際消費中心城市」。

三、主題樂園的蓬勃發展

如同國際零售業湧入中國市場，西方主題樂園也大舉進入中國。

上海迪士尼樂園開幕五年後，北京環球影城也在 2021 年 9 月開幕。北京環球影城是全球第五座且世界最大的環球影城，其中有七座主題公園，包含第一座「功夫熊貓蓋世之地」。

英國默林娛樂（Merlin Entertainments）正在中國興建三座樂高主題公園。預計在 2023 年開幕的四川樂高主題公園將融合當地文化元素，像是熊貓主題區；而深圳和上海的主題公園將於 2024 年開幕，分別以中國的高科技數位體驗和水鄉古鎮建築為核心主題。

值得關注的原因：

隨著各國紛紛封閉國界，中國的旅遊經濟轉向了內需市場，因此吸引了海內外的合作夥伴投注大量資金在中國的旅遊零售業和娛樂產業，除了看好中國國內觀光產業的長期發展，同時期盼國界開放後也能吸引許多外國旅客。

“隨著各國紛紛封閉國界，中國的旅遊經濟轉向了內需市場。

30

復興航海復興時代

具環保意識的旅客開始轉向海上旅行。

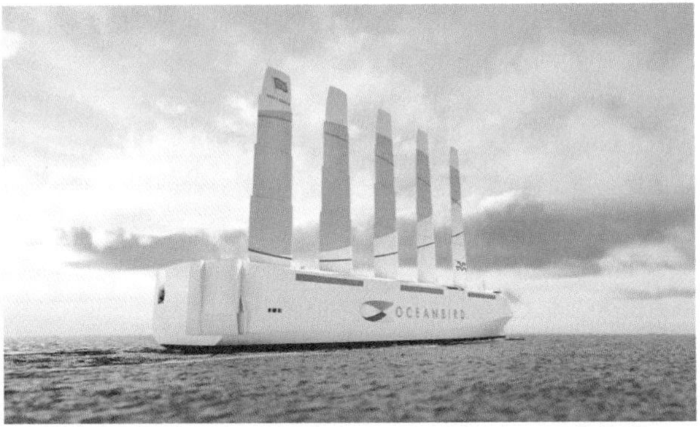

2019 年，環保少女葛瑞塔・桑柏格（Greta Thunberg）為了避免飛機所產生的溫室氣體，選擇搭乘帆船橫跨大西洋。從此，愈來愈多的個人與組織也開始轉向風力，以尋求更環保的交通方式。

瑞典的造船公司 Wallenius Marine 與瑞典政府和研究機構的合作，設計出完全由風力驅動的遠洋貨運船來載運汽車，希望降低汽車貿易產業的碳足跡。「海洋鳥」（Oceanbird）貨運船具備五個鋼製風帆，能夠運送超過 7,000 輛汽車。

設立於法國的貨運公司 TransOceanic Wind Transport 目標是打造並使用完全由風力驅動的貨船。該公司正在為國際貿易航線打造四艘貨船，能夠承載 1,100 噸的貨物，並減少 90% 的碳排放量。

The Oceanbird by Wallenius Marine and Alfa Laval

體育競賽將透過推廣電動交通工具，協助加速能源轉型，朝向潔淨能源發展。E1 系列賽是全世界第一場電動賽艇錦標賽，將於 2022 年在全球各地的海岸地區舉行。參賽隊伍將駕駛以大自然為靈感的 Racebird 電動帆船。除了驚心動魄的比賽之外，此系列賽帶來最深遠的影響是留下可持續使用的設施。主辦單位將在每個城市的碼頭留下基礎充電設備，並舉辦為期一週的活動來推廣永續發展。

E1 系列賽的共同創辦人和執行長 Rodi Basso 向偉門智威智庫表示：「正如汽車產業逐漸轉向電動化與潔淨科技一樣，海洋產業也必須如此，以避免對地球重要的生態系統造成不可挽回的破壞。」

對於個人來說，許多組織正致力於推廣帆船運動。法國公司 Sailcoop 正在建立帆船合作社，客戶可以從 2022 年 1 月開始預定行程。藉由創造航海專業人士、旅客與船東的合作網絡，Sailcoop 提供由私人水手導航的在地與國際水上旅行。

值得關注的原因：

陸地與空中旅行不再有往昔的光彩，因為碳排放與氣候變遷的不良後果與日俱增。精心設計的電力與風力船舶讓每個人都有機會落實碳中和運輸，舉凡企業、競賽水手到沒有船舶的個人皆如此。

Top: Sailcoop
Bottom: Oceanways, the world's first zero-emisson submarine conceptv

E1 Series. Image by Mark Lloyd

31
品牌&行銷
4.0

31

品牌廣告的反思

劫持廣告空間的破壞行為，揭露品牌邪惡的一面，
要求他們做出改善。

Ford poster by Brandalism

關注氣候議題的社運人士正將目標從製造最多污染的大企業，擴大到賦予他們權力的政府、銀行以及廣告公司。

在 2021 年 11 月於英國格拉斯哥舉辦的第 26 屆聯合國氣候大會（COP26），Brandalism、Badvertising、Adfree Cities 在內的社運組織策畫了游擊式的抗議行動。

《Drum》報導，2021 年 10 月匿名組織 Brandalism 在英國 20 座城鎮及城市各地的廣告看板、公車站張貼超過 100 張海報，指控奧美（Ogilvy）、競立（MediaCom）和 VCCP 等廣告代理商協助殼牌石油（Shell）、英國石油（BP）和英國航空（British Airways）等高碳排企業「漂綠」（greenwash），替他們營造環保的正面形象。Brandalism 日前曾批評巴克萊銀行（Barclays）和滙豐銀行（HSBC）為化石燃料企業提供融資服務。

智庫 New Weather Institute 發起了「Badvertising」行動，將廣告業視為「污染大腦」的元兇，並呼籲政府管控高碳排企業的廣告活動。

「長久以來，從來沒有人檢討廣告業在氣候危機中所扮演的角色。」Adfree Cities 的 Robbie Gillett 在接受《Drum》採訪時表示：「無論是透過創意人才來行銷高碳排產品、為大型石油公司營造環保的假象，或用高耗能的廣告螢幕填滿我們的公共空間，這些高污染的大型公關活動必須停止。」

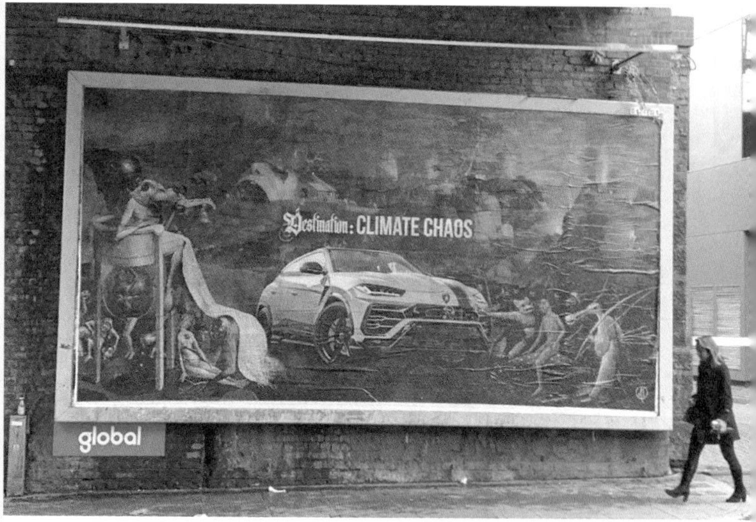

另一項常見的批評是，廣告公司在購物節期間透過炫耀性消費推廣非永續的生活模式。就連地方政府也未能倖免。歐洲公民倡議組織（European Citizens' Initiative）呼籲地方議會仿效荷蘭阿姆斯特丹，立法禁止汽車、航空及化石燃料公司的廣告活動並取消他們的贊助商資格。

值得關注的原因：

近年來，廣告業已做出不少努力，利用自身的營運策略來達成碳中和的目標。但社運人士認為，與旗下大客戶所造成的碳足跡相比，廣告公司的努力仍遠遠不夠。

Posters by Brandalism

32

從原始到先創

新一代的數位平台正將創造力賦予使用者。

IMVU social network. Image courtesy of Together Labs

IMVU 稱創造力爲未來數位時代的「新地位象徵」。

科技逐漸成為創意的來源，為新一代的數位平台和創意影響力鋪路。創意技術專家及數位設計師 Helena Dong 向偉門智威智庫表示，數位工具「啟動了全新的創意世界」，讓「創作能夠超越實體限制」。

根據偉門智威智庫委由偉門智威數據團隊在 2021 年 7 月進行的〈進入元宇宙〉(Into the Metaverse) 報告顯示，在美國、英國和中國的 Z 世代和千禧世代中，72% 的人認為今日的創造力必須仰賴科技，92% 認為科技打開了全新的創意世界。

「對 α 世代和 Z 世代來說，客製化和創造是遊戲體驗中錯綜複雜的一環。」《衛報》(The Guardian) 的遊戲編輯 Keith Stuart 指出。「對他們來說，量身訂做和遊戲元素同樣都是自我表達與探索的一部分。」

Snapchat 認為創造力是推動未來數位參與的動力。身為使用者，「你不是在創造內容讓人們使用，而是創造內容讓其他人進行再創造。」Snap 公司的產品組合行銷經理 Carolina Arguelles Navas 告訴偉門智威智庫：「這個力量非常強大。你創造的內容可以讓大家再利用，每個人會將其個人化並得到獨特的個人體驗。」

這股動力源自於數位創造力的雪球效應。「擴增實境 (augmented reality, AR) 最大的契機是催化劑的角色，能讓其他人利用自己研發的擴增實境體驗進行再創造；接著他們分享給身邊的好友，好友們發現了這樣的東西，再持續分享出去。你創造了一個觸媒，能夠擴大自己的創作規模。」

IMVU social network. Image courtesy of Together Labs

IMVU social network. Image courtesy of Together Labs

IMVU 是以創造力為核心的「新世代社交網絡」，IMVU 社交應用程式及母公司 Together Labs 執行長 Daren Tsui 表示，「我們的平台擁有超過 20 萬名創作者。多年來，我們的目錄已累積了 1,500 萬個項目」，並且幾乎都是由使用者推動而成。「我們只創造了其中的 0.001%；其他都是由創作者完成的。」IMVU 稱創造力為未來數位時代的「新地位象徵」，取代了原先的影響力和收入。執行長解釋，使用者進入平台後，「賺錢對他們來說並不是最重要的事情，重點在於他們的創作能否受到認可。」

值得關注的原因：

網路使用習慣持續改變。根據數位時裝公司 The Fabricant 表示，在數位世界中，「人們不再是被動的消費者，而是具創造力的使用者，能夠盡情表達自我並策畫自己的虛擬身份。」

33

超級粉絲經濟圈

藉由社群平台新的訂閱制度，數位創作者能透過內容產出來賺取收入。

在不使用第三方應用程式的情況下，社群應用程式讓使用者將創作內容商品化，在創作者社群建立了新的階層。

推特（Twitter）在 2021 年 9 月推出 Super Follows 的新功能，讓付費的推特使用者能夠觀看訂閱用戶專屬的內容。這項功能讓內容創作者能為超級粉絲發送獨家推文，但目前此服務仍在測試階段，僅開放給美國地區的部分 iOS 使用者。使用 Super Follows 功能的創作者可以自行決定每月收取 2.99 至 9.99 美元的費用，並透過付款平台 Stripe 進行收款，在扣除第三方費用後，最高可獲得 97% 的訂閱收入；一旦在 Twitter 上的各種收入加總超過 5 萬美元，扣除第三方費用後，創作者則可獲得 80% 的訂閱收入。

另外，推特也在測試為企業所打造的「Professional Profiles」。自 2021 年 4 月開始，企業的推特帳號多了特殊的設定，能直接在檔案中顯示品牌或公司的特定資訊。新的功能包括驗證徽章、企業類別，以及更大的企業資訊欄位，像是營業時段和地點等。

湯博樂（Tumblr）在 2021 年 9 月推出新的訂閱功能，並開放給全美的使用者。Post Plus 的功能可以讓創作者只向訂閱者發布貼文，和推特的 Super Follows 功能類似。湯博樂的使用者可以每月收取 1.99 至 9.99 美元的費用，並可針對現有的內容進行收費，不僅限於新的貼文。

值得關注的原因：

社群平台持續發展，提供的不僅是多媒體形式的娛樂內容。平台功能獲得強化，也多了吸引、提升並維持大量追蹤人數的誘因，激發出創造力並增進創作者和消費者在社群平台上的對話。

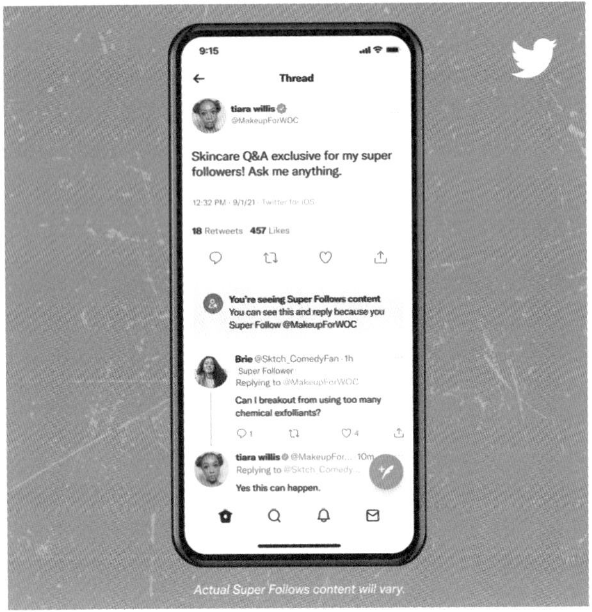

Left: Twitter Super Follows feature
Right: Tumblr Post Plus

34

虛擬世界玩品牌

遊戲是廣告和行銷產業的未來嗎？

WUNDERMAN THOMPSON

Top: Ralph Lauren Winter Escape on Roblox
Bottom: Nikeland on Roblox

根據市調公司 Technavio 在 2021 年報告推估，遊戲內置廣告的市場規模預計在 2021 至 2025 年間成長 35.4 億美元，使得各大品牌紛紛投入遊戲領域，在其中打造品牌的虛擬世界。

許多品牌開始與著名的 Roblox 等遊戲平台合作，創造出全新的遊戲內廣告體驗，希望吸引平台 4,600 萬名的每日活躍使用者。

Ralph Lauren 於 2021 年 12 月在 Roblox 平台推出數位體驗 Winter Escape。這項節慶主題的虛擬體驗包含了溜冰、烤棉花糖、尋寶遊戲以及購買 Roblox 獨家的數位時裝 The Ralph Lauren Digital Collection。此外，Nike 也在 2021 年 11 月於 Roblox 推出 Nikeland 虛擬樂園。在虛擬樂園裡，使用者可以替他們的虛擬化身穿上 Nike 的服飾及配件，盡情探索 Nikeland 不同的競技場、球場和建築，裡面還有各式各樣的小遊戲。2021 年 9 月推出的 Vans World 是 Roblox 的虛擬滑板公園，玩家可以在此練習滑板技巧、設計自己的 Vans 鞋款與滑板，並試穿各項虛擬裝備。現代集團（Hyundai）同時於 Roblox 平台推出 Hyundai Mobility Adventure 的虛擬空間，其中包含五個「主題公園」，讓使用者體驗賽車、玩遊戲、了解現代汽車的各項技術，並參與不同的節慶活動。

其他品牌則是在自家平台打造虛擬品牌世界。在 2021 年 9 月的德國國際車展 IAA Mobility 2021，寶馬（BMW）推出了 Joytopia 虛擬世界。除了展現寶馬未來的願景，Joytopia 更帶來酷玩樂團（Coldplay）的獨家演唱會，增添不少節慶氣氛。日本美妝品牌 SK-II 也在 2021 年 5 月推出虛擬城市 SK-II City，讓訪客可以漫步其中，自由購物、了解公司產品，甚至在 SK-II 電影院看場電影。

「以遊戲作為行銷管道的做法愈來愈常見也相當特別。」偉門智威的遊戲及電競主管 Grant Paterson 告訴偉門智威智庫。「我們將遊戲視為連結新型消費模式的管道。」

值得關注的原因：

遊戲正逐漸取代平面媒體和電視等廣告管道，特別是針對年輕世代。「對年輕族群而言，許多傳統的行銷手法早已不管用了。」《衛報》（The Guardian）遊戲編輯 Keith Stuart 告訴偉門智威智庫，「遊戲才是年輕世代生活的一部分。」隨著企業和行銷人員持續踏入遊戲這項不斷成長的領域，我們將在未來看見更多由品牌打造的虛擬世界。

BMW's Joytopia virtual world

35

終結品牌的獨裁

在去中心化組織的推動及鼓勵下，新一波的消費型創作者正逐漸掌握品牌故事的主導權。

無人帶領品牌是建立在社群對產品、資產和溝通的集體決策之上，如今去中心化科技與去中心化金融也在為無人帶頭品牌鋪路。成員通常透過購買加密代幣的方式進入社群，進而獲得參與品牌決策的權力，甚至能享有公司的分紅。

「無人帶頭品牌」（headless brand）一詞是由策略研究公司 Other Internet 在 2019 的文章中首次提出，文中將這些品牌形容為「自我強化、自我激勵且敘事方式具感染力的品牌，其出現與演化的方式出人意料且無人能擋。」文中將比特幣視為第一代的無人帶頭品牌，因為比特幣缺乏中心化的控制實體，是根據眾多投資者的決策來運作、發展。「無人帶頭品牌就像是網路迷因，」文章作者 Toby Shorin、Laura Lotti 和 Sam Hart 表示：「不屬於任何人，可以由所有人任意組合。」

近期 NFT（Non-fungible tokens，非同質化代幣）市場已然浮現，正式將文化、社群和加密貨幣的趨勢整合起來。自稱「無人帶領品牌工廠」的 Metafactory 於 2020 年推出，目標是建立藝術家、消費者和品牌之間的夥伴關係，創造出由社群經營的時尚品牌。例如，義大利數位藝術家 Van 和印尼 NFT 藝術家 Twisted Vacancy 會提交他們的設計，讓會員投票選出最受歡迎的作品，並由 Metafactory 統一進行生產。隨後由品牌成員和投資者共享利潤，以及專屬的 NFT 折扣和促銷活動。

在 2021 年 4 月推出的「無聊猿猴遊艇俱樂部」（Bored Ape Yacht Club）是擁有猿猴角色 NFT 的人所組成的社群。重要的是，各個猿猴角色的擁有者有該角色所有權，可以運用創意將

Metafactory

其資產商業化。許多擁有者已開始生產品牌精釀啤酒、滑板和 YouTube 系列短片等各項商品。《紐約客》(The New Yorker)的 Kyle Chayka 解釋,「這些文化創作能在使用者的努力下自然擴展,同時保有品牌的識別度,打造出一種使用者原創的神話。」

值得關注的原因：

「無聊猿猴是愚蠢的收藏品,還是挑戰 Supreme 地位的去中心化競爭者?」推特用戶 @punk6529 在 2021 年 10 月如此寫道。如果無聊猿猴生態系統的市值如報導所述已達十億美元,答案很有可能是後者。目前在街頭服飾和音樂等文化商品中,無人帶領新創公司或許是最強的競爭者,但隨著消費者對品牌敘事越來越有話語權,所有品牌都必須密切關注這項趨勢。

36

廣告正能量

在品牌廣告和消費者互動中，快樂的片刻能讓人精神振奮。

由於消費者渴望具有價值、更愉悅的內容，他們在元宇宙和數位平台的主動參與已經超過以往的被動消費。如今品牌也調整他們的廣告手法，增添更多鼓舞且溫暖人心的時刻，邀請觀眾加入他們的喜悅歡騰。

TikTok 充滿了舞蹈影片、搞笑的惡作劇和特技潮流，是現代生活快樂的泉源，也為品牌帶來了機會，能讓他們與受眾建立既輕鬆又真實的互動。根據 Flamingo Group 的研究指出，73% 的 TikTok 使用者表示在打開 TikTok 後感到更快樂。由於品牌將行銷重點放在營造正向的空間和平台，正面情緒與品牌形象的結合仍是行銷人員的重要策略。

情緒智能是 2021 年 10 月凌志汽車（Lexus）廣告的核心精神。廣告目的在宣傳凌志 ES 車系的油電混合車，利用臉部辨識科技來讀取消費者的情緒，並隨之調整廣告內容。〈Feel Your Best〉企劃的目標是透過個人化體驗來讓觀眾產生正面的感受。

Gap 在 2021 年的節慶廣告〈All Together Now〉當中，著重在愛、仁慈以及品牌的核心價值之一──「現代美國的樂觀主義」。該廣告由歌手凱蒂・佩芮（Katy Perry）主演，並以披頭四的〈All You Need is Love〉作為背景音樂。團結、愛與快樂的主題符合品牌的正向行銷策略。

Target 在 2021 年節慶期間推出新版〈What We Value Most Shouldn't Cost More〉廣告，其中由 Black Pumas 和 Sofia Reyes 演繹情感合唱團（The Emotions）的〈Best of My Love〉。「今年的節慶廣告讓 Target 有機會和所有的顧客建立連結，同時幫助他們在節慶期間找到日常生活中觸手可及的幸福。」行銷與數位長 Cara Sylvester 如此表示。

值得關注的原因：

消費者持續尋找真實且令人振奮的內容，品牌也在樂觀正向的平台來滿足他們的需求，目標是藉由各種行銷策略創造出快樂的情緒。樂觀與團結的主題對消費者而言相當重要，而關注這些共同價值的品牌也為顧客帶來正面的情緒，並提升品牌社群內的互動參與度。

The Lexus ES "Feel Your Best" campaign

> 品牌調整廣告手法，
> 增添更多令人振奮
> 且溫暖人心的時刻，
> 邀請觀眾加入
> 他們的喜悅歡騰。

37

再生品牌

綜觀各行各業，許多品牌正抓緊機會實踐再生行動，
加大品牌推進永續目標的力道。

PepsiCo regenerative farming

再生不僅僅是減少對地球的危害，而是透過修復、再利用資源來徹底改變對環境的負面影響，根據偉門智威智庫 2021 年的〈再生崛起〉報告，全球 84% 的受訪者認為必須由企業擔任領頭羊，否則再生行動難以落實。為回應此議題，各品牌也承諾朝向再生目標發展。

為了發展「農場到衣櫥」（farm-to-closet）的模式，加州永續時尚品牌 Christy Dawn 在 2021 年 9 月推出著重於再生農業的土地管理新計畫 The Land Stewardship。透過此計畫，顧客可以投資 200 美元，協助一塊棉花田由傳統種植方式改為再生農耕。棉花收成後，顧客可以根據其所認養的棉花田之產量，得到相應的店內折扣作為報酬。如此一來，Christy Dawn 的顧客就確實能推動該企業真正達成再生目標。

世界知名的時尚品牌也紛紛投入再生農業。2021 年 10 月，Ralph Lauren 宣布與土壤健康研究所（Soil Health Institute）合作，創立了「美國再生棉基金」（US Regenerative Cotton Fund）。在此之前，保護國際基金會（Conservation International）和全球奢侈品牌開雲集團（Kering）已共同成立「再生自然基金」（Regenerative Fund for Nature），並公布首批獲得基金支持的七個計畫，目標是在未來五年內讓 100 萬公頃的土地改採再生經營方式。

零售業者也加入實踐再生的行列。2021 年 10 月，英國連鎖超市 Morrisons 宣布與麥當勞（McDonald' s）、哈珀亞當斯大學（Harper Adams University）以及全國農民聯盟（National Farmers' Union）合作，成立了英國第一所永續飲食與農耕學校，最終目標是改變國內的農業實踐方式。日前，沃爾瑪（Walmart）在 2020 年 9 月誓言將成為再生公司，其中包含在 2030 年前至少要修復 5,000 萬英畝土地的承諾。

過去數年間，大型食品業者逐漸發展再生農業，跨國企業如達能（Danone）、雀巢（Nestlé）和通用磨坊（General Mills）皆公布相關計畫，要協助部分供應商採行再生做法。2021 年 4 月，百事公司（PepsiCo）宣布雄心勃勃的目標，希望在 2030 年前將再生技術推廣到 700 萬英畝的土地，相當於其農業足跡的所有總和。

值得關注的原因：

許多品牌認知到，僅僅減少對地球的危害早已不夠。如何再利用全球的資源，修復數個世紀以來累積的損害，才是現今的永續發展目標。

PepsiCo regenerative farming

37

WUNDERMAN THOMPSON

The US Regenerative Cotton Fund, a Soil Health Institute partnership with Ralph Lauren

38

未來企業宣言

許多企業正在更新其內部品牌訊息，以保持文化關聯性並與現代員工建立聯結。

為了全球 130 萬的員工，亞馬遜（Amazon）希望成為世界上最好的雇主。亞馬遜在 2021 年 7 月新增了兩條「領導原則」，共計 16 條原則。第一條，「努力成為世界上最棒的雇主」，表示亞馬遜的領導階級應致力於「創造更安全、生產力更高、績效表現更佳、更多元且公平的工作環境。」第二條著重在擴展規模的過程必須合理並負起企業責任，內容點出「公司規模很大，能夠影響全世界，但我們絕非十全十美。」接任傑夫·貝佐斯（Jeff Bezos）執行長一職的安迪·賈西（Andy Jassy）希望未來亞馬遜能成為員工優先並且負責任的企業。

隨著居家辦公的趨勢持續擴大，讓不少人感到挫敗，無法在工作和生活之間取得平衡，因此谷歌（Google）發布了健康宣言，內容引人共鳴，像是「把家庭擺在工作之前是沒問題的」以及「說出內心的負面感受是沒關係的」。

值得關注的原因：

一些公司正經歷品牌重塑，希望藉由更新內部政策，回應當今的需求並將員工放在首位。這項轉變展現出企業對於員工健康與幸福的重視，以及雇主必須設身處地為員工著想。

39

夢境行銷

許多品牌和廣告商主在設法引導我們的夢境。

夢境的商業開發正在逐漸成為現實，同時引發了科學界的疑慮。要求政府監管的聲浪四起，大眾開始關注利用夢境孵化作為廣告手法的企業。雖然新一波的潛意識行銷擁有無盡的可能，但仍有許多不確定因素。

「夢境孵化」（Dream Incubation）或「目標夢境孵化」（Targeted Dream Incubation,TDI）是擁有古老根源的現代科學領域，可透過如聲音等感官提示，來形塑或「促發」人們的夢境。在臨床上，目標夢境孵化可用來改善人們負面的習慣，例如吸菸；在行銷領域則是用來提升品牌親和力。

安海斯—布希公司（Anheuser Busch）獲得超級盃的獨家廣告代理權，Molson Coors 公司在 2021 年 1 月找到極為不同的方法來瞄準超級盃粉絲。與微軟（Microsoft）Xbox 廣告〈Made From Dream〉中的目標夢境孵化類似，Molson Coors 與哈佛大學的夢境心理學家 Deirdre Barrett 共同設計 Coors Big Game Dream 的畫面與音效，讓觀眾在做夢時徜徉在山景之間，正好讓他們對 Molson Coors 的產品產生興趣。該公司的新聞稿寫道：「透過引導夢境的科學技術，Coors Light 啤酒和 Coors Seltzer 氣泡水將帶給您沁人心脾的美夢。」

這些廣告聽起來或許令人愉快，但麻省理工學院(Massachusetts Institute of Technology）的神經科學家 Adam Haar 認為這種做法運用在行銷領域是相當可怕的。廣告商已經開始介入我們自然的睡眠記憶，未來還可能會發展出更邪惡的計畫。例如，早在 2018 年，漢堡王（Burger King）就有許多驚人的計畫。漢堡王在

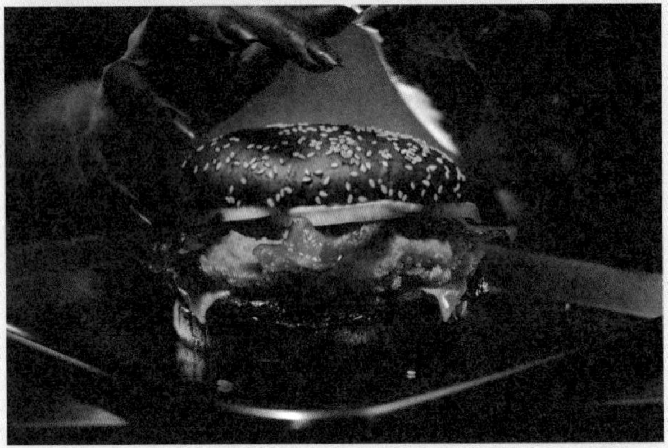

Top: Xbox Series XS global launch events
Bottom: Burger King's "nightmare" burger

高達 77% 的美國行銷人員表示他們計畫在未來三年內於廣告中運用夢境技術。

萬聖節推出的「夢魘」漢堡廣告已透過「臨床證實」會引發惡夢。在不同學術領域的 40 位專業人士署名支持下，Haar 為 DXE 撰寫的專欄在 2021 年 6 月刊出，內容提到：「社會急需積極的行動和新的保護政策，來阻止廣告商繼續操縱我們早已困擾不堪的意識及潛意識，保護大腦的最後一片淨土之一：我們的夢境。」

值得關注的原因：

各大品牌對於左右夢境的科技愈來愈有興趣：美國市場行銷協會（American Marketing Association）在 2021 年的研究指出，高達 77% 的美國行銷人員表示他們計畫在未來三年內於廣告中運用夢境技術。雖然目前並沒有相關的禁令加以管制，但有些消費者將此技術視為反烏托邦。在我們深入了解其科學技術之前，各品牌應謹慎使用「夢境行銷」。

40

擴增實境廣告

品牌正透過擴增實境來升級數位廣告。

擴增實境（Augmented reality，AR）逐漸成為市場主流，消費者也愈來愈有興趣在擴增實境中與品牌進行互動。根據 Statista 公司在 2021 年 8 月的研究，目前全球有 15 億擴增實境的活躍使用者，預計在 2025 年將達到 43 億人。值得注意的是，根據愛立信（Ericsson）在 2021 年 7 月的調查，70% 的消費者表示希望看到更多的擴增實境廣告。

各品牌開始採用擴增實境，來和數位消費族群互動。2021 年 11 月，福斯汽車（Volkswagen）在亞馬遜的紙箱外嵌入擴增實境廣告。只要一掃紙箱上的行動條碼，使用者便能透過擴增實境的駕駛體驗，深入了解福斯 2022 年的全新休旅車款 Taos。

WUNDERMAN THOMPSON　AR Labs WPP partnership with Snap

2021 年 9 月，Snap 和廣告巨頭 WPP 推出擴增實境的合作項目 AR Labs，為品牌提供擴增實境的行銷方案。AR Labs 將為 WPP 的客戶研發訂製計分卡，用來打造更有效率的廣告宣傳活動。2021 年 10 月，Snap 也成立新的創意工作室 Arcadia，目標是創造擴增實境廣告，並幫助品牌在 Snapchat 和其他數位平台上開發擴增實境的行銷模式與體驗。Arcadia 工作室已經與 Shake Shack 漢堡、寶僑美妝（P&G Beauty）和威訊通訊（Verizon）等公司展開合作。

未來的購物商場將充滿著漂浮在空中的擴增實境廣告。2021 年 7 月，資產管理公司 Brookfield Properties 和媒體業者 The Aria Network 合作，將擴增實境廣告引入商場中的開放空間。這項新的協議讓 The Aria Network 享有 Brookfield Properties 虛擬空間的獨家使用權，空間總面積超過 1.5 億平方英尺，涵蓋 100 個不同的地點。The Aria Network 將運用這些空間，讓品牌得以使用擴增實境來行銷，消費者可以透過手機來收看這類廣告。

「擴增實境在未來的行銷與商業領域扮演了重要角色。」WPP 戰略發展與夥伴關係執行副總裁 Sanja Partalo 表示。

值得關注的原因：

擴增實境廣告的出現，為數位行銷和廣告的新世代奠定了基礎，特別是消費者感興趣的互動廣告。

"

擴增實境
在未來的行銷與商務
扮演了重要角色。

41
食品&飲品
50

41

專屬特調自己採

以自然界為靈感的永續雞尾酒。

Visit Sweden's elderflower vinegar. Photography by Martin Vallin

調酒師利用從當地採集的原料，精心製作獨一無二的雞尾酒，提供消費者各式各樣的永續飲品。

2021 年 9 月，瑞典觀光局（Visit Sweden）宣布要將國內的重返自然之旅推廣至英國、美國與德國。以瑞典觀光局的「暢飲之國」計畫（Drinkable Country program）為基礎，新的「瑞典夏日滋味」廣告（Taste of Swedish Summer）展示了瑞典夏季可找到的雲杉芽和野花等 22 種天然原料，並介紹醃漬、發酵等食物保存方法以及創新食譜。瑞典觀光局與廣告公司 Forsman & Bodenfors 以及傳立媒體 Mindshare 合作，將行銷活動著重在當地的農產品。「暢飲之國」計畫鼓勵遊客盡情探索瑞典鄉間，也就是「世上最大的戶外酒吧」，並在全國 14 個地點安排當地導遊，協助旅客採集野莓和各種植物來製作他們的專屬特調。

烈酒品牌 Hangar 1 利用 2020 年納帕谷（Napa Valley）「玻璃大火」（Glass Fire）中受損的梅洛和馬爾貝克葡萄來製作伏特加。這款酒精濃度 40% 的 Smoke Point Vodka 由不宜釀製葡萄酒的葡萄蒸餾而成，帶有一絲八角和香草氣息，為伏特加增添了獨特的風味。隨後，該公司也將銷售收入捐給加州消防基金會（California Fire Foundation）。

值得關注的原因：

無論是強調回歸自然或再生利用，自然永續、精心特調的雞尾酒都都令人身心舒暢。當代的創新者以本地植物為原料，推出了創新的酒單，且這些在地供應食材所製成的特調也減少了資源的浪費。

Visit Sweden. Image by Niklas Nyman

42

喝出免疫力

在解渴的同時，養生族群也在增強自身的免疫力。

2021 年 10 月，洛杉磯的兒童零食品牌 Bitsy's 推出可提升兒童免疫力的飲料「Swish」，內含電解質、維他命 C 和鋅，可以加入孩子的水瓶中，隨時隨地增強免疫力。

2021 年秋季，荷蘭的 Ful Foods 公司則是利用微藻類螺旋藻，在英國推出 Ful Revive 系列富含維他命的飲料。飲料獨特的藍色是來自於螺旋藻中的天然抗氧化劑藻藍素，特色是能促進免疫力。除了增進健康，該品牌還聲稱微藻能吸收其本身重量 1.5 ~ 2 倍的碳，並進行光合作用、釋出氧氣，因此這款飲料能夠「改善氣候變遷」。

美國食品及飲料品牌優鮮沛（Ocean Spray）也開始研發健康商品。2020 年 11 月，優鮮沛創立了 B1U 功能飲料品牌，並推出一款名為「我需要免疫力」（I Need Immunity）的檸檬洋甘菊水。除了飲料之外，該品牌也在 2021 年 3 月推出了新的綜合果乾品牌 Fruit Medley，內含能為人體帶來各種益處的果乾；其中一款主打免疫力的產品 Immunity Blend 含有 β- 葡聚醣，經證實可提升免疫力。

隨著人們持續關注疾病預防，增強免疫力食品的全球市場也跟著成長（根據 Stratagem Market Insights 顧問公司指出，2021 年至 2028 年的年複合成長率預計將達 8.2%），提升免疫力的飲品成為創新的重點。

值得關注的原因：

根據 Innova 市場諮詢公司的 2020 年消費者調查報告，全球每十位消費者中就有六位希望透過食物和飲品來提升免疫力，這也讓品牌更有動力創造出對整體健康有益的產品。

42

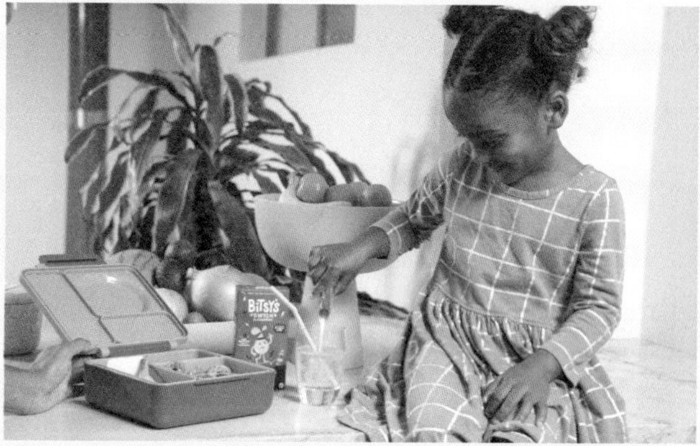

Left: Ocean Spray's B1U functional-beverage brand
Right: Bitsy's Swish is an immunity-boosting drink for kids

43

米其林瘋素食

純素飲食以庶民之姿晉升到上流社會。

Mushroom dish at Eleven Madison Park. Photography by Evan Sung

許多米其林餐廳和頂尖廚師正轉向純素飲食，讓蔬菜享有以往肉品在美食界的霸主地位。

米其林三星餐廳「麥迪遜公園 11 號」(Eleven Madison Park) 過去以鴨肉、龍蝦和肥肝佳餚聞名，在封城結束後的 2021 年 6 月重新開張，推出完全採用植物性食材的菜單。「對我來說，未來是植物性飲食的世代。」身兼主廚及老闆的 Daniel Humm 表示。

丹麥的米其林三星餐廳「天竺葵」(Geranium) 在 2021 年 11 月宣布將刪除菜單中的肉類料理。「天竺葵」在 10 月時獲選為世界排名第二的餐廳，如今他們將重心轉向植物性食材和海鮮為主的料理。「我認為我們需要全新的開始。」主廚兼合夥人 Rasmus

Kofoed 向《貝林時報》(Berlingske)表示。「我們揮手告別以往的招牌料理，我認為這是很重要的一步。」

英國倫敦的米其林餐廳 Gauthier Soho 去年 6 月時重新開張，推出了全蔬食菜單。ONA 餐廳(店名的三個字母代表 origine non-animale，意即無動物來源)在 2021 年 1 月成為法國第一間摘星的純素食餐廳。美國加州餐廳 SingleThread 幕後的米其林團隊，在 2021 年 5 月宣布將成立一間沒有肉類料理的休閒餐廳。

値得關注的原因：

知名主廚與餐廳老闆正將純素飲食提升為高雅精緻的用餐體驗。

Left: Tonburi dish at Eleven Madison Park. Photography by Evan Sung
Right: Geranium. Photography by Claes Bech-Poulsen

44

未來咖啡

繼人造肉和人造海鮮之後，咖啡有可能是下一個在實驗室誕生的產物。

2021 年 9 月，芬蘭科技研究院（VTT Technical Research Centre）宣布他們成功製造出第一杯「人造咖啡」，無論香氣還是口感都和正常的咖啡沒有兩樣，且毋需種植任何咖啡作物。這款咖啡是在實驗室的生物反應器中透過細胞培養而成，鋼製容器裡裝滿了富含營養物質的培養液。

「品嚐第一杯人造咖啡的感覺讓人相當興奮。」該研究團隊的負責人 Heiko Rischer 博士說。「預計在四年後就能進行量產，並獲得監管機關的批准。」

Coffee produced in a bioreactor through cellular agriculture by VTT Research

發明人造咖啡的誘因和發明人造肉、人造海鮮類似：全世界對咖啡的需求與日俱增，為地球的自然資源帶來極大的負擔。根據 Mordor Intelligence 市場調查，全球咖啡市場在 2020 年的市值超過了 1,020 億美元。舉凡咖啡豆、咖啡粉、即溶咖啡，到咖啡包、咖啡膠囊，咖啡市場不斷推陳出新，競爭激烈。

隨著世界各地的咖啡產量及需求量不斷提升，人們開始關注森林砍伐和咖啡加工過程造成的河川污染問題。傳統的咖啡作物生長在樹蔭之下，隨著需求大幅提升，咖啡農開始砍伐林木，以種植出一排排收益較高的咖啡作物。科學家警告，未來氣候變遷也可能導致咖啡栽種面積縮減，特別是衣索比亞等地的高級品種，因此人們開始尋找能取代咖啡豆的替代方案。

Rischer 表示，未來仍須進行加工和配方的研究，並通過監管機關核准。「即便如此，我們已證明實驗室培育咖啡是可行的。」他補充道。

值得關注的原因：

科學家已經可以在實驗室培育出動物和植物細胞，但培育過程相當辛苦且費用昂貴，也容易引發消費者對「科學怪食」（Frankenfood，由《科學怪人》中的 Frankenstein 和 food 所組成的複合字）的恐懼。世上第一款人造肉是由矽谷公司 Eat Just 生產的雞塊，雖然在 2020 年底於新加坡取得銷售許可，但之後仍無法拓展至其他市場。咖啡則沒有這種包袱。對於這些將人造咖啡商業化的品牌，最大的考驗在於是否能訂出合理的價格，讓消費者願意每天掏錢喝杯人造咖啡。

Coffee produced in a bioreactor through cellular agriculture by VTT Research

45

環保釀酒愛地球

全球烈酒品牌紛紛立下碳中和目標來應對氣候變遷。

烈酒品牌正在改造他們的生產過程，以追求永續、減少浪費，藉此對抗氣候變遷。除了 Air Company 和 Bespoken Spirits 等新的碳中和酒廠外，傳統烈酒公司也承諾將透過營運改革為地球盡一份心力。

2021 年 9 月，帝亞吉歐（Diageo）在北美設立旗下第一間碳中和酒廠，目標是在 2030 年前全面採用再生電力，不再使用化石燃料進行生產，並採用虛擬測量技術。另外，該酒廠也提供 30 個全職工作機會以支持社區，甚至 100% 採購當地非基因改造玉米。帝亞吉歐集團在 2020 年宣布將於 2030 年實現淨零碳排放的目標，作為其烈酒改革倡議「2030 社會：進步精神」（Society 2030: Spirit of Progress initiative）的行動方案。目前，帝亞吉歐旗下的酒廠如歐本（Oban）和皇家藍勳（Royal Lochnagar）已達成碳中和目標。

Air Company 則是捕集空氣中的二氧化碳，將其轉化成酒精，並在過程中多捕集一磅的碳。Air Company 在 2020 年推出此技術後，也在 2021 年 8 月拿下美國太空總署碳轉化競賽（NASA CO_2 Conversion Challenge）首獎。

絕對伏特加（Absolut Vodka）在 2021 年 5 月宣布將改革生產過程，目標是 2025 年後不再使用任何化石燃料。絕對伏特加領先業界，早在 2013 年就宣布達到碳中和，生產過程運用 85% 的再生能源，達成零垃圾填埋，並將衍生的副產品重新用作燃料或動物飼料。

值得關注的原因：

隨著知名烈酒公司加入對抗氣候變遷的陣營，食品與飲品產業正逐漸減少生產過程的廢棄物和碳排量。

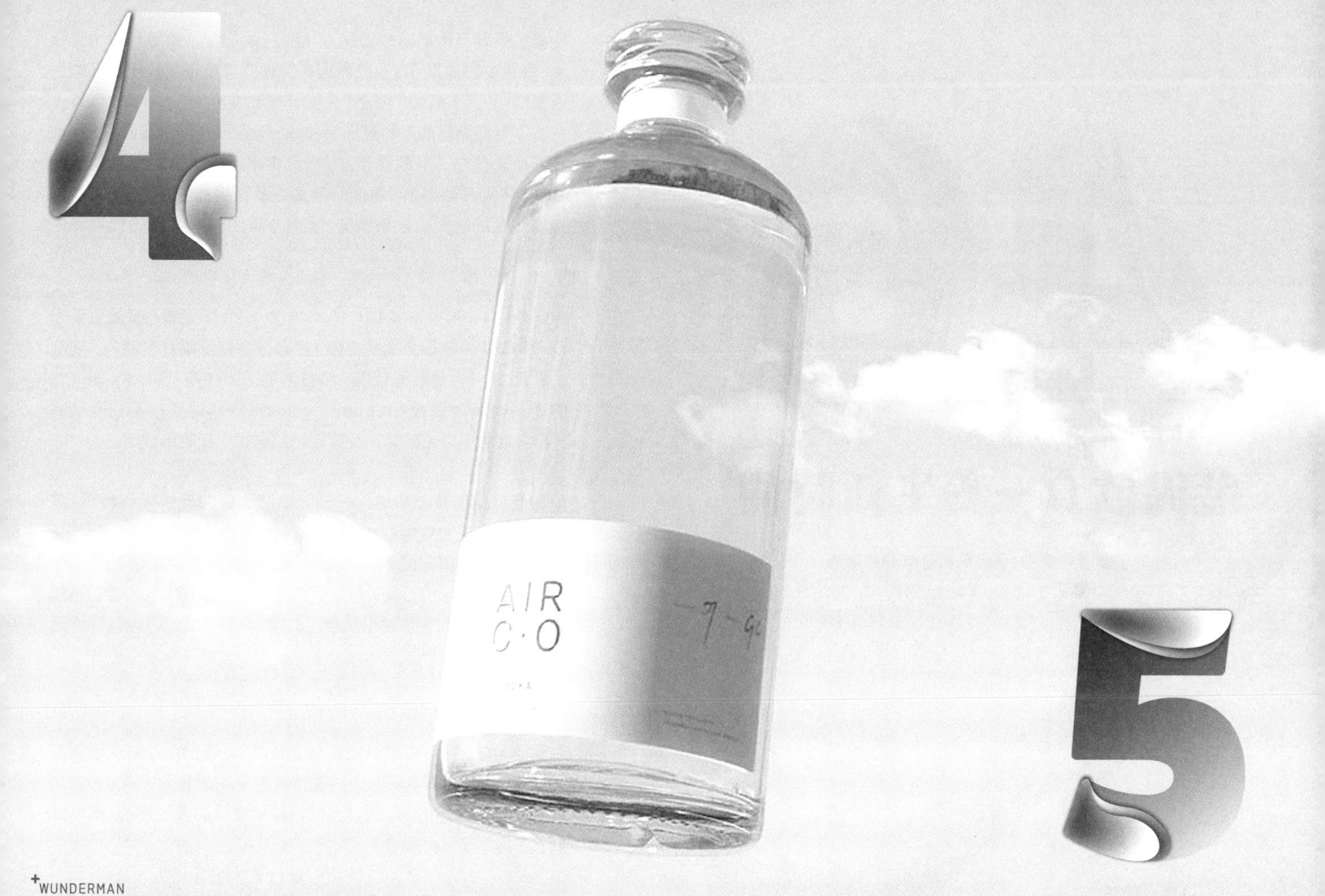

Air Company's recaptured CO2 vodka

46

藍區飲食－養生新時尚

為了健康與養生，各品牌與社群開始擁抱「藍區」（Blue Zone）飲食。

相較於世界其他地區的居民，「藍區」的居民活得更長壽也更健康，種種的跡象顯示，主要原因在於他們擁有各式各樣良好的生活習慣。五大「藍區」包含了希臘伊卡利亞島、日本沖繩島、義大利薩丁尼亞半島的奧利亞斯特拉省、美國加州的洛馬林達區，以及哥斯大黎加的尼科亞半島，研究指出這些地區的居民能融入社群，注重集體關懷、適度的飲食以及永續的生活方式。如今，其他地區的居民也能學習讓「藍區」居民保持健康的飲食與生活習慣。

Bush's Beans 在 2021 年 10 月推出一系列「藍區」有機蔬菜配料，能夠加在餐點與湯品之中。豆類被各個藍區社群視為「明星長壽食物」，也是藍區社群合作生產的主力作物。Bush's Beans 的資深行銷副總裁 Stephen Palacios 表示這次的系列產品將「讓各地的所有人都能像長壽聖地的居民一樣吃出健康」。

位於亞利桑那州土桑市的一個社區將廢棄的學校重新利用，搖身一變為社區食物中心，靈感來源便是藍區社群所展現的合作精神。另一個小型團體 The Midtown Farm 則是在當地社區種植平價作物，作為拉丁裔與原住民居民的食物來源。他們透過雨水回收系統和共同工作坊來吸引社群參與，真正實踐了藍區的生活方式。

值得關注的原因：

有意識地生活、注重節制以及融入社群，藍區的生活方式逐漸成為主流，因為世界各地的人試圖追求更全面的養生方式。由於消費者愈來愈注重健康，他們也開始尋找集體的養生實踐，而藍區飲食正提供了一種解答。

Bush's Beans的全新系列產品將「讓各地的所有人都能像長壽聖地的居民一樣吃出健康」。

Bush's Beans Blue Zones Zesty Black Bean organic plant-based meal toppings

47

2022 最熱門食材

2022 年盛行的新食材有益我們的健康及環境。

多年生小麥（Kernza）

這是一款友善環境、永續且經改良化的小麥品種，由美國的土地研究所（The Land Institute）培育而成並享有專利，如今也推出啤酒與麥片的相關製品。傳統的小麥為一年生穀物，需要每年重新播種，而 Kernza 是多年生植物，播種一次就能有多次收成。此外，Kernza 還能滋養土壤，減少周圍植物對肥料的需求，也是天然的碳捕捉器。

2021 年 9 月，Patagonia Provisions 與奧勒岡州波特蘭的釀酒廠 Hopworks Urban Brewery 合作，推出第三款以 Kernza 釀製的啤酒。食品大廠通用磨坊（General Mills）旗下的 Cascadian Farm 也利用 Kernza 製作烘烤蜂蜜麥片。

Kernza. Image courtesy of the Land Institute

燈籠果（Peruvian gooseberry）

燈籠果又稱為秘魯苦蘵、黃金莓，是原產於安地斯山脈的漿果，味道又苦又甜。這種水果因為有益健康而愈來愈受歡迎，其中包含大量的抗氧化劑、維他命 A 和 C 以及礦物質。Freehand 飯店品牌旗下最新的拉美餐廳 Comodo 在 2021 年10月於紐約開幕，最近也推出了燈籠果料理。

茶籽油

在亞洲生產且使用了幾個世紀的茶籽油，近期成了風靡西方的食用油。茶籽油因為味道淡、發煙點高，又稱為「東方的橄欖油」。由原產於東亞的開花植物大果油茶的種籽製成，茶籽油內含豐富的抗氧化劑、Omega-3、礦物質和維他命 E、A 和 B。創立於 2021 年 10 月的新品牌 Yóu Yóu 正將茶籽油引入美國市場，並同時維護茶籽油的歷史傳統。共同創辦人 Anthony Chen 告訴《Well & Good》，他們花了八年的時間才製作出第一瓶 Yóu Yóu 茶籽油。「我們和湖南地區的生產者合作，這項技術已在當地流傳了好幾個世代。」

Left: Comodo at the Freehand. Photography by Gentl and Hyers
Right: Yóu Yóu tea seed oil

48

加速陳年新技術

既然能在幾天之內喝到陳年好酒，何必等上數年？

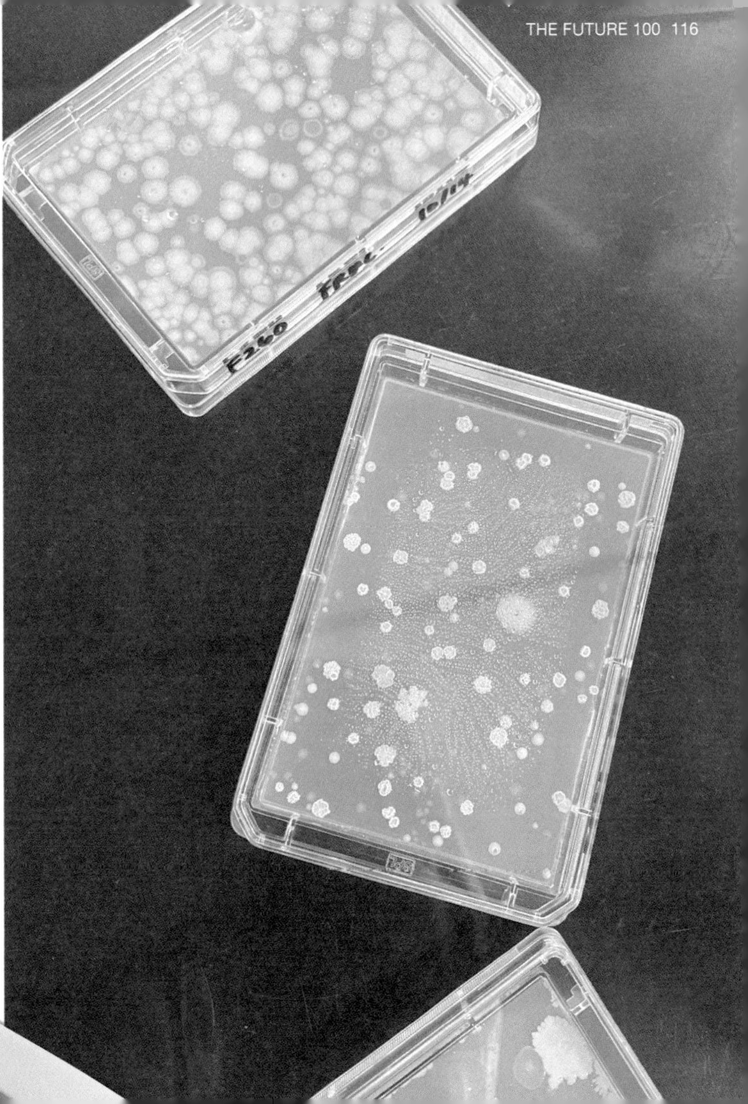

Kingdom Supercultures

烈酒公司 Bespoken Spirits 希望透過環保永續的新熟成方式，顛覆步調緩慢、浪費資源且過時的烈酒產業。透過現代科技、材料科學和數據分析，這間加州公司在一週內便能生產出香氣、顏色和風味都屬精緻上乘的烈酒，相較之下，傳統的威士忌熟成往往需要數年的時間。

加速熟成的過程涉及 200 多億種不同的配方，撼動了全球的烈酒市場，根據市調公司 Research & Markets 的數據，其市價預計從 2020 年的 1,430 億成長至 2025 年的 2,090 億。「從一開始，我們就想要顛覆這個產業，但目的是幫助產業成長。」與 Martin Janousek 共同創立 Bespoken Spirits 的 Stu Aaron 向偉門智威智庫表示。

> 從一開始，
> 我們就想要顛覆這個產業，
> 但目的是幫助產業成長。

位於紐約的生物設計公司 Kingdom Supercultures 希望透過科學來加速植物性食品、飲品和天然產品的發酵過程。這間新創公司是由 Kendall Dabaghi 和 Ravi Sheth 在 2020 年設立，目前已推出許多新口味的醬料，並被 Eleven Madison Park 和 Gramercy Tavern 等米其林餐廳搶購一空。在 2021 年 10 月，該公司更獲得 2,500 萬美元的 A 輪融資。

值得關注的原因：

野心勃勃的新創公司顛覆耗時的酒類熟成與食物發酵製程，希望提升生產效率及產量，並探索新的味覺體驗。

Bespoken Spirits

49

風土新產出

氣候變遷為全球農業帶來巨大的影響，雖然肥沃的土壤變得貧瘠不堪，但同時北方也出現了新的農地。

雖然氣候變遷造成全球農業浩劫，但原先寒冷的氣候區溫度升高，也讓一些品牌看見了新的契機。

葡萄酒產量在北方出現大幅的成長，因為溫度上升讓該區越來越適合種植備受喜愛的葡萄品種。在加拿大各地，新的葡萄酒莊如雨後春筍般出現，根據《Wine Industry Advisor》引用的聯合國糧農組織數據，當地在過去二十年的產量已增加超過 75%。在 2019 年，加拿大卑詩省酒廠 CheckMate Artisanal Winery 的 2015 年 Little Pawn 夏多內葡萄酒獲得葡萄酒作家、侍酒師以及作家 John Schreiner 的滿分肯定，創下加拿大史上最佳紀錄。該酒莊的成立是受到該區氣候變遷的影響，讓當地能夠種植品質優良的舊世界葡萄品種。

The Morettino family's Sicilan-grown coffee, served in antique Arabian coffeeware

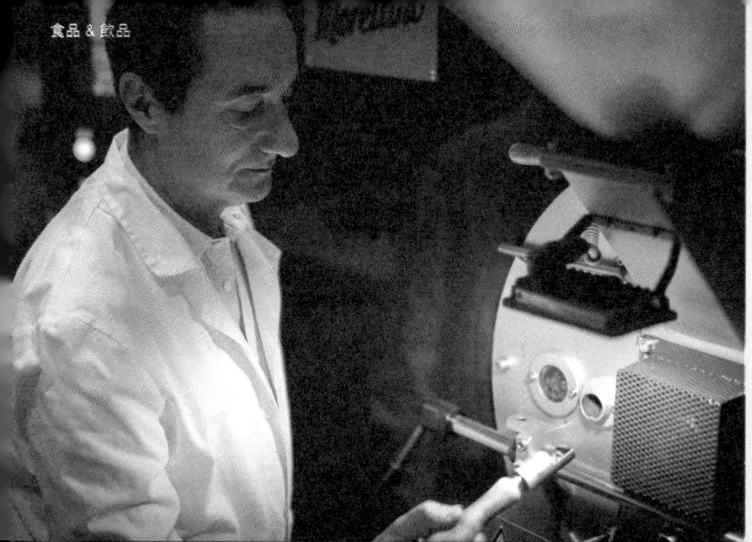

WUNDERMAN THOMPSON

Top: Alberto Morettino
Bottom: Coffee plant in Palermo. Images courtesy of the Morettino family

其他農作物也開始向北方移動。2020 年 12 月，《紐約時報》（The New York Times）和非營利媒體 ProPublica 描述了俄羅斯地貌的變化，由於氣溫升高，該國東部地區的不毛之地如今成了肥沃的農地。俄羅斯現在能在更多地區種植大豆、小麥和玉米，未來可望成為大型的糧食生產國。

雖然過往義大利並不屬於寒冷氣候帶，但當地也開始出現新的農產品。西西里島的農夫 Andrea Passanis 如今在他祖父的土地上種植酪梨，取代了以往的葡萄。隨著天氣變得越來越熱，不再適合種植葡萄，當地卻為酪梨、荔枝和百香果提供完美的生長環境。Passanisi 致力於西西里酪梨的永續實踐，透過順應不斷變化的氣候，來繼承農耕的傳統。2021 年，另一個西西里作物終於開花結果－咖啡豆。Morettino 家族在嘗試了三十年後，終於成功獲得第一批的咖啡豆收成。Morettino 家族的最終目標是創立土生土長的義大利咖啡品牌。

值得關注的原因：

氣候變遷迫使農夫和農業企業家必須適應和接受新的作物，而這些作物在十年前根本無法在當地生長。新的風土條件很有可能徹底改變我們對食物傳統和原產地的想像。

50

跟著味蕾去旅行

為了替理想的旅遊生活尋找出路，旅人將目光轉向廚房。

Counter of Joy 餐廳敬邀各位食客「讓味蕾恣意暢遊在中國的山巒、西非的海岸線、土耳其市區的麵包店以及不列顛群島的鄉村牧場。」自 2021 年 11 月 11 日至 12 月 18 日止，Old Selfridges Hotel 的盛宴嘉年華（Great Feast festival）會中，由米其林星廚推出七道菜的味覺饗宴，讓倫敦的食客踏上環遊世界的美食之旅。

倫敦人若想以更平易近人的方式了解外國美食，不妨逛逛城裡隨處可見的美國糖果店。據《NBC》報導，在倫敦著名的牛津街（Oxford Street），不到一平方英里的範圍內，就有九間專門販售美國糖果的大型糖果店，例如 2021 年初開張的 American Candy Land 和 Candy Surprise。

2021 年 6 月出版的食譜書《哥倫比亞：重新發現哥倫比亞靈魂深處的食譜與儀式》（The Colombiana: A Rediscovery of Recipes and Rituals from the Soul of Columbia，暫譯）帶領讀者和家中大廚探索這個南美國家。除了傳統的哥倫比亞食譜外，該書還包含主持宴會的妙招、知名藝術家的作品照片（包含陶藝家、紡織藝術家、時尚與珠寶設計師），以及哥倫比亞女性美食英雄的簡介，讓讀者深入了解哥倫比亞的文化與餐飲。

值得關注的原因：

對於許多人來說，出國旅行仍難以實現或不具吸引力，因此人們選擇踏上味覺之旅，這也推動了一波以全球為靈感的飲食體驗。

WUNDERMAN THOMPSON The Great Feast by Counter of Joy

51
美容
60

51

標籤新顯學

美妝保養品牌開始重新思考產品標示內容，公開呈現產品對環境造成的影響。

有越來越多美妝保養品牌開始在產品包裝上闡明生產流程的永續性，藉此滿足消費者對環境影響資訊透明的期許。

2021 年 9 月，幾家知名的美妝品牌聯合開發了一套系統，用以追蹤自家產品的環境影響和永續指數。這套系統不會獨厚特定品牌，消費者能清楚了解手中產品帶來的環境影響，也能透過產品標示來比較此計畫中各品牌的品項。目前參與的品牌包含聯合利華（Unilever）、漢高（Henkel）、萊雅（L'Oréal）、Natura & Co 和 LVMH，他們的目標是要支持永續發展，並邀請更多品牌加入，以實現美妝產業的資訊透明化。

美妝保養品牌 Tata Harper 的幾款產品獲得永續林業倡議（Sustainable Forestry Initiative）標籤，代表它們的包材符合永續和責任開採原則，且該包裝也可回收。可回收與否是很明確的指標，也可能影響注重永續議題的消費者的購買決策。

2021 年間，保養品牌 Cocokind 也為提升產品標示的資訊透明度下足功夫。他們在每件產品標示上加入一組資訊欄位，呈現該產品的永續指數和碳足跡，讓消費者可以清楚看到各產品對環境的影響。

值得關注的原因：

越來越多美妝保養品牌選擇在產品標示上呈現出環境影響資訊，公開他們在永續實踐方面的成績。消費者對此亦相當關注，表示這些倡議對市場而言也很重要。

> “越來越多美妝保養品牌
> 選擇在產品標示上
> 呈現出環境影響資訊。

Left: The Henkel brand collaborated in the development of a brand-agnostic system to track the environmental impact of beauty products. Right: Image courtesy of Unilever

52

明日之星礦物

肌膚保養融入了金屬元素，品牌從印度和亞洲的古老美容秘方汲取靈感，將貴金屬融入旗下產品的保養配方中。

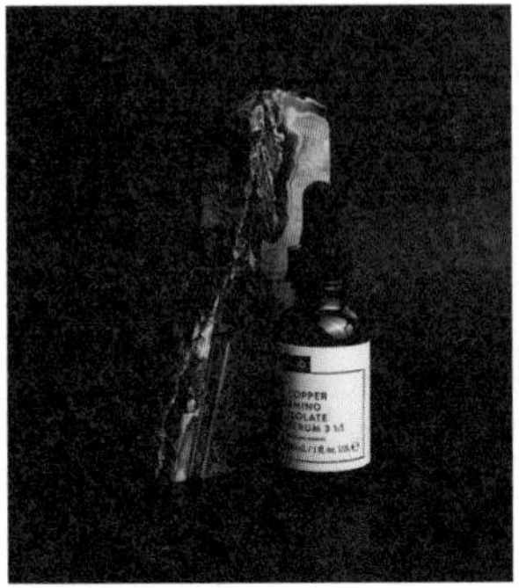

Niod（The Ordinary 的姐妹牌）在 2021 年 9 月推出藍銅胜肽保養精華液，該成分可促進傷口癒合、對抗發炎反應，對肌膚生成具有重要功效，也能促進膠原蛋白和彈性蛋白的增生，成為肌膚保養界的明星成分。

波蘭熱賣的藥妝品牌 Tolpa 在 2021 年 7 月推出一款導入銀微粒的面膜，具有去角質、抗菌、改善色素沈澱等功效。2021 年 5 月，African Botanics 推出修護乳霜 Silver Rescue Cream，內含具有抗菌、修護功能的銀膠。

值得關注的原因：

度過兵荒馬亂的兩年後，消費者在自我照護方面尋求的是能讓他們倍感呵護的儀式感，礦物保養正巧符合他們追求的奢華寵愛感受。

Left: Copper peptide serum by Niod
Right: Silver face mask by Tolpa

53

美容保養不再「正常」

品牌正在逐步重塑美容產業。

2021 年 3 月，聯合利華（Unilever）宣布要在旗下所有美容和個人護理品牌的包裝和廣告中，刪除代表「正常／一般／中性」的「normal」一詞，藉此促進多元包容價值。此一作為彰顯了聯合利華的全球影響力，也反映出消費者不斷演變的價值觀。

「每天有 10 億人在使用我們的美容和個人護理產品，而接觸到我們廣告的人又更多，所以我們有能力為人們的生活帶來真正的改變。」聯合利華美容和個人護理事業部總裁 Sunny Jain 如此說道。「我們致力於對抗會帶來傷害的規範和刻板印象，為美麗塑造更廣泛、更多元的定義。」除了刪除「正常」一詞外，該品牌還表示他們不會對廣告模特兒的照片過度修圖。

歌手 Harry Styles 流動的性別氣質廣為人知，他在 2021 年 11 月推出全新美妝品牌 Pleasing，首波主打商品為四款指甲油、一支滾珠眼唇雙效精華以及一款精華液。品牌廣告的主角有男有女，因為 Harry Styles 希望能為「社群中每個獨特的你發聲」，並致力於「消除二元迷思」。

露得清（Neutrogena）於 2021 年 4 月公開「為所有膚色存在」（For People With Skin）計畫。該品牌成立於 1930 年，他們希望抗衡各種造成肌膚保養不平等的因素，包括社經地位、種族、健康護理產品的取得難度等。時任總經理的 Kerry Sullivan 對《女裝日報》（WWD）表示：「我們想要為所有膚色、所有的人存在。」

值得關注的原因：

彰顯多元價值的全新詞組重新界定了美妝保養產業，帶來更加個人化的想像，對美的解讀也更多元。「所有人都適用」的美妝思維已被屏棄，且再也回不去了。

Images courtesy of Pleasing

54

妝怪不怪

以實驗性妝容表達自我。

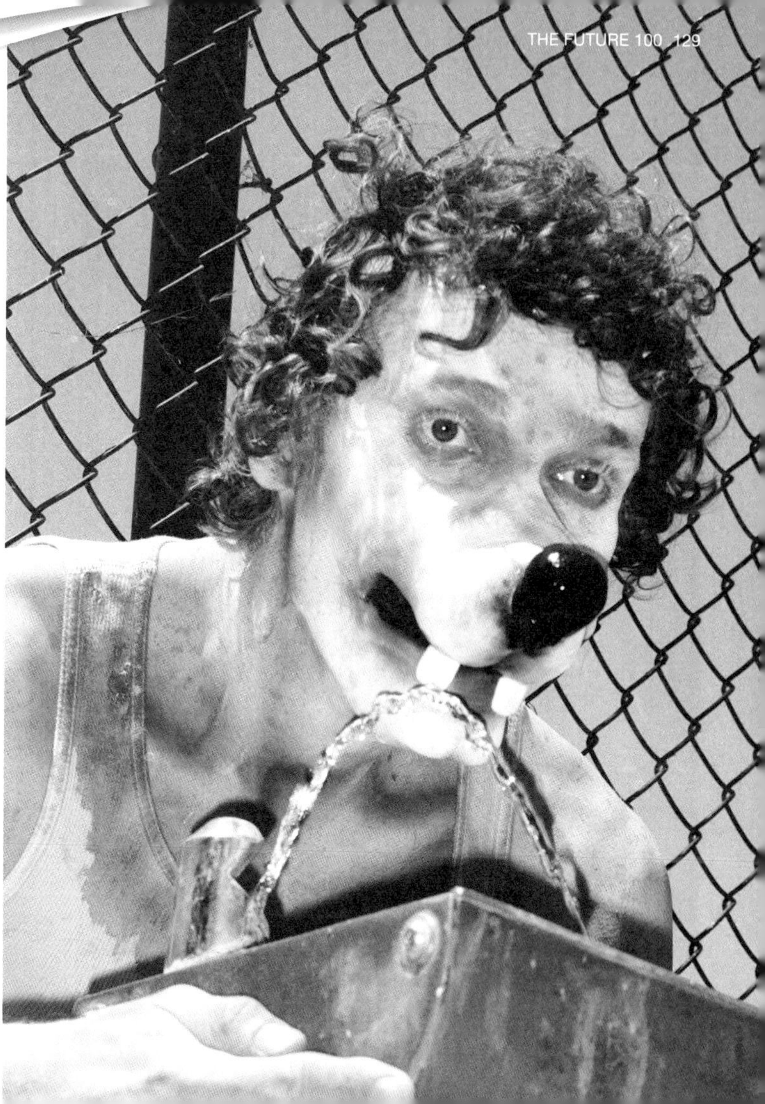

Image from the first issue of Jackson Bowley's Circus magazine

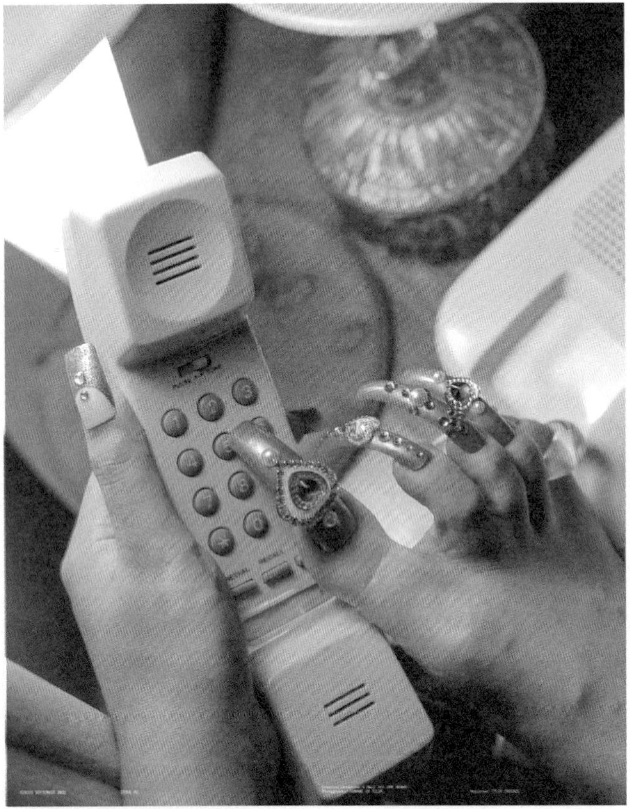

經歷過去幾年的辛苦生活後，美妝愛好者此刻在找尋大玩特玩與實驗的機會。《Circus》是新型美妝刊物，希望「大家不用看得太認真」。此刊物於 2021 年 9 月發表，強調荒謬和玩樂之美。《Dazed Beauty》將其評為「輕鬆的美妝平台，專為超級怪咖存在」。刊物中充滿各種前衛的打扮，從眼花撩亂的瘋狂牙齒，到酷似壓克力顏料的愚蠢足部美甲，再到小丑般的樣貌。

「現在每件事好像都太嚴肅了，」《Circus》的創作者兼總編 Jackson Bowley 對《iD》如此表示。「我只是想做一本好玩、簡單、受到矚目的刊物。然後呢，我也想做一本可以透過美妝圖像來真正推動一些事情的美妝雜誌，包含我們看待這些圖像的方式，以及我們可以用這些圖像來做什麼。」

據《Vogue》報導，在 Schiaparelli 的 2022 春夏線上時裝發表中，模特兒的超現實妝扮「怪得恰到好處」，有人做了鍍金的延甲飾物、戴上傘型帽，也有人提著以臉孔為主題的包包。

值得關注的原因：

消費者的審美觀點再次解放，追求狂野的自我表達。現在，他們拿起刷具不見得是為了「變美」，而是在追求有趣、實驗性的妝容，挑戰創意的界線。

Image from the first issue of Jackson Bowley's Circus magazine

55

元宇宙玩美

電競業者在遊戲中展示虛擬妝效與實體美妝產品，
提高玩家的參與度，也為美妝品牌與
創意人才帶來機會。

遊戲玩家以虛擬化妝品來妝點虛擬替身，除了為遊戲增添創意，也讓角色更有個性。就算是《俠盜獵車手》（Grand Theft Auto）或《要塞英雄》（Fortnite）這類血腥或動作類的遊戲，玩家還是會選配虛擬時裝和妝髮來展現個人特色，也因此更能投入遊戲。「裝扮自己的角色可以讓你進一步發揮想像力」《黎明死線》（Dead by Daylight）的執行製作人 Jo-Ashley Robert 對《Vogue》如此說到，「而且這越來越受歡迎。」

Nars、Gucci 等傳統美妝品牌也開始推出虛擬化妝品供玩家使用。Nars 在 2021 年 10 月，為 Drest 這款應用程式新增 30 項虛擬產品，並邀請虛擬模特兒展示產品；Gucci 也在 10 月為 Drest 的美妝模式增加 29 款虛擬化妝品，產品組合超過 40 種，且可以在應用程式中直接透過連結來購買實體商品。

《模擬市民 4》「水療日」組合包在 2021 年 9 月美麗升級。玩家可以選擇「細心呵護」模式，讓角色去做瑜伽、冥想、做臉和新款美甲，擴充包裡還包含 100 種以上的膚色、髮型、妝容。

> 玩家以虛擬的高級時裝和妝髮來展現個人特色。

3D 數位藝術家 Nathalie Nguyen 以 Photoshop 為其自畫像加上不同的特效，包含受外星人啟發的數位美妝效果和 3D 美甲，模糊觀眾眼中現實和虛擬的界線。Nguyen 以實體物件搭配 3D 渲染妝容的美學重新定義真實，也凸顯出我們的網路形象和現實生活有何不同。

值得關注的原因：

數位美妝已經從 CGI 模特兒 Perl 的 AI 美妝產品線再次升級（我們早在《改變未來的 100 件事：2019 年全球百大趨勢》的〈另類審美：CGI 虛擬美人〉章節中就已預探此一趨勢），品牌開始將實體商品搬上數位舞台。遊戲玩家熱衷元美妝的同時，品牌也開始在元宇宙找尋可以銷售、推廣產品的機會。

Gucci Beauty added 29 virtual products to Drest's Beauty Mode feature

56

有酸才夠美

保養品牌鎖定三大酸類成分及其功效。

酸類保養佔領美容櫃位，因此我們想將焦點帶到 2022 年重要的三大酸類成分上。

傳明酸

Topicals 於 2021 年發表首款產品 Faded 亮白潔淨精華，內含傳明酸來修復曬傷或傷疤。傳明酸可防止黑色素沉澱與黑斑生成，調理膚質使其均勻透亮。

My Topicals Faded serum with tranexamic acid

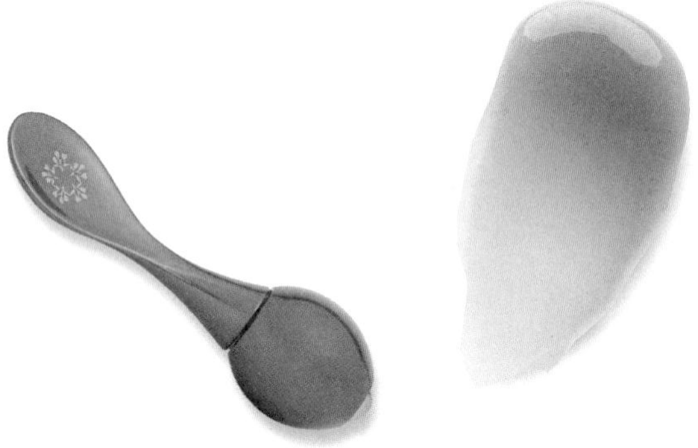

杜鵑花酸

2021 年 10 月，肌膚保養品牌 Bloomeffects 推出黑色鬱金香系列保養品，其中的眼部凝膠以杜鵑花酸為主成份，可以讓眼周肌膚更緊實，減少黑眼圈、浮腫與眼周細紋。

葡萄糖酸

Juvia's Place 於 2021 年 9 月推出全新保養系列，在去角質棉片中加入葡萄糖酸，讓肌膚淨白透亮。嬌生（Johnson & Johnson）在 4 月發表的研究報告中特別提及葡萄糖酸，指出該成分可以讓肌膚吸飽水份、去角質、抑制黑色素生成，敏感膚質的人也適用。

值得關注的原因：

酸類成分是最新的美容熱搜關鍵字，在美妝商品的陳列架上，也早已是相當受歡迎的新品項。

Black Tulip Eye Treatment with azelaic acid by Bloomeffects

57

適性包裝

美妝品牌為多元的消費客群提供適性的產品包裝設計。

美容與保健業者重新包裝品牌，提供對肢體障礙或行動不便的消費者更友善的產品包裝。

寶僑（Procter & Gamble）於 2021 年 11 月公開發表歐蕾（Olay）新生高效系列護膚霜的新包裝，使用容易開啟的瓶蓋，讓過去不便使用該產品的消費者也能輕鬆取用。新的瓶蓋多了側翼並且加高，讓蓋子更易抓取；產品標示的色彩對比度也調高，使內容更易讀；包裝上還以點字符號寫上「護膚霜」的字樣。歐蕾也和其他業者分享該設計，希望鼓勵更多品牌改用這類包裝，讓各家產品都能更符合無障礙原則。

聯合利華（Unilever）於 2021 年 3 月打造全球首款專為體香膏設計的適性包裝，旗下體香膏品牌 The Degree 與身障人士合作，共同開發出真正符合身障人士需求的產品。他們的產品可以單手

Easy Open Lid by Olay

使用，瓶身加上收納用的提手，磁吸瓶蓋可輕鬆替換，包裝上還有以點字符號標示的產品標籤。此概念由偉門智威共融設計與數位輔助全球總監 Christina Mallon 首先提出，她告訴偉門智威智庫：「每個消費者一生中都有可能經歷幾次不便，但多數產品設計都沒有把這些障礙納入考量。」

同樣在 3 月，沐浴與身體保養品牌 Cleanlogic 重新打造產品包裝，為全產品加入點字符號，產品的部分利潤也會捐給支持視障者的機構，包括美國盲人基金會（American Foundation for the Blind）。

值得關注的原因：

「品牌必須考量適性包裝，才能真正以消費者為核心」，Mallon 如此說道。消費者開始要求各界美妝業者提供更易近用的包裝設計，品牌也採納此建議，重新設計產品包裝來服務行動不便的使用者。

> 品牌重新設計產品包裝
> 來服務行動不便的使用者。

58

微劑量保養

皮膚保養專家以少量的有效成分來完成「少即是多」的全新保養程序。

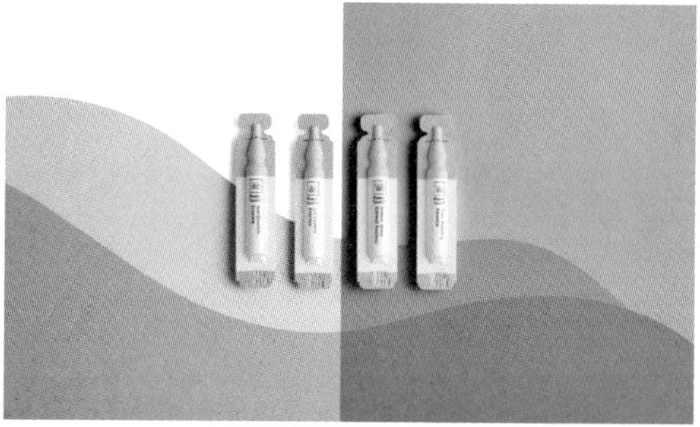

微劑量成為肌膚保養的選項之一。美妝保養愛好者深受吸引，在肌膚上搽以較少量或者精萃後的成分，並改以長期效果為訴求，以避免強烈的副作用。

保養品牌 The Wo 主打一系列「單次份」的產品，氣泡袋裡的內容物剛好是一次的用量，讓消費者可以根據每日膚況來打造自己的保養流程，也只需購買符合需求用量的產品。

訂閱制保養品牌 Skin & Me 搭起消費者與皮膚科專家的橋樑，皮膚科醫師提供低劑量或劑量合適的客製處方，讓微劑量保養變得輕鬆簡便，且也能納入專業意見。

Wō packages its skincare products in single-application blister packs

WUNDERMAN THOMPSON Spectacle Skincare's Performance Crème comes in a microdosed formulation

Spectacle Skincare 在旗下乳霜產品 Performance Crème 中使用微劑量配方，裡面加入視黃醛、葡萄糖酸和維他命 C。少量的成分不會致敏，因此可長期使用以達最佳效果，且不會因為持續使用而讓效力減弱。Spectacle Skincare 的共同創辦人與調劑師 Andre Condit 告訴偉門智威智庫，美妝消費者「要把保養當成馬拉松而不是賽跑，肌膚保養的步調應該要緩慢、穩定，這是一趟長達一生的旅程。」

保養精萃最近變得很受歡迎，更是微劑量保養的熱門選項之一。這些低濃度的保養精萃可以添加到日常保養品項當中（例如可以加入保濕霜中混合使用），增強肌膚保養功效。理膚寶水（La Roche-Posay）販售 0.3% 的低劑量視黃醇，而寶拉珍選（Paula's Choice）則推出維他命 C 強化精萃，可以逐滴添加到保濕霜中使用。

值得關注的原因：

Andre Condit 提到，微劑量保養重回舞台，是因為這是「導入關鍵營養成分、前導物質和活化細胞最有效的日常做法。生物利用度高，各種膚質的適應狀態最佳，刺激度也最低。」長期使用低劑量保養品所帶來的功效，吸引了追求風險低、效果好的消費族群。

59

共融美髮

以往髮品並未重視不同人種的髮絲特性，但現在商品架上出現養護不同髮質的商品，而且銷售成績極佳。

WUNDERMAN THOMPSON

The Pressed Roots hair salon in Dallas, Texas

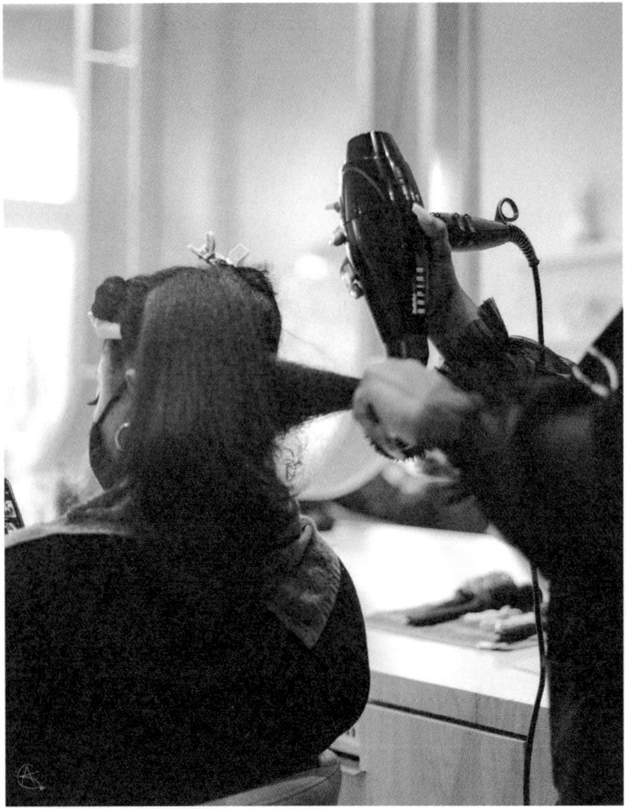

髮型師與名人開始擁護多元共融的美髮生態，希望護髮商品可以符合所有人的需求，也更易取得。髮品市場經常排除特殊髮絲的需求，黑人女性於是開始打造非洲中心的髮廊，成立專屬沙龍，並為有色人種尋覓合適的產品。

位於德州達拉斯的 Pressed Roots 先前曾經開設過快閃店，後來於 2021 年 10 月正式開業，致力為非洲髮質提供專業的吹整和頭髮護理服務。創辦人 Piersten Gaines 畢業於哈佛商學院，她想為供應嚴重不足的市場推出這項服務，並對《Wallpaper》表示，她正在「改寫美容美髮業，因為過去幾十年來，它們一直忽略其他人種的特殊髮質。」

Tracee Ellis Ross 的 Pattern Beauty 髮品於 2021 年 9 月在絲芙蘭（Sephora）上架，商品流通範圍因此變得更廣也更易取得。Ross 對《InStyle》表示，Pattern 的成功挑戰了「黑人護髮只是小眾市場」的思維。

Gabrielle Union 的 Flawless 系列產品現在可以從沃爾瑪（Walmart）和亞馬遜（Amazon）入手。他們與知名髮型師 Larry Sims 共同開發 Flawless 系列商品，內含 12 款專為非洲髮質設計的奢華滋潤髮品，包括洗髮乳、護髮乳、護髮精華等等。

值得關注的原因：

品牌的論述持續圍繞多元、共融等議題，新的品牌也加入戰場，為黑人品牌提供機會與服務。店家賣起多元髮品，新型護髮服務也如雨後春筍出現，為特殊髮質護髮市場帶來全新局面。

The Pressed Roots hair salon in Dallas, Texas

The Pressed Roots hair salon in Dallas, Texas

60

美甲新創奇招

科技新創公司正以美甲機器人顛覆美甲生態。

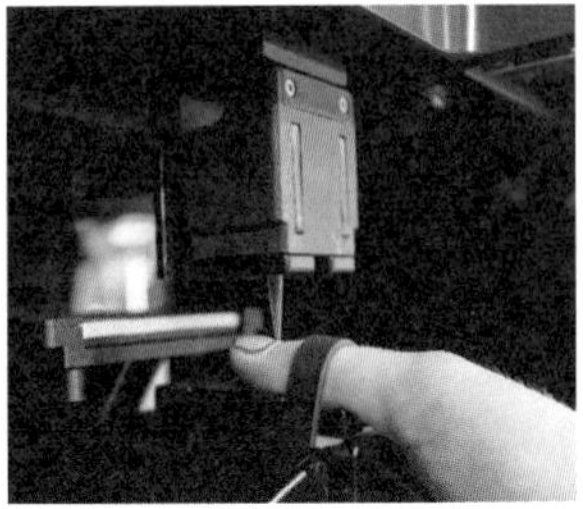

「不會出錯，不會變慢，不會聊些有的沒的。」這是總部位於舊金山的 Clockwork 所做出的商品承諾，聲稱該產品是世界上第一部美甲機器人。這款產品於 2021 年 3 月推出，且這家美甲科技新創在同年秋季也於紐約洛克斐勒中心（Rockefeller Center）開設實體店面。便利、精準是 Clockwork 的兩大訴求，該款機器人在 10 分鐘內便能畫好漂亮的美甲。「可以把我們想成速食店，然後把美甲沙龍想成正式的餐廳。」Clockwork 的創辦人 Renuka Apte 對《Alllure》如此說道。「這兩種型態的店家，在消費者的生活中都有一定的需求。」

Nimble 是一款家用美甲機器，預定於 2021 年底上市。該公司在 Kickstarter 的集資目標是 25,000 美元，而截至 2021 年 11 月，他們已獲得超過 180 萬美元的資金。Nimble 的產品也和 Clockwork 一樣，只需 10 分鐘就能快速完成美甲。

值得關注的原因：

科技新創公司發現越來越多消費者對美甲沙龍或是居家美甲機器的訴求都轉向便利，於是快速美甲市場也轉往機器人的方向發展。從商業的角度來看，根據《Reportlinker》2021 年 4 月的報導，全球美甲市場的規模在 2027 年前預計會成長到 116 億美元。

WUNDERMAN THOMPSON

Clockwork in San Francisco offers robot manicures

61

零售&商業

70

61

虛擬消費熱潮

從 B2B、DTC 到 DTA——最新的商業模式是將數位商品直接發送至消費者的數位裝置上。

Adidas and Karlie Kloss collaboration. Image courtesy of The Fabricant

2021年有許多時尚品牌將商業模式從「企業對企業」(business-to-business,B2B)和「直接面對消費者」(direct-to-consumer,DTC),轉向「直接發送數位商品」(direct-to-avatar,DTA)。2021年12月,Nike收購虛擬球鞋市集RTFKT。時間再往回推3個月,Balenciaga在《要塞英雄》(Fortnite)中推出專屬遊戲時裝。Ralph Lauren在夏季推出一組包含50件時裝的數位衣櫃,可以透過社交軟體Zepeto購入;American Eagle也為個人表情貼Bitmoj推出首款DTA服飾。Gucci和The North Face在年初便以《Pokémon Go》的遊戲時裝設計展開合作。數位時尚品牌The Fabricant也和Adidas、Puma、Tommy Hilfiger等品牌合作,將各品牌的服飾虛擬化。

高級汽車廠也帶動這波潮流。瑪莎拉蒂(Maserati)、奧斯頓馬丁(Aston Martin)、特斯拉(Tesla)都在2020年至2021年間,於「中國版的《絕地求生》(PUBG)」,也就是騰訊推出的手遊《和平精英》中推出虛擬車款。勞斯萊斯(Rolls-Royce)同樣在2020年於騰訊的《QQ飛車》中推出首款虛擬汽車。

值得關注的原因:

The Fabricant的創辦人暨執行長Kerry Murphy預測,消費主義的未來在於虛擬商品市場。「大家會開始看到數位商品的價值,並了解提供數位商品或者款式無限的數位時裝,會比推出限量款的實體商品還更好。」Murphy對偉門智威智庫如此表示。

Puma, featured with digital fashion house The Fabricant

Puma. Image courtesy of The Fabricant

62

零售業大變身

長期以來的困境迫使零售業者重新思考核心定位，
有些企業決定開始多角化經營。

過去幾年間受到最大衝擊的產業當屬零售業。2020 年時尚品牌碰壁，店家關門，銷售額也大減；時間快轉至今，零售業者還是受到供應鏈中斷與勞力短缺所影響。這些危機催生新的發展。

在什麼都不確定的年代，適應力即是關鍵。大型零售業者開始轉換跑道，以更有創意的方式多角化經營企業。

2021 年 7 月，英國零售品牌 John Lewis & Partners 和 Waitrose 的母集團 John Lewis Partnership 宣布要出租集團名下的不動產。自 1864 年成立至今，該集團於 2021 年 1 月首次發布全年虧損的消息，多角化經營於是成為延續企業生命的重要選項。該集團的土地調查資料顯示，當前閒置的商場空間可以改造成 7,000

戶住屋。他們計畫要蓋不同的房型，從小套房到四間房的房型都涵蓋其中，這表示屋主可以住在 Waitrose 超市樓上，或者緊鄰該集團的物流中心。John Lewis Partnership 希望在 2030 年前，會有四成的獲利來自零售以外的事業，其中主要來自金融服務、房產、戶外生活事業。

為了實現氣候正效益的目標，瑞典家具公司宜家家居（Ikea）也開始拓展事業範疇，將再生能源賣給一般民眾使用。過往以組合家

具起家的 Ikea 希望推動全球規模最大的再生能源運動，希望綠電在全球都是容易取得且價格合理的能源選項。

值得關注的原因：

在新零售時代，消費者不再將品牌視為單一服務的供應者，而是希望能與信任的品牌有更深入的互動，這也是新的商機所在。多元化經營可能是實體零售業者能否復甦的關鍵。

Left: John Lewis & Partners
Right: Ikea Strömma sells renewable energy to households

63

小窗開啓新關係

通訊平台成為建立品牌忠誠度的新戰場。

對話式商務(Chat commerce，可以縮寫成 ccommerce、c-commerce 或 cCommerce)廣泛出現在通訊平台上，這種商務模式也被稱為私人網域商務，藉此和品牌官網或網路商城(例如天貓和亞馬遜)等公開網域有所區別。

在中國，微信的每月用戶數高達 12 億人，該公司擅於和奢侈品牌搭建關係，主要以直播和私人訊息為管道。據波士頓顧問集團(Boston Consulting Group)和騰訊發表於 2020 年的市場洞察報告顯示，消費者在微信上的年平均開銷是 17 萬人民幣。

廣州消費彩妝品牌「完美日記」結合世代文化來提供低價美妝，該品牌出現在其目標用戶(Z 世代)生活的各個角落，從社群媒體兼電商平台「小紅書」，一路到短影音平台「嗶哩嗶哩」和「抖音」(中國版 TikTok)。

完美日記也邀請顧客加入官方微信帳號(微信公众号)或是品牌虛擬大使「小完子」的帳號，這些帳號中都匯集了上千名的關注者，品牌除了會在裡面提前曝光新品資訊，這些平台同時也扮演私人購物助理的角色。

偉門智威中國區策略長凌嘉表示：「小完子不只可以讓你一窺新品和折扣，還可以讓你從群聊當中找到靈感。雖然看起來有點假，有點像作秀，但其實縮短了消費者從關注、消費，一路到建立忠誠度的整趟旅程。」

對話式商務也拓展到中國以外的地區。據《日經亞洲評論》(Nikkei Asia)2021 年 6 月的報導，若從商家與買家間的訊息

量來判斷，越南和泰國使用臉書（Facebook）訊息來經營網路零售事業的成績傲視全球。在泰國，Burberry、Louis Vuitton、Chanel 等國際品牌都推出 LINE 官方帳號，設計專屬貼圖來吸引消費者，並透過直播功能來播放品牌時裝秀和數位廣告。「LINE 購物」是 LINE 推出的商務平台，光是在泰國就坐擁 700 百萬名用戶，這是 2021 年 7 月泰國 LINE 電商部總經理 Lertad Supadhiloke 告訴《曼谷郵報》（Bangkok Post）的數據。

值得關注的原因：

因為大家越來越常在 WeChat、Whatsapp 和 LINE 等通訊軟體上聊天，品牌也就加入了聊天平台，想和消費者建立更親密、一對一的關係。

> 品牌開始使用聊天平台，想和消費者建立更親密、小而美的關係。

+WUNDERMAN THOMPSON AI bot Xiao Wanzi chats with consumers about Perfect Diary cosmetics on WeChat

64

虛擬旗艦店

數位旗艦商店佔據了電商平台的首頁。

偉門智威數據 2021 年 7 月的調查顯示，全球有 81% 的消費者認同品牌的數位形象和店面形象一樣重要，這也促使品牌開始升級網購平台上的店面設計，以及成立虛擬的品牌旗艦商店。

2021 年 7 月，奢侈品牌芬迪（Fendi）開設 360 度的數位旗艦店，店面設計仿效位於紐約 57 街的實體店，為顧客提供虛擬導覽和商品選購服務。愛馬仕（Hermès）在新加坡、阿拉伯聯合大公國和泰國也成立了數位旗艦店。

美妝品牌也在提升數位門面的形象。蘭蔻（Lancôme）於 2020 夏季在新加坡開設首間虛擬快閃旗艦店，以「超未來肌因賦活露」和 #LiveYourStrength 為主題，為顧客提供 3D 購物體驗、購物諮詢與教育活動，裡面還包含「探索專區」，讓顧客可以透過性格測驗（由心理學家 Perpetua Neo 所設計）來找出自己的優勢；這家隸屬萊雅集團（L'Oréal）的保養品牌在澳洲、韓國、美國都有開設虛擬快閃店。2021 年 4 月，Nars 成立線上旗艦店，讓顧客可以沈浸在 3D 購物環境當中。

值得關注的原因：

據《eMarketer》預測，全球電商市場的產值會從 2021 年的 4.89 兆美元成長到 2022 年的 5.42 兆美元，虛擬旗艦店成為吸引消費者目光的新所在，同時也讓品牌的整體數位形象再次升級。

Fendi's 360-degree digital flagship on 57th Street in New York City

65

Alpha 世代登場

Alpha 世代用以下三種方式，帶起新一波零售風潮。

出生於 2010 至 2025 年的 Alpha 世代比 Z 世代又更年輕了一些，他們目前也已開始改寫零售產業的樣貌。

多元包容陳列

品牌與零售業者捨棄傳統的性別框架，讓產品更加中性。PacSun 於 2021 年 6 月推出全新的中性兒童服飾品牌 PacSun Kids，於 9 月發表另一中性服飾品牌 Colour Range，11 月時又開設品牌首間無性別兒童服飾店。同年 10 月，加州成為美國第一個強制零售業者販售無性別商品的州別，新法令要求大型商家不能將玩具與嬰幼兒商品按性別分開陳列。推動此法的民主黨議員 Evan Low 表示：「以社會觀念判斷哪些玩具適合何種性別，是現代進步思想的反指標。」

PacSun Kids gender-neutral clothing. Photography by Chris Martin

共融性商品

品牌與零售業者也提供更多元的商品來照顧各類身心障礙人士的需求。JCPenney 於 2021 年 7 月推出適性設計兒童服飾，並與適性商品專賣店 Patti & Ricky 合作，提供更多元的兒童專用適性配件。2021 年 6 月，Headspace、芝麻街與企鵝藍燈書屋（Penguin Random House）合作推出「怪獸冥想」系列書籍，一套六本，「幫助小朋友學習正念、冥想與社會情緒學習的基本概念」。

WUNDERMAN THOMPSON Patti & Ricky collaborated with JCPenney to make children's clothing with adaptive features. Photography by Alexis Buatti-Ramos/Hyphen Photography

永續型玩樂

玩具品牌也高度重視永續價值，希望藉此吸引年輕世代的消費者。2021 年 5 月，美泰兒（Mattel）啟動產品回收計劃，消費者可將舊的產品送回美泰兒回收再製。樂高（Lego）於 2021 年 6 月發表首款以回收塑膠製成的積木產品打樣。

值得關注的原因：

跟隨 Z 世代的腳步，Alpha 世代持續強化 Z 世代在零售業中帶起的重要價值觀。

百貨公司生活圈

零售業者重新反思傳統百貨的經營模式。

近來，與其說百貨公司是零售業，還不如說它們是市民廣場，而這也反映了零售場景從奢侈品牌的大型展示間轉型成為社群微型生態系的狀況。

Beales 於 2020 年關閉位於英國的所有店面，但目前已在易主後重新開設三家分店，他們的目標不限於零售。位於普爾的分店頂樓將會轉型成由英國國家健保署（National Health Service）經營的「健康村」，裡面配有皮膚科、骨科、眼科以及乳癌篩檢科，針對長期飽受新冠疫情（Covid-19）所苦的民眾，也設有特別的諮詢室。

全新百貨概念進駐先前由英國百貨品牌 Debehams 經營的空間。新品牌 Bobby's 於 2021 年 9 月插旗英國波恩茅斯鎮，除了購物、當地工匠進駐之外，還設有華美的大廳、藝廊、冰淇淋和咖啡店，取代滿是服裝、飾品、家居選物的陳設。未來他們還計畫要加入美髮沙龍、牙醫門診、微型烘焙坊和燻烤室。

Beales 的執行長 Tony Brown 對《衛報》（The Guardian）表示：「我沒有再看過新的大型連鎖百貨了。未來會有小型的在地連鎖企業出現，開設八家、十家的店面。商業模式在未來幾年內會有大幅的變動，因為大眾追求的是更在地的服務。」

值得關注的原因：

很顯然傳統百貨的經營模式已不再合適。我們在《改變未來的 100 件事：2020 年全球百大趨勢》當中，已經報導過精品百貨公司的消逝，後來也有許多老牌的大型業者宣告關店和破產。現在，新一代的百貨公司需要重新思考並調整經營模式。

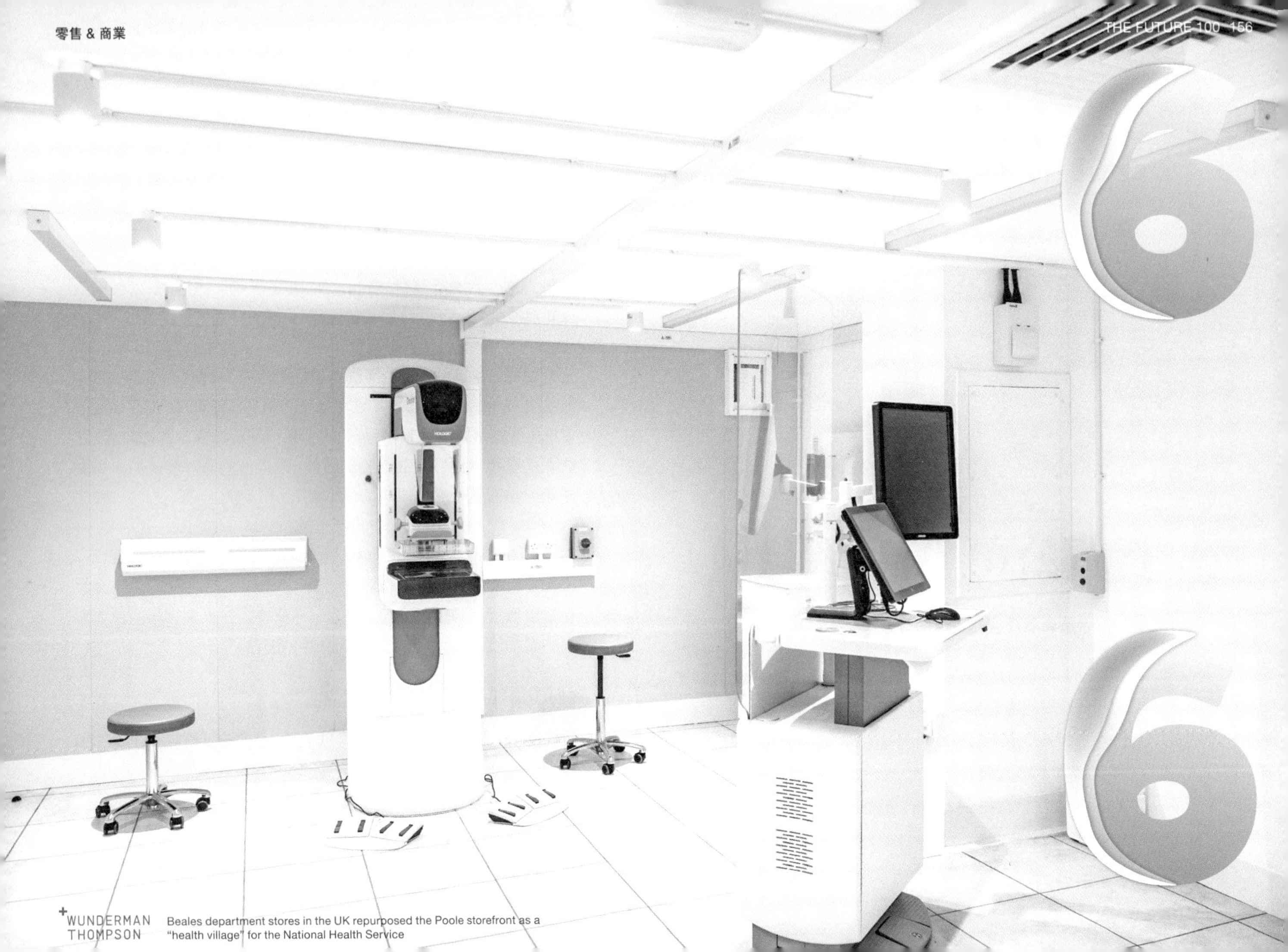

WUNDERMAN THOMPSON

Beales department stores in the UK repurposed the Poole storefront as a "health village" for the National Health Service

67

數位雙胞胎

實體零售商店和工廠都多了一個存在虛擬世界的雙胞胎兄弟，目的是要提升親切度與工作效率。

WUNDERMAN THOMPSON BMW and Nvidia are partnering to create a digital twin of the carmaker's factory in Regensburg, Germany

「未來每一家工廠、每一棟建築都會出現數位雙胞胎，模擬並追蹤實體工廠和實體建物的狀況。」輝達（Nvidia）執行長黃仁勳於 2021 年 4 月對《時代雜誌》（Time）如此說道。而黃仁勳口中的元宇宙「完全就是虛擬和現實世界的融合」。輝達正和寶馬（BMW）攜手，為寶馬於德國雷根斯堡的工廠打造數位雙胞胎，讓工作團隊能夠先以虛擬的方式規劃並模擬新的物流作業，再帶回實體的汽車工廠執行。

科技公司也讓數位雙胞胎的生成變得更加容易。2021 年 11 月 30 日，亞馬遜（Amazon）公開發表 AWS IoT TwinMaker，讓企業可以簡便、快速地生成模擬實體運作系統的數位孿生系統。微軟（Microsoft）的 Azure Digital Twins 提供建造虛擬建築、基礎設施、甚至整座城市的技術，希望能「促成更優質的商品，優化工作流程，降低成本，並驚豔客戶。」

零售業者也將實體店面複製到虛擬介面上，希望讓消費者感到親切，也讓購物體驗更自然。2021 年 3 月，Burberry 以東京銀座的旗艦店為範本，推出數位版旗艦店。Coach 則與虛擬店面開發公司 Obsess 合作，複製出 Coach 位於紐約第五大道的旗艦店。「數位展示間讓批發商可以欣賞我們每季的最新款式，同時又不需要親身飛來看商品，減少我們事業的碳足跡，同時加快採購流程。」Coach 的全球視覺體驗資深副總 Giovanni Zaccariello 解釋道。

值得關注的原因：

數位孿生店面為零售業帶來創新，除了保證解決真實世界的物流問題，同時也完美複製了實體逛街的樂趣。

Left: Burberry Ginza virtual store in collaboration with Elle Digital
Right: Coach cloned its New York Fifth Avenue flagship store with Obsess

68

科技巨頭跨界現身

科技巨頭近期拉攏消費者的方式已跨出螢幕之外。

據《華爾街日報》(The Wall Street Journal)2021年8月的報導，亞馬遜（Amazon）計劃開設百貨公司。亞馬遜曾於 2017 年收購全食超市（Whole Foods），於 2018 年開設第一家四星商店，於 2020 年開設首家無人商店，而最新計畫也顯示他們持續跨足實體零售版圖的意圖。據報導，這些店面特別販售亞馬遜自有品牌服飾與家居商品，同時也作為退換貨與客服中心。

谷歌（Google）於 2021 年 6 月開設首家實體店鋪，吸引了眾人的目光，地點位於紐約市。與傳統零售賣場相比，這家店有更多的展示間，販售谷歌從 Nest 到 Fibit 的全系列產品，並包含工作坊教室，提供給旗下品牌舉辦活動，例如 Pixel 的攝影課，Nest 的烹飪示範，還有 YouTube 音樂會等。

蘋果（Apple）的零售與群眾部門資深副總 Deirdre O'Brien 於 2021 年 6 月對路透社（Reuters）表示，他們也將透過實體店面拓展美國零售市場，包含持續貫徹疫情前的行銷策略，例如舉辦店面活動並提供消費以外的體驗機會。

值得關注的原因：

科技巨頭將目光轉向實體零售產業，這可能會持續提升實體消費與線上購物的跨域體驗。

WUNDERMAN THOMPSON

Google's first physical store in New York City

69

進擊的 NFT

品牌開始從不斷進化的非同質化代幣（NFT）
領域尋求新的獲利方式。

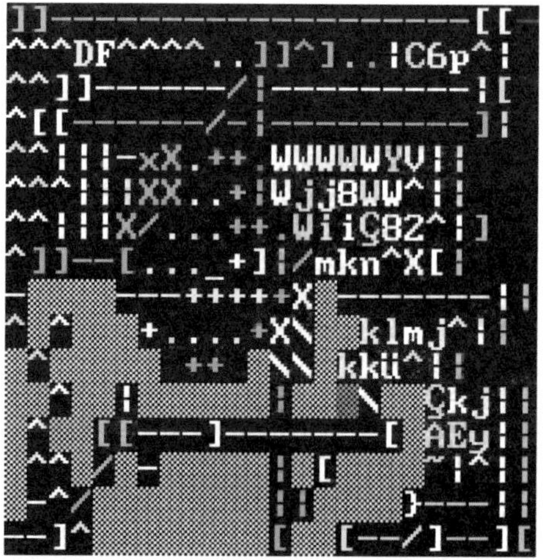

企業開始在這個最新的數位疆域中追求獲利成長。藝術家和品牌隨時準備好要鑄造新的 NFT，來滿足消費者對收藏、交易的各種需求，各方人士也已在元宇宙新興的論壇當中碰頭。

蘇富比（Sotheby's）是第一家推出 NFT 專屬拍場的拍賣公司。2021 年 10 月，該公司發表旗下專屬的元宇宙，除了有名人背書，也支持許多過去一年曾與其合作的數位藝術家。管理總監 Sebastian Fahey 告訴《Hypebeast》，蘇富比計畫運用其「專業和策展能力來服務迅速發展的藝術市場以及數位原生世代」。

Series 4 Glitchbox from Sotheby's Natively Digital NFT collection

同月，加密貨幣交易所 Coinbase 宣布要推出 NFT 賣場，並將有興趣的投資客加入早鳥等候名單當中。Coinbase 的 NFT 平台會包含「社交功能」，藉此支持「創作者經濟」，也就是透過創作影片和數位內容來獲利。

值得關注的原因：

大品牌和重要產業持續投資 NFT 並參與相關交易，元宇宙也隨其獲利潛能與發展機會而持續演進。踏入這個全新疆域的品牌，若善用機會，就有可能在發展中的市場找到新的商機

> 大品牌和重要產業持續投資NFT並參與相關交易，元宇宙也仰賴其獲利與發展潛能而持續演進。

Left: MoonCat from Sotheby's Natively Digital NFT collection
Right: Yuga Labs' Bored Ape Yacht Club from Sotheby's Natively Digital NFT collection

78

復古零售

近期設計商店紛紛以懷舊裝潢來將時光倒流。

Superette's Sip 'n' Smoke cannabis dispensary. Photography by Alex Lysakowski

Superette 位於多倫多的最新大麻診療所，以復古雜貨店為裝潢靈感，使用繽紛色彩、搶眼圖像，以及《Dezeen》稱為「普普藝術」的風格，讓人聯想到上個世紀中期的零售店鋪。2021 年 8 月，該公司開設免下車服務窗口 Sip'n' Smoke，一樣使用復古裝潢，以懷舊咖啡廳為靈感來源。

洛杉磯超市 Wine & Eggs 於 2021 年開設，部分室內裝潢以公立學校為靈感，空間和品牌形象皆使用飽滿的藍黃色系為主調，搭配亮綠色共同呈現。圓弧形木櫃和展示台讓人想起學校建築，而藍綠色格子地板則以商用乙烯基瓷磚鋪設而成。「我喜歡乙烯基地板，因為看起來很活潑，也讓我想起在公立學校的兒時生活，」負責室內設計的 Adi Goodrich 對《Dezeen》如此說道。

創意廣告公司 Saint of Athens 設計了一間珠寶店，於 2021 年 8 月在希臘的米克諾斯開幕，風格類似舊時代華麗的奢華泳池。室內以淺藍色磁磚和紅白條紋為主要裝飾，該公司的創辦人 Nikos Paleologos 告訴《Dezeen》：「淺藍色讓人想起 60 年代的豪華都會泳池，金屬家具、復古元素和客製藍色磨石子展示櫃既復古又現代，很像魏斯 • 安德森（Wes Anderson）導演創造出來的世界。」

值得關注的原因：

過去兩年，許多設計以自然元素為靈感，希望創造舒適、安穩的感受。現在，最新的店面選用俗氣、有趣的設計來打造復古的迷人角落。

Superette's Sip 'n' Smoke cannabis dispensary. Photography by Alex Lysakowski

71
OCEANSKY
CRUISES
奢華
80

71

心靈療程興起

提供身心療癒服務的場所開始意識到催眠的潛在療效。

奢華旅館正開始將身心靈療程從全身熱成像按摩（thermal body mapping）、睡眠教練（sleep coaches）拓展到催眠療程（hypnotherapy）。

香港文華東方酒店於 2021 年 6 月聘僱了催眠治療師 Christine Deschemin，推出放鬆身心、改善飲食習慣的工作坊，並提供客製化的催眠治療服務。2021 年春季，倫敦飯店業者 Belmond Cadogan Hotel 與催眠治療師 Malminder Gill 合作，推出免費的睡眠住房管理服務，在房內提供 Gill 錄製的冥想引導住客入睡，也在晨間播放鼓舞人心的錄音讓住客醒腦；除此之外還有一對一的諮詢以及專屬的催眠療程。

紐約市中心四季飯店（Four Seasons）的水療中心於 2018 年推出駐館治療師計畫，他們發現客人要的不只是傳統的水療體驗，還包含療癒心靈的放鬆活動。前幾年駐館的師資包含聲音治療師 Michelle Pirret 和水晶療癒師 Rashia Bell。2020 年 12 月，以旅行催眠師身份為人所知的 Nicole Hernandez 也進駐館內，提供獨特的催眠課程，幫助來賓舒緩焦慮與克服恐懼。Hernandez 獨特的「時光旅人計劃」引導客戶重新回到過去的時光，藉此改善現在的生活。

值得關注的原因：

旅宿業者在養生療程中提供更多的心靈療癒服務，不只透過水晶、塔羅牌，還有據說能促進健康、改善習慣並提升正念的催眠體驗。

> 旅宿業者開始在養生療程中提供更多的心靈療癒服務。

Left: The Spa at the Four Seasons New York Downtown Resident Healer Program
Right: Mandarin Oriental Hong Kong

72

簡約奢華風潮

面對中國的「共同富裕」政策，奢侈品牌重新調整經營策略。

在 2021 年的中國國慶連假期間，上海某一市場成為社群媒體的熱議話題。上千名顧客湧入昔為法國租界的烏中市集購買蔬果和雞蛋，不過這些基本的料理食材，這次是裝在Prada的包裝袋裡。

這個快閃活動是為了宣傳 Prada 2021 年秋冬全新企劃「Feels Like Prada」。不論這個企劃到底算不算成功（到處都有人在自拍，攤商的包裝袋、包裝紙也都完全用盡），還是這是中產階級化的指標，或如上海社會科學院的助理研究員朱天華對《第六聲》所言，是「日常生活中的消費主義」，該企劃都在全世界持續籠罩於新冠肺炎（COVID-19）、氣候變遷、經濟不平等加劇的危機時刻，輕輕地以平實的步調躍上檯面。

2021 年中，在中國針對大型科技公司進行長達一個月的科技整肅後，國家主席習近平宣布了「共同富裕」政策，要求企業一起為縮小該國的貧富差距而努力。

中國政府承諾會讓更多勞工躋身中產階級，並讓就學、居住、健康照護等基本需求變得更平易近人。某些中國的億萬富翁已同意捐出數十億元來資助慈善事業。

除了中國，也有其他地方在反制奢靡生活。2021 年 11 月，某位越南高官在社群媒體上遭到撻伐，因為有外流影片顯示他在英國被餵食金箔牛排，地點在知名主廚「灑鹽哥」Nusret Gokce 位於倫敦騎士橋的餐廳。

消費主義之后金· 卡戴珊（Kim Kardashian）出席 2021 年大都會藝術博物館慈善晚宴（Met Gala）時，並未身著以往那種金光熠熠的禮服，而是將全身上下、從臉到腳以黑布緊緊包裹。

值得關注的原因：

據貝恩策略顧問公司（Bain & Company）的 2021 年的奢侈品研究報告顯示，個人奢侈品市場在 2021 年重新回溫，市值達到 2,830 億歐元，比 2020 年的低谷上升了 29%。這股回升力道主要來自中國，目前佔了全球市場的 21%。然而，疫情也激發人們重新評估奢侈的意義。貝恩公司該份報告的主筆 Claudia D'Arpizio 認為：「疫後復甦對奢侈品牌來說是某種文藝復興，以前名牌代表身份地位、品牌 logo、限量供應，現在他們則重新找回使命感與責任，參與社會對話。」

Prada's "Feels Like Prada" fall/winter 2021 campaign. Photography by David Sims

73

虛擬擁有權的菁英

現在有新的方式可以彰顯你的社會地位，那就是利用炙手可熱
且所有權專屬於你的數位資產：
NFT（Non-fungible tokens，非同質化代幣）
虛擬人物角色。

WUNDERMAN THOMPSON

Gutter Cat Gang Pigeon avatar

從明星運動員到饒舌歌手和科技公司老闆，富貴名流都在搶購NFT人物。NBA 球星柯瑞（Steph Curry）以 18 萬美元買下「無聊猿猴遊艇俱樂部」（Bored Ape Yacht Club）的第 7990 號角色，昔日拳王泰森（Mike Tyson）購入 Cool Cat，而科技公司創辦人 Alexis Ohanian 則持有 Pudgy Penguin。Ohanian 還花了 28 萬美元，為他的妻子也就是網壇傳奇小威廉絲（Serena Williams）購入 CryptoPunk 創造的 NFT 角色。以 CryptoPunk 來說，這樣的價位其實不算貴；2021 年，CryptoPunk 旗下稀有的NFT人物在佳士得拍賣(Christie's)和蘇富比拍賣(Sotheby's)都漲到了 700 萬美元。就連金融巨頭 Visa 都出手，以 15 萬美元買下 CryptoPunk 的龐克頭造型 NFT。入手 NFT 後，把大頭貼換成自己持有的 NFT 角色當然是必要工作。

NFT 的市場在 2021 年呈現爆炸性成長，出售限量角色的相關社群數量也跟著暴增。這些虛擬人物會以動畫風格出現在個人檔案的大頭貼，通常由演算法依特定主題自動生成，顏色、髮型、服裝、配件各異，也有某些稀有、獨特的款式。除了猿猴、龐克風、企鵝之外，對此感興趣的買家也可以購買貓貓（Gutter Cat Gang）、狗狗（The Doge Pound）、鴨子（Sup Ducks）、外星人（Lonely Alien Space Club）還有各式各樣的女性人物（Fame Lady Squad）。

雖然 NFT 虛擬人物的核心概念是具備實質市場價值且可轉移的資產，但他們也是持有者展現財富與地位的管道，彰顯自己是幣圈的精英貴族。除了擁有這項數位資產，投資人還能以社群會員的身份，加入收藏家專屬的 Discord 和 Telegram 頻道，獲得非常寶貴的社群交流機會。由於渴望躋身上流社會但無法獨力負擔一紙 NFT 的人數眾多，所以現在也出現了可租借及碎片化的 NFT 權狀。

加密商品投資客 Cooper Turley（Coopahtroopa）對此也頗有心得，他在《WAGMI》的一集播客節目中談到，他以 300 美元購入的一款CryptoPunk NFT，現在已漲價到50萬美元。他提到「擁有 CryptoPunk 所帶來的社會資產，遠遠不是金錢所能衡量的。這項商品是你加入藏家和會員專屬私密社群的門票，能為你的人生帶來長遠的好處。我認為持有這類商品所帶來的社會聲望永遠不會消退。」

值得關注的原因：

NFT人物長期下來會不會仍然受歡迎，這點目前還有待商榷，但是以這項虛擬產品來彰顯社會地位的趨勢似乎越演越烈，這點更值得我們探討。偉門智威智庫在〈進入元宇宙〉（Into the Metaverse）這份報告中，提到消費者對「虛擬擁有權」具有強烈的興趣。虛擬擁有權象徵的意義和地位，也似乎等同於真實世界中的名車和名錶。在我們邁入元宇宙之際，虛擬人物確實會成為重要的投資標的。

Left: Gutter Cat Gang Dog avatar
Right: Gutter Cat Gang Cat avatar

SpottieWiFi avatar

74

長住型醫療會所

這些長住型醫療會所對於邀請客人「多逗留一段時間」是認真的。

水療和養生度假會館在漫長的新冠疫情之中推出新的療程，希望賓客多停留一會，好好休養身心靈。

位於曼谷外圍的 RAKxa 醫療會所針對新冠肺炎（COVID-19）推出新的健康療養方案，近期相當受到關注。該集團提供為期三天的全方位療程來修復肺部功能，包含高壓氧壓力艙、血氧注入，並於奧運規格的運動場進行胸肌強化訓練，且每種療程都會依據賓客的需求量身打造。

地處西班牙海岸的養生會所 The SHA Wellness Clinic 於 2021 年 5 月推出為期七天的後疫情方案。賓客來到會所時會先接受篩檢，然後根據檢測結果來客製療程。檢測項目包含壓力測試、頸動脈超音波、抽血檢查，療程則包含反射療法、水中指壓按摩療程，以及刺激腦細胞並幫助腦細胞再生的腦部光生物調節療法。

奧地利阿爾卑斯山上的 The Lanserhof 度假會所，宣稱他們為期兩週的調養方案可以治療新冠肺炎的長期症狀。The Lanserhof 度假會所過往提供的是高檔、昂貴的全身排毒療程，現在全新的

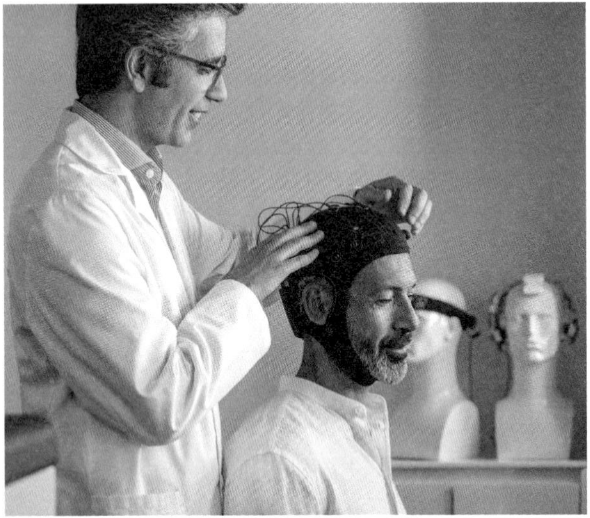

方案則包含個人化的能量餐、咀嚼訓練師、按摩療程、呼吸治療、驗尿（找出感染或腎臟問題），並依照病患症狀來設計個人化的訓練課程。

值得關注的原因：

在觀光旅遊業停擺了好一段時間之後，度假會所重新設計療程，希望滿足消費者新一波的養生療養需求。醫療會所和復健療程提供長期方案，改寫了旅宿業的常規。

Left: The SHA Wellness Clinic offers a seven-day post-COVID program
Right: RAKxa wellness and medical retreat

The Lanserhof Resort in the Austrian Alps. Photography by Alexander Haiden

75

郊區奢侈品天地

郊區會是新的奢侈品賣場嗎？

由於奢侈品消費族群積極地尋找第二個據點及新的度假聖地，精品品牌與零售業者也跟緊他們的腳步，從市中心移動到郊區。

2021 年夏季，Gucci 在紐約漢普頓地區開設該區第一家常設店，並在同年秋季於伊利諾州的橡樹溪展店。Dior 在亞利桑那州的斯科茨代爾開設店面，LV 也在德州的普拉諾開始營運，Hermès 則於 2021 年 6 月插旗密西根州的底特律（這是他們在該州的第一家店面）。

以往消費者對於度假與郊區購物的需求不夠高也不夠穩定，所以遲遲不見非快閃型的店面，但現在局勢已經有了轉變。在科羅拉多州的小鎮阿斯本，任職於地產公司 Setterfield & Bright 的 Angi Wang 對《華盛頓郵報》（The Washington Post）表示，「以前我們都說這裡的市場太小了，但現在大家都想要進駐。大家爭相來到阿斯本，現在我們真的完全找不到任何空地了。」

值得關注的原因：

奢侈品牌不再將焦點放在城市熱區裡。市場研究公司 Luxury Institute 的總執行 Milton Pedraza 向《華盛頓郵報》表示：「疫情讓精品零售走向去中心化。好像每個人都搬到郊區或者度假小屋了，所以店家也就跟著搬了過去。」

“疫情讓精品零售走向去中心化。

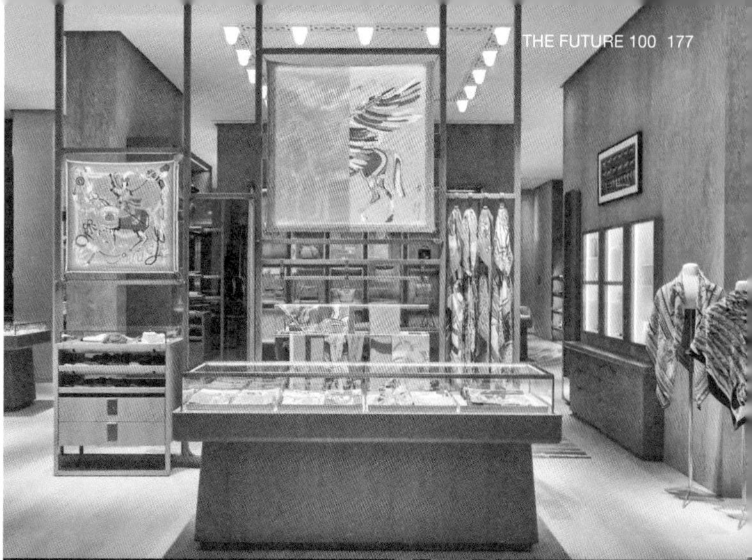

Top: Hermès store in the greater Detroit area
Bottom: Louis Vuitton store in Plano, Texas

76

假貨辨識升級

透過區塊鏈的技術，保證精品的真實性，
讓假貨逐漸成為過去式。

人工智慧（AI）和區塊鏈技術正被用來追蹤流通於市面上的假貨，以及對抗二手市場的仿冒品。

2021 年 4 月，LVMH、Prada、Richemont 三大集團為了維護精品業的真實性和可信度，他們組成 Aura 區塊鏈聯盟，利用區塊鏈技術來驗證全球精品的貨源、交易，這些紀錄甚至涵蓋到二手市場。2021 年 10 月，OTB 集團也加入 Aura 區塊鏈聯盟，成為創始成員之一，該集團旗下包含高端時尚的精品品牌，例如 Diesel、Marni 等。

以 AI 技術為核心的精品驗證機構 Entrupy 成立於 2016 年，總部位於紐約，稱自己是「第一套且是唯一一套能夠提供精品驗證真偽的解決方案」，準確率達 99.1%。此套方案採用深度學習與比較圖像的技術，藉此判定精品的真偽。

根據經濟合作與發展組織（Organization for Economic Cooperation and Development）報導，2019 年的假貨交易達到 4,640 億美元，Certilogo 的研究也顯示，線上假貨市場在疫情期間創新高，在 2020 年 5 月至 2021 年 4 月之間成長了 5%。這也和日趨熱門的二手交易市場的走勢不謀而合，ThredUp 預估，二手市場的交易量在 2025 年前會達到 770 億美元。

值得關注的原因：

二手精品未來還是會很受歡迎，尤其在有意識的消費族群當中更是如此，且這個族群的人數也不斷上升。精品業與科技業的聯手打造快速辨識假貨的工具，藉此保護精品品牌的真實性和可信度。

快樂處方箋

現在，獲得快樂是一種奢侈！

WUNDERMAN THOMPSON

Dior Spa Cheval Blanc Paris's Happiness Shots offer 30- to 45-minute concentrated "bursts of pleasure."

精品品牌推出照顧情緒健康的新產品，透過提升身心狀態的服務來寵愛顧客。

位於巴黎白馬莊園飯店（Cheval Blanc Paris）的 Dior 水療中心於 2021 年 9 月開張，他們為賓客提供「快樂處方箋」，運用 30 至 45 分鐘的密集療程，帶給賓客滿滿的愉悅和寵愛的感受。此外，針對顧客的個人狀況來搭配不同的療程，以求達到最佳功效。這劑快樂處方箋可以添加按摩、輕煥膚、輕型去角質等療程中使用。

雅詩蘭黛（Estée Lauder）推出全新的奢華香氛系列，希望能觸發各種不同的正向情緒。為了滿足來自世界各地的消費者，該品牌參考腦科學研究，了解不同香氣對情緒的影響，並據此打造出八款不同的香氛，可以促進「正向情緒和喜悅」或者帶來「沈靜而愉快」的感受。

值得關注的原因：

不管是在水療中心或是品牌店面，各大精品品牌都為消費者提供了更多元且不同以往的產品或服務。從正向情緒和身心健康的角度出發，精品品牌下定決心，要讓顧客在步出大門時，能懷抱著比進門時還更愉悅的心情。

Estée Lauder's luxury fragrance collection. Image courtesy of Facebook

78

奢華長住體驗

長住型度假空間轉型成能與家族成員和好友共享的奢華旅宿。

焦慮不安的旅人正在尋找某種特定的場域來作為新的度假基地，那就是：為大型團體設計的長住型旅宿。度假空間提供長住方案，希望幫助旅客重置生活，而非只是短暫停留。

伊塔富士島（Ithaafushi）為 24 人的好友團體提供奢華的住宿方案，每晚要價 85,000 美元。旅客可以霸佔整座小島，得到完全私密且可長住的度假空間。這座私人島嶼位於馬爾地夫的華爾道夫飯店（Waldorf Astoria Maldives），有海景、度假屋、水療池、健身房、水上運動，並配有私廚，甚至還有 24 小時的個人門房服務。

渴望童話般住宿體驗的旅客，現在可以租下義大利翁布里亞山區的整棟古堡好好體驗一番。古堡飯店 Castello di Reschio 每晚要價 29 萬歐元，住客可以帶朋友和家人一起入住，整座城堡有 36 間房間，至少有 11 間可供住宿，全包式的價格不只涵蓋餐飲和音樂娛樂，旁邊還有橄欖樹園、壯麗美景以及葡萄園等可供遊覽。因為租下了整座城堡，賓客可以在住宿期間恣意享受水療池、烹飪與藝術課程、馬術體驗等豐富的活動。

值得關注的原因：

旅客在尋找有趣的住宿地點，同時也想帶上摯愛的家人朋友一同前往，因此旅宿業者重新設計大型空間，將其改造成豪華的秘密基地，讓賓客可以和家族成員與一眾好友共聚一堂。旅客鎖定眾人都能同享的度假空間，並暫居其中，好好放鬆享受長假。

The private island of Ithaafushi, part of the Waldorf Astoria Maldives, offers luxurious stays for guests and 24 of their closest friends

79

奢華走進音響界

從時尚精品到豪華名車，奢侈品牌紛紛開始投資音響設備，
讓耳朵也能享受奢華體驗。

WUNDERMAN THOMPSON

The Louis Vuitton portable Horizon Light Up speaker, modeled after the brand's Toupie handbag

> 對奢侈品牌來說，音響會是品牌成長的關鍵趨力

Horizon Light Up Speaker，開賣售價近 3,000 美元，外型類似該品牌的飛碟包 Toupie，並搭配 LV 經典花樣。

賓士（Mercedes-Benz）是最新一家與高檔音響品牌合作的豪華汽車廠，他們宣布自 2022 年夏季開始，賓士最頂級的車款一律會搭載杜比全景聲音響系統。

蘋果（Apple）的聆聽裝置在過去五年的進化史是很值得研究的案例。蘋果原本在販售 iPhone 時都會附贈一款有線耳機，但現在他們積極鼓勵 iPhone 用戶購買檔次越來越高的耳機。從 2016 年推出第一代 AirPods 耳機（售價 159 美元）以來，蘋果不斷提升耳機的功能與售價，最高價的商品是 2020 年 12 月推出的 AirPods Max，售價為 549 美元。自 2020 年底開始，蘋果也不再隨機附上免費的耳機。

值得關注的原因：

音響設備正在逐漸升級。對奢侈品牌來說，音響會是品牌成長的關鍵趨力，同時也是打造奢華體驗時必須納入考量的重要元素。

Mercedes-Benz will add Dolby Atmos speakers to its models from summer 2022

80

空中豪華遊艇

飛船旅行以低碳、奢華的形象重新回歸。

根據預測，航空旅遊業很快就能重回疫情前的水準，因此業者有必要降低碳排放量，且漸進式的減碳已經不夠了，現在需要的是全新解決方案。

飛船能重返天際嗎？飛船的定位是比客機和郵輪更環保永續的高檔運輸工具，有些專家甚至認為，未來十年內飛船會引發飛航革命。

飛船帶給旅客獨特的奢華體驗，寬大舒適的座艙、客廳、精緻用餐區和全景觀景窗，這些都是顯而易見的特色優勢。

奢華旅遊公司 Ocean Sky Cruises 已開始規劃 2024 年的北極飛船探險旅程。該公司在售票時發起「真正的世界領航者」的口號，他們會成為第一間讓飛船在北極著陸的公司，寫下歷史性的新篇章。這趟 38 小時的旅程會包含野外探查、觀賞極光、享用機上調酒等行程。

以色列航空公司 Atlas LTA 也想進軍高端消費市場，該公司的豪華機艙提供能鳥瞰窗外的觀景座位，讓乘客的觀光體驗再升級。

WUNDERMAN THOMPSON

Top: Ocean Sky Cruises
Bottom: Airlander, the world's first hybrid aircraft, by Hybrid Air Vehicles
Right: Flying Whales

英國製造商 Hybrid Air Vehicles 打造了全球第一架混合動力飛機 Airlander，最新一代的機種使用氫燃料的電池電動馬達，搭載豪華座位，並利用落地窗的設計讓觀景體驗順暢無阻。

飛船也是較為環保的選項。Airlander 的製造商希望飛船能在 2025 年前，提供跨城市的短程飛航服務，同時也可以將飛船應用於貨物運輸。同樣的，法國公司 Flying Whales 也在發展飛船船隊，做為環保的空運選項；該飛船可飛抵全球各地遺世獨立、難以進入的區域，且維持少量的碳足跡。

值得關注的原因：

全新打造的飛船能讓旅程更加環保同時又不失奢華。這些高檔次、低碳排的體驗，預示著豪華飛航旅程的下一個黃金世代。

The Pressed Roots hair salon in Dallas, Texas

81
健康
90

81

數位遊戲新處方

接受治療的最新媒介是什麼？透過螢幕。

新興「科劑」(techceuticals）開啟了健康管理的未來。醫生在處方箋中加入電動遊戲和虛擬實境（VR），希望治療腦霧、注意力不足過動症（ADHD）、憂鬱和創傷後壓力症後群（PTSD）等症狀。

2021 年 11 月，美國食品藥物管理局（Food and Drug Administration，FDA）核准使用虛擬實境療法 EaseVRx 來治療慢性背部疼痛。同年 10 月，該局處已先行核准將虛擬實境療法應用於弱視兒童的治療上。

2021 年 4 月，數位治療公司 Akili Interactive 與美國康乃爾大學威爾醫學院（Weill Cornell Medicine）、紐約長老會醫院（NewYork-Presbyterian Hospital）、范登堡大學附設醫學中心（Vanderbilt University Medical Center）合作，共同評估電玩遊戲 EndeavorRx 對新冠肺炎患者腦霧症狀的治療功效。開始 EndeavorRx 是要用來治療患有 ADHD 的兒童，該遊戲在 2020 年 6 月寫下歷史紀錄，因其成為首款由 FDA 核准且具處方箋等級的電玩遊戲。Akili Interactive 描述道，攝入推薦劑量以後（每天玩 25 分鐘，一週 5 天，持續一個月），有三分之一的兒童「在接受客觀注意力評估時，至少會有一次的評估報告沒有出現可量

測的注意力缺失現象」。2021 年 5 月，該公司於募資中獲得 1.6 億美元的資金，主要用於開發更多處方箋等級的遊戲。

值得關注的原因：

醫學的未來會仰賴遊戲化的科技產品嗎？身為數位營養師的 AeBeZe Labs 創辦人暨執行長 Michael Phillips Moskowitz 認同此一說法。他向偉門智威智庫表示，數位內容「有強大的策展潛能，數位療法會成為醫藥界的新興研究範疇」。未來，我們將會看到更多的處方箋級數位內容以及數位療法

Left: AppliedVR's EaseVRx prescription treatment
Right: EndeavorRX by Akili Interactive

82

男性生育新創企業

生物科技新創公司開始鎖定男性生育問題。

長久以來，生育率下降的議題經常聚焦於女性，而現在生技新創開始鎖定男性，提供精液分析以及冷凍精子的服務。部分男性因職涯考量而決定晚點生育，也有人單純想要買個保障，以免日後受傷或者生育力下降，這些人便是冷凍精子的客群。

波士頓新創企業 Legacy 販售居家精液分析套組，並與冷凍精子中心合作。該公司從 Y Combinator 和 Bain Capital Ventures 等創投募集了兩千萬美元的資金，創辦人 Khaled Kteily 表示，他之所以有這樣的創業念頭，是因為他某次坐在車上時，不慎把熱茶灑到自己的大腿上，造成二度灼傷，讓他擔心起自己未來的生育能力。Kteily 心中預設的冷凍精子目標客群範圍很廣，包含即將外派的軍人、需要代理孕母的同性伴侶、想在變性以前保有生育機會的跨性別人士等。Kteily 向《TechCrunch》表示，「我們認為每個男人離開家進入大專院校時可能都需要此一服務，投資人也看見了這個大好機會。」

位於布魯克林的品牌 Dadi 於 2019 年推出，這是一組溫控精液運輸套組，讓人能把精液從家裡送往實驗室；該產品從創投募集了一千萬美元。洛杉磯的 Yo 和倫敦的 ExSeed Health 等其他業者，提供可與智慧型手機結合的裝置，讓用戶在家就可檢測精液。

值得關注的原因：

為女性僱員提供凍卵福利的雇主，可能也會開始為男性僱員提供冷凍精子的健康福利。低生育率對男性來說也是一種健康警示，及早做精子分析也可協助了解整體健康狀況。

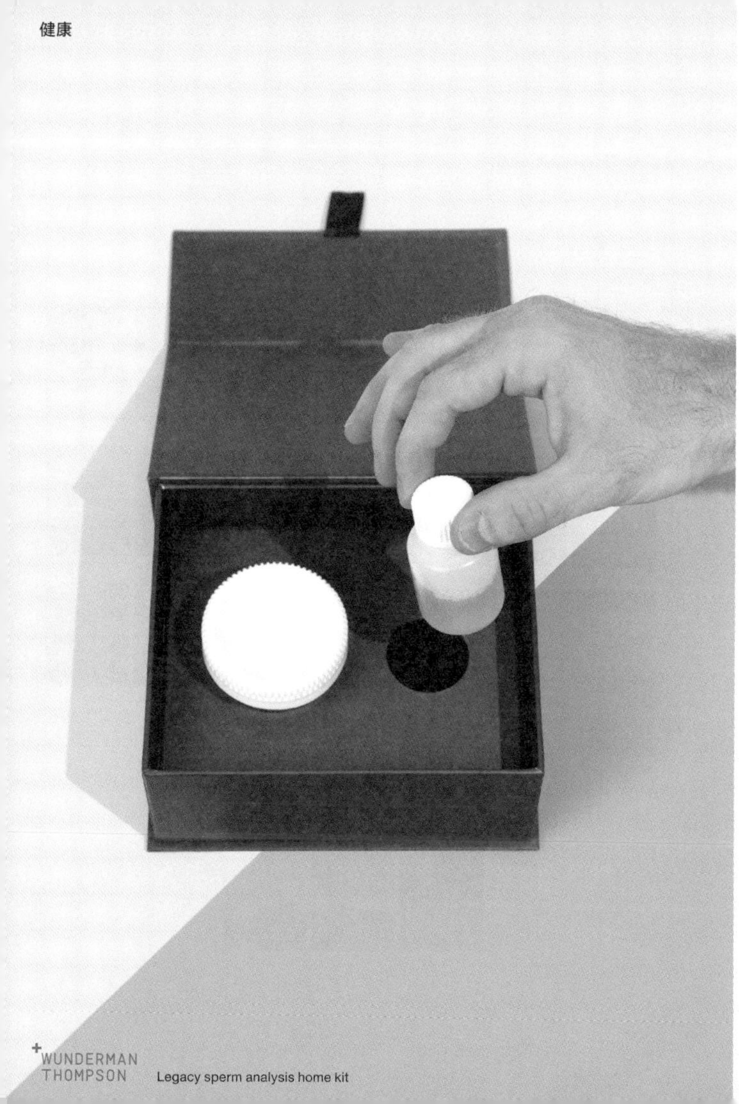

+WUNDERMAN THOMPSON Legacy sperm analysis home kit

而現在生技新創
開始鎖定男性，
提供精液分析
以及冷凍精子
的服務。

83

TikTok 化身心理治療

Z 世代開始從 TikTok 尋求心理健康建議。

Images courtesy of TikTok

心理健康專家開始利用 TikTok 來為焦慮的世代提供指引。心理師以俏皮的影片搭配流行音樂與舞蹈來回答和壓力、創傷、心理治療有關的提問，也提供一系列建議，讓觀眾學習如何健康地表達情緒，吸引了上百萬的追蹤者與點閱數。

持有牌照的心理治療博士 Courtney Tracy 的 TikTok 帳號（@the.truth.doctor）截至 2021 年 12 月累積了 170 萬名追蹤者，她在上面分享跨世代創傷、以健康的方式表達憤怒等不同議題。Micheline Maalouf 是持有牌照的創傷治療師，她為她的 110 萬名追蹤者提供自我療癒的秘訣，也談及未排解的創傷會有哪些徵兆。

2021 年 12 月初，TikTok 上與心理健康（#mentalhealth）、心理治療（#therapy）有關的標籤分別有 216 億和 53 億次瀏覽，抖音心理治療（#therapytiktok）和抖音心理治療師（#therapistsoftiktok）的觀看數也分別有 4 億 4750 萬與 3 億 5760 萬。

值得關注的原因：

TikTok 是 Z 世代愛用的應用程式，使用人數比 Instagram 和 Snapchat 還多。Z 世代對心理健康的議題持有相當開放的態度，也開始把 TikTok 視為接收簡短資訊、教育內容、專業諮商的管道。

@the.truth.doctor. Images courtesy of TikTok

84

促進代謝的品牌

代謝能力是關心身體健康的消費者用來監測和增進健康狀況的最新指標。

根據一篇 2021 年 8 月刊登於《科學》(Science)期刊的研究指出，在 20 歲至 60 歲間，代謝速度都維持在穩定的範圍，因此代謝緩慢不是中年肥胖的成因。這份研究為腸道健康、體力、消化能力之間的連結指出新的研究方向。現在新的健康品牌開始提供好消化的健康促進產品，協助消費者改善代謝能力並解決代謝問題。

英國無酒精飲料品牌 OhMG 在 2021 年 5 月推出一系列富含鎂離子的飲用水。鎂可以減緩焦慮、協助放鬆、調節神經系統，也能透過強化代謝能力來增強體力。販售益生菌蘇打水的新創公司 Mayawell 於 2020 年面世，使用有機、人工採收的龍舌蘭為原料；龍舌蘭可以促進代謝、強化免疫系統、改善消化能力。

健康領域的重要人物也對代謝能力帶來的影響有正向評價。葛妮絲・派特洛(Gwyneth Paltrow)非常相信 Will Cole 博士直觀的節食計畫，該計畫旨在促使代謝能力和腸道健康恢復原本的水準。葛妮絲・派特洛的健康管理公司 Goop 也販售促進代謝的超級粉末。

監測代謝狀況成為衡量身體健康的新指標，相關的追蹤工具也受到越來越多的關注。Lumen 在募集到超過 1,700 萬美元的資金

後，於 2020 年 5 月上架，承諾會「解決代謝問題」。位於紐約的 Levels 打造了監測並強化代謝能力的穿戴式生醫裝置，讓使用者能享有「更長壽、更充實、更健康的生活」。赫爾辛基的 Veri 是另一款製造穿戴式醫療裝置的新創公司，成立於 2020 年。Veri 的穿戴式裝置可追蹤血糖並連接可作為「代謝指南針」的 Veri 應用程式。

值得關注的原因：

據 2018 年由北卡羅來納大學教堂山分校（University of North Carolina at Chapel Hill）的吉林全球公共衛生學院（Gillings School of Global Public Health）研究指出，只有 12% 的美國人擁有良好的代謝能力。健康成為所有人關注的重點，因此提升代謝能力的品牌紛紛上市，以便觀察在意身體健康的消費者對於整體健康的種種需求。

Left: OhMG offers a range of magnesium-enriched waters
Right: Levels created a biowearable that monitors metabolic fitness

85

心理健康藥局

消費者現在可以在同一個地點就買齊 OK 蹦、藥物、心理治療療程。

Top: CVS Health connects customers with licensed therapists
Bottom: Image courtesy of Aetna

> 這些便利的心理服務模式
> 大幅改變了大衆
> 尋求心理治療的方式。

據 Aetna 於 2021 年發布的〈員工心理健康調查〉(Mental Health Pulse Survey)顯示，美國 18 歲至 34 歲的人口中，有 65% 曾在新冠疫情爆發後，擔心起自己或家人朋友的心理健康。這反應出 2020 至 2021 年間，焦慮或憂鬱的狀況大幅增加，而為了回應這些求助的需求，大型藥妝業者如 CVS、Walgreens、Rite Aid、沃爾瑪(Walmart)等，紛紛透過線上、應用程式內和實體的門診來為顧客提供心理健康服務。

2021 年 1 月，CVS Health 透過旗下提供免預約服務的店面 CVS MinuteClinic，來媒合持有牌照的心理師與年滿 18 歲的顧客。消費者可以在特定的 CVS 店鋪內尋求評估、轉介，甚至私人諮商服務。一開始的服務範圍包含德州、賓州、佛羅里達州，現在也進一步延伸到紐澤西。CVS 計畫要把實體門診和電話諮商服務的範圍，拓展到 34 個地區。

Walgreens 的照護計畫 Find Care 始於 2021 年 3 月，由持有牌照的心理師提供線上治療服務，目前也為尋求心理治療的顧客安排門診時段。由於該品牌與心理健康組織 Mental Health America 合作，顧客可以預約電話諮商公司 BetterHelp 和 Sanvello 提供的線上心理健康檢查服務。

沃爾瑪(Walmart)以旗下健康事業 Walmart Health 提供心理諮商服務，並於 2021 年 5 月收購遠距醫療平台 MeMD 後，增加了線上心理健康照護服務。2021 年 6 月，Rite Aid 也開始在以下十個州別提供電話諮商服務：德拉瓦州、愛達荷州、馬里蘭州、新罕布什爾州、紐澤西州、俄亥俄州、賓州、德州、維吉尼亞州、華盛頓州。

值得關注的原因：

這些便利的心理服務模式大幅改變了大眾尋求心理治療的方式。諮商服務與傳統醫療和藥物販售服務接軌，這樣的新模式將會重塑消費者對自身心理健康照護的需求，讓身體與心理健康都能得到同等的照護。

Walmart and MeMD

86

療癒之音

音訊平台和聲響科技化身成為養生會所，
讓人得以放鬆並修復心靈。

ASMR（Autonomous sensory meridian response，自發性知覺神經反應）在音樂、養生、紓壓領域都成了耳熟能詳的詞彙。消費者現在開始利用 ASMR、聲響和音訊，來做為自我身心照護的方式。

Sona 是一款專為焦慮而設計的音樂治療應用程式，於 2022 年的美國消費電子用品展（CES）亮相。Sona 的創辦人 Neal Sarin 對偉門智威智庫表示：「我們正在努力讓音樂成為核准療法。」他接著解釋，程式中的音樂皆為原創，由該公司挑選的作曲家和獲頒葛萊美獎的音樂工程師創作而成，他們採用 Sona 特有的作曲流程來增加大腦的 α 波，讓聆聽者得以放鬆。

2021 年 10 月，聲響體驗新創品牌 Spatial 和 Catalyst by Wellstar 與非營利數位串流平台 HealthTunes 合作，利用聲音的修復力來守護醫護人員。這些平台將攜手打造聲音庇護所，參考有科學根據的音樂治療期刊《MusicMedicine》來為前線醫護人員打造舒緩壓力與焦慮的空間，讓他們可以在工作中稍微喘口氣。Spatial 的營運長 Darrel Rodriguez 告訴《Fast Company》，「沈浸式聲響有機會成為一種治療方式」，且該公司「希望能對社會發揮影響」。

音訊應用程式 Dipsea 結合療癒的聲音與情慾故事來引導聆聽者入睡。Dipsea 豐富的睡眠曲目為使用者提供大量的選擇，除了助眠、放鬆，甚至還能提高性慾。Kama 這類關注情慾發展的應用程式以及類似 Maude 的養生品牌，都在開發情慾音效來為平台打造額外的特色。

值得關注的原因：

強力音效已經超越聲響行銷的範疇，化身新的療癒會所。在自我照護、療癒、養生的領域中，音效的影響力與日俱增，因此品牌也開始整合不同的聲效產品，來滿足消費者的需求與渴望。

WUNDERMAN THOMPSON

Dipsea combines soothing sounds with erotic stories to guide listeners to sleep

87

抗體療法

新冠肺炎（COVID-19）患者開始以計算卡路里的方式計算抗體數，抗體療法相關的研究也正如火如荼地進行。

隨著新冠肺炎的變種病毒持續感染全球人口，醫療機構急著探討抗體是否能成為通用疫苗或療法的關鍵解方。

醫療門診開始為患者提供新冠肺炎抗體數目測量的額外福利。《紐約時報》（The New York Times）指出，全球各地前往高檔醫療機構求診的患者，紛紛開始以「計算卡路里的方式」計算抗體數，以圖個安心。提供這類服務的機構包含比佛利山莊的 My Concierge MD、曼哈頓的 Sollis Health，以及加州蒙特斯托的私人保健中心 Montecito Concierge Medicine。

2021 年 11 月由北卡羅來納大學和杜克大學發表的突破性研究指出，使用分離抗體有機會治療新冠肺炎與其變種病毒引發的疾病。該研究認為，一種名為 DH1047 的抗體不僅可以預防感染，還可以在確診後對抗病毒。此一結果指出了通用疫苗的設計方向，通用疫苗為可以對抗多種變種病毒的疫苗。

AZ 公司（AstraZeneca）同樣於 11 月宣布，要為疫苗與抗體治療另立專屬研究部門。新部門會著重研究該公司的新冠肺炎治療方針，除了結合抗體治療的研究、開發與製造，也希望對抗未來的變種病毒。抗體治療的試驗結果相當不錯，讓人看到此一療法的潛力，目前也有更多的研究正在進行。

值得關注的原因：

由於抗體治療出現了一絲曙光，醫療機構可能會持續鎖定新冠肺炎抗體測量、監測以及維持抗體數目的商機。

88

下個世代的心理健康

兒童心理健康危機促使應用程式與線上遊戲發行商
改寫平台的使用限制。

需轉介至心理治療門診的兒童越來越多，讓線上平台與社交應用程式不得不承認他們對年幼用戶造成的影響，並因此將心力放到適當的保護措施上。

英國皇家精神醫學院的資料顯示，英國在疫情期間需要轉介至心理治療門診的兒童數目，幾乎加倍成長至 20 萬人。特別是緊急轉介的人數，在 2019 年 4 月至 6 月共有 5,219 人，但在 2021 年則來到 8,552 人。

#kidsoftiktok. Image courtesy of TikTok

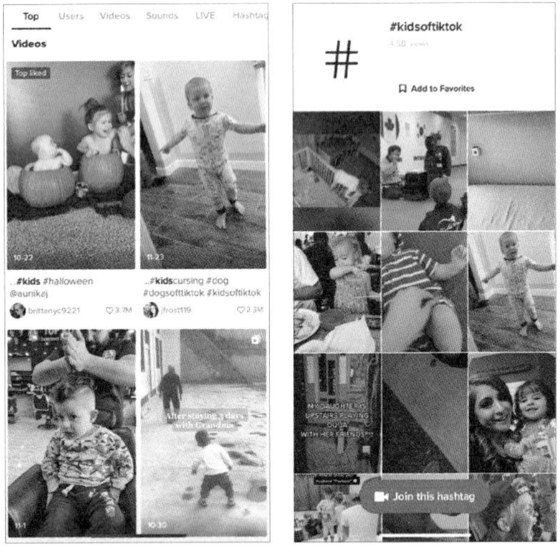

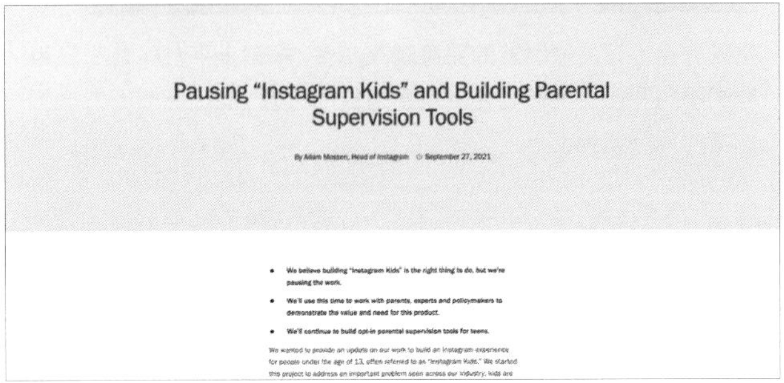
Pausing "Instagram Kids" and Building Parental Supervision Tools

By Adam Mosseri, Head of Instagram · September 27, 2021

- We believe building "Instagram Kids" is the right thing to do, but we're pausing the work.
- We'll use this time to work with parents, experts and policymakers to demonstrate the value and need for this product.
- We'll continue to build opt-in parental supervision tools for teens.

We wanted to provide an update on our work to build an Instagram experience for people under the age of 13, often referred to as "Instagram Kids." We started this project to address an important problem seen across our industry: kids are

美國兒科學會、美國兒童醫院協會、美國兒童與青少年精神醫學會的專家認為，兒童心理健康危機是國家危機，「且與兩個因素密不可分，一是新冠肺炎（COVID-19）造成的壓力，另一個因素則是種族正義帶來的難題」。他們的數據顯示，與 2019 年相比，2020 年因心理問題緊急求診的人數，在 5 至 11 歲的兒童中增加了 24%，在 12 至 17 歲的兒童中則增加了 31%。

有些平台則開始重新制訂策略，例如 2021 年 9 月，Instagram 暫緩兒童專屬平台 Instagram Kids 的相關設置工作，希望在改制平台之前，先讓焦點重新回到家長、立法人員與專家的作為上。Instagram 的母公司 Meta 希望為 10 至 12 歲的兒童打造這個獨立、無廣告的平台，呈現兒童適宜的內容，讓家長可全權監督，並得在家長同意下才能加入使用。

2021 年 9 月，字節跳動公司在中國的抖音應用程式上推出兒童模式，限制 14 歲以下的兒童一天最多只能使用 40 分鐘，符合中國政府針對 14 歲以下兒童所制定的電玩限制。此前一個月，中國國家新聞出版署宣布了針對 18 歲以下青少年與兒童的遊戲限制，規定他們只能在週五、週末及國定假日的晚上 8 點至 9 點之間打電動。

值得關注的原因：

社交媒體和電玩對兒童造成極大的影響，政府與家長紛紛要求保護兒童的上網安全。科技公司因此開始重新調整策略，藉此保護年輕世代的心理健康。

Top: Images courtesy of TikTok
Bottom: Instagram announces work on Instagram Kids has been paused

89

5G 醫療

中國搭建 5G 基礎建設的速度領先全球，醫療照護產業成為第一波受惠的對象之一。

中國與亞洲其他市場的遠距醫療服務已不限於基本的視訊諮詢，現在還能提供類似實體門診的完整醫療服務。前一代的 4G 網路可能會出現延遲、連接不穩的狀況，因此限制了遠距醫療的使用範圍；5G 的部署則改善了視訊諮詢的畫質、遠距病患監測的成效，甚至還提升了機器人遠距手術的品質。

早在 2020 年 1 月，中國的中興通訊和中國電信已針對新冠肺炎（COVID-19）部署了中國最早的 5G 遠距醫療門診。總部位於深圳的中興通訊表示，此技術以四川大學華西醫院的醫師為中央節點，為 20 多家不同醫院的新冠肺炎患者提供遠距醫療診治服務。

廣州位於中國的「大灣區」內，該區因與矽谷所在的美國「灣區」發展情形類似而得名。廣州的廣東省第二人民醫院使用了 5G 技術來收集、傳送、監測病患的醫療數據。該醫院的護理師陳曉芳（音譯）在美聯社一則發表於 2021 年 11 月的影音報導中，示範如何使用智慧手錶來監測靜脈注射等流程，並表示「這樣我們就能節省很多時間」。根據美聯社的報導，該醫院上萬台的裝置與感測器都已連上 5G 網路，可以即時收集心電圖等醫療資訊以供醫護人員監測。

香港中文大學醫院攜手香港電訊集團，於 2021 年 6 月宣布成為香港第一間部署 5G 網路的私人醫院，可即時傳送內視鏡檢查、超音波、電腦斷層掃描和其他高解析度的醫療影像來進行遠距醫療諮詢。

值得關注的原因：

中國的病患已經可以利用手機應用程式（例如「平安好醫生」和騰訊的「微醫」）來預約門診時間、接收掃瞄影像和檢查報告，並獲得醫生的簡單建議。未來 5G 還有更多發展可能，「最後會變成任何事情都可以在線上進行 …… 醫生可以在世界各地執業，病患也可以向世界各地的醫生求診」。IHH 醫療集團管理中國東部業務的執行長 Kenneth Chung 對《美國全國廣播公司商業頻道》（CNBC）如此說道。

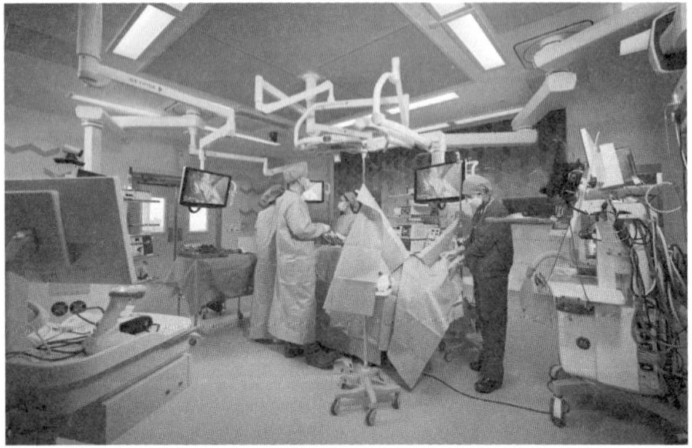

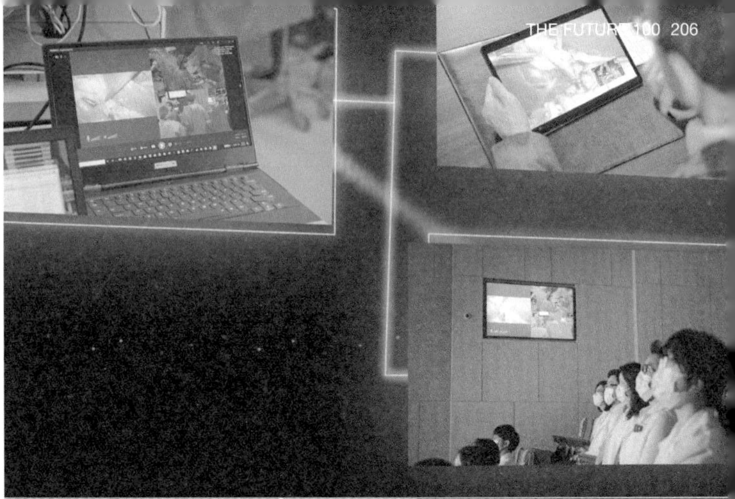

+WUNDERMAN THOMPSON

HKT has partnered with CUHK Medical Centre to bring 5G technology to the hospital, enabling live remote consultation with participants at different locations

90

情緒健康

情緒充電站開始出現在世界各地的公共空間中。

Dwight White. Image by Jaylen Prater, courtesy of Pinterest Havens

隨著與心理健康有關的污名開始褪去，為心理和情緒健康設計的公共空間紛紛浮現。

馬德里有座公共藝術空間能讓觀眾表達並描繪他們的心理狀態，這個空間名為 La Lloreria（意即「哭泣室」），旨在消除與心理健康有關的禁忌，提供讓人思考、肯認並以藝術表達情緒的空間。2021 年 10 月，西班牙首相桑傑士發布了一項一億歐元（約台幣 31 億元）的心理健康計畫，並指出該國民眾相當關注心理健康。

社交平台 Pinterest 於 2021 年 10 月推出 Pinterest Havens，希望讓「社區所激發的靈感，能有線上和實體的展示空間」。該公司也在芝加哥委製裝置藝術作品《避風港：你值得放鬆一下》（Havens:Invest in Rest），其中包含了當地藝術家 Dwight White 的壁畫、讓人身心放鬆的紙本圖像、沈浸式藝術以及社區計畫，希望幫助觀眾對抗生活中的疲勞，並鼓勵觀眾關注自身的情緒健康。

2021 年 10 月，紐約市魯賓藝術博物館（Rubin Museum of Art）開設了療癒型文化空間「曼陀羅實驗室」，透過佛教宗義來促進情緒健康與人際連結。參觀者可以探索自身的複雜情緒，並加以面對、轉化。執行董事 Jorrit Britschgi 表示，該空間希望能「讓我們有力量面對當今的挑戰：拓寬我們的想像力，理解並管理我們的情緒，增加我們的同理心，並幫助我們與他人建立聯繫。」

值得關注的原因：

這些充滿情感的空間會成為未來的遊樂場嗎？能夠建立連結、休息和冥想的獨立空間開始融入社區的公共場所之中。

The Rubin Museum of Art's Mandala Lab. Image by Rafael Gamo

The Rubin Museum of Art's Mandala Lab. Image by Rafael Gamo

91
工作
100

91

啓動元宇宙辦公

虛擬傳送門、全息投影和能夠自在漫遊的虛擬化身——辦公模式的未來面貌已然成形。

虛擬辦公室開始成為主流，因為遠距工作和虛實整合的工作風潮可能會持續下去。微軟（Microsoft）計劃在 2022 年為其協作工具 Microsoft Teams 推出混合實境服務 Mesh，用戶除了能以客製化的虛擬化身參與會議，還能一同使用全息投影來協作專案。Mesh 還為企業提供可打造沉浸式虛擬環境的功能，微軟將該功能形容為「通往元宇宙的大門」。

微軟技術研究員 Alex Kipman 解釋道：「我們公司注重生產力和知識型員工的需求，而這項服務是消費者向我們提出的真實要求，也和我們過去 12 年來為混合實境設定的願景相符。」Kipman 接著說，「一切都兜在一起了。」

Meta 於 2021 年 8 月推出了虛擬工作室 Horizon Workrooms。透過虛擬實境（VR），同事們可以在同一個虛擬工作空間中互相合作、共同創作，「即使分處天涯海角，您也能與團隊成員在桌邊會面，並將您的居家辦公室變成您最愛的遠距會議室」，Horizon Workrooms 如此承諾。

Mesh for Microsoft Teams. Image courtesy of Microsoft

建立品牌專屬的虛擬工作空間也越來越受歡迎。偉門智威在2022 年美國消費電子用品展（CES）上推出虛擬會議中心。Sinespace 的 Breakroom 於 2020 年 4 月發表，是「遠距工作團隊的新型社交中心」；該公司還能在 24 小時內為品牌設立專屬辦公室。Gather 在其後一個月推出，旨在讓「虛擬互動更具人性」。Kumospace 和 Z 世代新創品牌 Branch 的運作方式與 Gather 類似，其中的虛擬房間是由模擬實體世界的方式設計而成，可加強自然互動，讓用戶的虛擬化身能在裡面四處走動並互相交流。

值得關注的原因：

多虧了元宇宙，我們彼此連結、生活和工作的方式正在改變。未來的辦公模式將會強化虛實整合，且使用對象不只限於少數人；虛擬工作空間更會帶頭實現新形態的創造力、協作與沉浸體驗。

WUNDERMAN THOMPSON
The Wunderman Thompson Metaverse in collaboration with Odyssey

> 元宇宙改變了
> 我們彼此連結、
> 生活和工作的方式。

92

「影響長」人氣攀升

領導階層中，有個人氣攀升的新職位：
影響長（Chief Impact Officer，CIO）。

Taco Bell named Lil Nas X as the chain's first CIO

企業領導階層開始讓「影響長」成為董事會的一員，其任務旨在彰顯品牌的社區和社會影響力。

饒舌歌手納斯小子（Lil Nas X）過去曾在連鎖速食店 Taco Bell 打工，他於 2021 年 8 月被指派成為這家企業的首位影響長。此榮譽職的派任恰逢納斯小子的專輯《Montero》發行日，Taco Bell 也同時推出鼓勵青年創意人才的獎學金計劃。納斯小子也現身 Taco Bell 的早餐廣告，並「以自己的親身經歷，來為所有 Taco Bell 的團隊成員帶來影響。」該品牌如此表示。

哈利王子於 2021 年 3 月開始擔任矽谷新創公司 BetterUp 的影響長。這個為客戶提供輔導與心理健康服務的平台表示，他們的任務是「釋放世界上所有人的潛力，而這需要靠創新、影響力、誠信來達成」。該公司的影響長需要制定產品策略並決定慈善捐款額度，而哈利王子本人也有公開倡導心理健康的重要。

值得關注的原因：

近年來，消費者對品牌的要求越來越高，領導階層的社會參與和誠信也因此被迫提升。影響長負責面向群眾發揮公司的影響力，致力於慈善事業，並確保品牌對社區和消費者發揮正向影響。

Taco Bell named Lil Nas X as the chain's first CIO

93

辦公室回歸自然

盆栽、蜂巢、賞鳥一最新的公司福利是讓員工能更親近大自然。

總部位於曼哈頓市中心的投資公司 Nuveen，讓員工可以在午休時段來到在被高樓環繞的陽台上採收蜂蜜。該公司設置了兩個蜂箱，同時也聘請了一名養蜂人來照顧蜜蜂，並為員工提供採蜜教學，這是他們斥資 1.2 億美元並於 2021 年完工的辦公室翻新計畫之一。

Springdale Green 是位於德州奧斯汀的全新開發區，他們把賞鳥小屋和吊床搬進辦公室，並在周圍種滿原生植物並鋪設土壤。房地產公司 Newmark 的執行副董 Philip Mahoney 對《紐約時報》（The New York Times）表示，他們的辦公室「比較像戶外空間，而非室內場所。」

房地產公司 Brookfield Properties 近期翻修了位於華盛頓的 Victor Building，在這棟大樓工作的員工現在可以在回家之前，先到屋頂的菜園摘一些西洋芹和羅勒等香料來烹調晚餐。

Uber 在舊金山的新總部於 2021 年 3 月開張，其中一個主要的設計理念是提供新鮮空氣：總共有 180 片 14 英尺高的玻璃窗全天不斷開合呼吸，讓空氣不會只在室內不斷循環，而是會往外排出，並讓戶外空氣也能流入室內。

值得關注的原因：

「辦公室飯店化（hotelification）是過去五年來的總體趨勢，」世邦魏理仕（CBRE）的執行董事總經理 Lenny Beaudoin 對《紐約時報》如此說道。在接下來的五年裡，這股趨勢會變成辦公室「戶外化」（outdoor-ification），主要因為企業正將自然元素視為未來辦公室設計的一環。

WUNDERMAN THOMPSON The Victor Building hosts a garden of herbs and vegetables that employees can harvest to cook with

94

區塊鏈決策模式

Web 3.0 經濟以 DAO（Digital autonomous organization，數位自治組織）的模式，提供受聘於企業以外的就業方案。

CryptoTwitter 對 DAO 深感期待。簡單來說，DAO 是一個數位原生社群或組織，而且可能可以代表未來的工作型態 - 你的下一個雇主可能就是某個 DAO。

嚴格來說，DAO 是一個由社群主導、建立在區塊鏈上的數位組織。它不是由執行長或董事會管理，而是由程式碼來定義其運作模式，也就是所謂的智能合約。在實務上，許多 DAO 尚未完全實現自治的目標，因此口語中也會用 DAO 來代指一般的數位組織。這些組織比較像具有共同興趣和目標的線上社團，並且通常以某個 Reddit 群組或 Discord 伺服器為集散地。

重要的是，DAO 還具有綁定加密貨幣的內建金庫，這代表組織成員在為社群做出貢獻以後，可以獲得代幣作為獎勵。這些新型礦工已開始受到 DAO 所吸引，並將 DAO 視為朝九晚五以外的替代型就業方案。

2021 年 9 月，社群發起人和顧問 Rafa Fernandez 在 Web 3.0 發布平台 Mirror 上發布了一篇長文，裡面提到他決定辭去他在科技新創公司的夢想職位，改為 DAO 效力。Fernandez 不是唯一的案例，而且參與 DAO 經濟的人數正在快速成長。根據追蹤該行業的平台 DeepDAO 的數據，2021 年 12 月持有加密貨幣的人數與會員數為 160 萬人，光是和前一個月相比，就增加了 35.6 萬人。可以彰顯這種爆炸性成長的另一信號，是新型 DAO 經濟的興起，例如 Opolis 等公司便為 DAO 員工提供醫療保健福利、薪資條和其他共享型服務。

從員工的角度來看，DAO 有很多優勢。它們是數位組織，因此沒有「實體總部」或「地理疆界的問題」- 但對許多 Z 世代來說，這兩個概念早已過時了。

在 DAO 當中階級幾乎不存在，因此當然也沒有老闆的概念。另一方面，它們為成員提供機會，可以透過集體力量影響決策，也能共享利潤。最重要的是，它們本來就由志同道合、充滿熱情和參與度高的人所組成，成員追求的是相同的目標。

「它最核心的概念，是一群真正關心某件事的人，想一起為之努力，」在波士頓大學教授區塊鏈和社會影響力的 Anne Connelly 向 WBUR 廣播電台如此解釋。

那麼問題來了，傳統公司能否轉型成 DAO 呢？其實這已經是現在進行式。ShapeShift 是一個成立於 2014 年的加密交易平台，他們計劃在 2022 年解構公司並轉型成 DAO。

當然 DAO 也面臨了某些挑戰。社群用戶了解其中還有許多議題需要釐清，像是 DAO 的法律地位，以及解決衝突的方式。儘管如此，社群基礎、作法彈性以及共同目標所提供的綜合吸引力，目前看來仍然相當強大。

值得關注的原因：

雖然不是每家公司都想複製 DAO 的模式，這個新模式也並非全盤適用，但在建立社群與文化和員工賦權方面，我們還是能從中學習到有趣的課題。Orca Protocol 的共同創辦人兼執行長 Julia Rosenberg 最近在加密貨幣會議 Mainnet 中說明，在這個時代，員工積極地提出倡議，希望能重塑職場環境以符合他們的價值觀：「如果你不同意，你也有機會促成改變，這是在中心化組織無法實現的事。」

Left: ShapeShift
Right: Mirror. Image courtesy of Twitter

95

微型創業家 2.0

美國人正重新評估他們的職場生活，推動了前所未見的離職潮和職業轉向。

2021 年底，許多美國人離開了原先的工作崗位。同年四月的單月離職總人數打破了美國的歷史紀錄，並持續呈現成長趨勢，僅九月份就有超過 440 萬名員工離職。根據微軟（Microsoft）在 2021 年 3 月公布的全球工作趨勢報告（Work Trend Index），全球有 41% 的人考慮在未來的一年內辭職，Z 世代的比例更增加至 54%。《華盛頓郵報》（The Washington Post）稱這項轉變為「對工作的全面重評估」。

那麼這些員工都去哪了？許多人開始追求高收入的工作，像是零售業或服務業員工轉向入門級工作，或職業生涯中期的專業人士轉換跑道。勞動力分析公司 Visier 認為，截至 2020 年 12 月，經理階層的離職率比去年增加了 12%。

其他人則是追求所愛或將斜槓創業發展為全職事業。微軟的研究指出，46% 的人正在計畫重大的職業轉換或職涯轉型。大批英國的員工開始成為自由工作者。根據自由接案平台 PeoplePerHour 在 2021 年 4 月的數據，約有五分之一的自由工作者同時從事斜槓創業並任職於企業，其中近五分之二的人在過去十二個月內開始自由接案。

在辭去了語言治療師的工作後，Jake Kenyon 決定在 2021 年 1 月將他位於羅德島州首府的手染紗線副業 Kenyarn 發展為全職事業。

這項模式延續了 2020 年疫情初期開始的新趨勢，員工紛紛辭去辦公室的工作，將自己所愛的副業轉換為全職事業。如今，這項趨勢讓全國民眾開始重新評估工作，促成了新的就業時代。

值得關注的原因：

如果說 2020 年讓消費者重新評估了他們的生活與價值觀，那麼 2022 年他們追求的就是符合這些價值觀的工作。根據《商業內幕》（Business Insider）表示，員工正在仔細思考自己想從職業生涯與職場中得到什麼，這將有可能帶來「全面的職場變革」。

Jake Kenyon's Kenyarn side hustle turned into a full-time career

96

女力復甦

為了協助女性對抗經濟衰退下的性別劣勢，全球企業正努力替女性打造友善的職場環境。

經濟衰退導致世界各地的女性大量退出勞動市場，而此問題至今仍未改善。如今，從金融服務業到飯店業等各行各業正上演前所未見的人才爭奪戰。而對女性友善的職場不僅能與時俱進，更能大幅提升競爭優勢。那麼，一年過去了，為了讓女性重回職場，企業又做出了什麼改變？

最大的轉變當然就是彈性工時，舉凡 Spotify、臉書（Facebook）、美國運通（American Express）等企業都採用了此方式。彈性工作對於兼顧工作和家庭的女性來說特別具有吸引力，儘管英格蘭銀行經濟學家 Catherine Mann 等評論家警告，如果男性沒有跟著採用遠距上班，那麼遠距上班的做法最終可能使女性付出代價。

展望未來，在企業文化中將彈性工作正常化將成為緩解不平等現象的必要手段。為此，英國建築公司 Multiplex 在 2021 年 10 月推出了新的彈性工作政策，希望能吸引更多女性投入職場。該公司的倡議名為 Multiplex Flex，提供員工一系列的彈性工作方案，像是每週上班四天、遠距工作以及休假代替加班費等。資誠

對女性友善的職場不僅能與時俱進，更能大幅提升競爭優勢。

（PwC）也致力於保障遠距上班的員工，不讓他們蒙受任何損失。四大會計師事務所在 2021 年秋季宣布，除了持續採用遠距工作外，更承諾將密切注意遠距上班員工與辦公室員工之間的加薪、薪水與獎金是否一致，並在發現差異時立即採取行動。

疫情期間仍在工作崗位上的女性則面臨了不同的挑戰。麥肯錫管理顧問公司（McKinsey & Co）以及非營利組織 LeanIn.org 發布的《2021 年女性職場報告書》（Women in the Workplace 2021）指出，自 2020 年以來，感到職業倦怠的女性與男性人數差距已經翻倍。針對北美地區 6 萬 5,000 名勞工的調查報告指出，三分之一的女性曾考慮降低職涯目標或直接離職，與疫情初期相較，當時僅有四分之一的女性有此考量。

報告更指出，女性主管在員工身心健康方面付出了更多的時間，但這項努力卻往往遭到忽視。此外，根據統計結果，女性比男性更有可能致力於多元、平等與包容性倡議，但僅有不到四分之一的受訪公司以正式制度認可這項成就。然而，領英（LinkedIn）卻採取截然不同的做法，除了承諾每年支付一萬美元給員工資源小組的主席，更建立了非財務性的獎勵機制來表彰員工的貢獻。推特（Twitter）則在 2020 年時採取了類似的做法。

值得關注的原因：

經濟衰退下女性困境可能持續影響企業未來數年的發展，突顯出雇主必須立即採取行動。如果公司願意採用各項政策，致力促進女性、家庭照護者以及員工的身心狀況，將能以最佳狀態度過這波經濟風暴。

Images courtesy of Multiplex

97

Z 世代徵才

品牌重新調整他們的徵才策略，希望能吸引 Z 世代員工擔任長期職位。

時尚品牌開始招募更年輕的求職者，希望號召多元人才加入公司，並讓從事入門工作的職員長期留任。

2021 年 9 月，法國奢侈品牌 LVMH 宣布將在 2022 年底前招募 2 萬 5,000 名 30 歲以下的員工。這波針對 Z 世代的長期徵才活動顯示了該品牌對於全球年輕人才的關注，以及擴大徵才範圍並招募多元人才的期許。LVMH 特別強調希望長期聘雇，並從四面八方廣納人才，不僅限於名校或富裕家庭出身的求職者。

服飾品牌 Hollister 在 2021 年 10 月宣布任命第一位的遊戲教頭。年僅 18 歲的 Kyle “Bugha” Giersdorf 不僅是《要塞英雄》（Fortnite）的世界冠軍，截至 2021 年 11 月止，他還擁有 490 萬名 Twitch 粉絲。目前他正在設計以玩家為靈感的服飾，替這個衝浪與海灘服飾品牌開拓全新的領域。Bugha 也將領導「Hollister 品牌隊」，希望帶領更多充滿潛力的實況主，讓品牌成為遊戲宇宙的中心，並吸引新一波的青年世代購買其產品。

值得關注的原因：

業界需要能洞悉 Z 世代年輕市場的人才。聘用年輕人才擔任永久職不僅有利於品牌徵才，同時也滿足了 Z 世代與千禧世代對於充分培訓與職業發展的需求。在品牌追求長期穩健經營之下，吸引了不少初入職場的優秀人才。

WUNDERMAN THOMPSON

Hollister appointed Fortnite World Cup champion Kyle "Bugha" Giersdorf as its first chief gaming scout

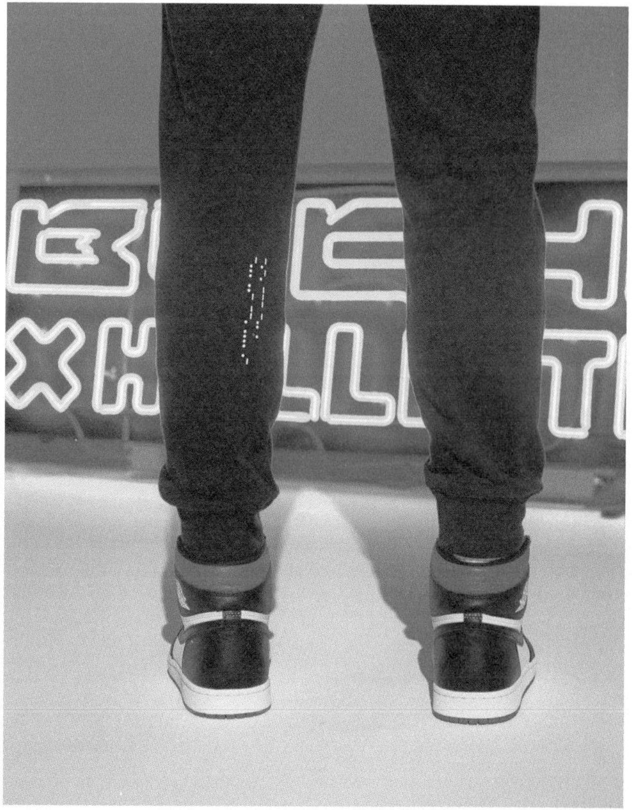

98

重新培訓

新一代的員工將面臨職場的技能再造。

企業不斷地變化，員工所需的技能也跟著改變。隨著數位革命的發展，品牌意識到為了跟上時代，最快且最有效的方式就是加強培訓現有的員工。專業的大學或碩士學位或許曾是求職的先決條件，但如今公司卻鼓勵員工做從中學。

Guild Education 公司的聯合創辦人兼執行長 Rachel Carlson 預測，這個趨勢將帶來新的教育模式，甚至可能取代大學學位。Carlson 向 podcast 節目 Masters of Scale 表示，以往的「4+40」——也就是到學校學習四年、工作四十年——已經過時，而被新的模式所取代。「現在的情況是每四年進修一次。」Carlson 表示。「每四年必須重新學習某種新的技能。」

Levi Strauss & Co 在 2021 年 5 月宣布了全公司員工的數位培訓計畫。此計畫的核心是機器學習訓練營（Machine Learning Bootcamp），這項為期八週的全天帶薪培訓將培養員工的數位技能，如撰寫程式或機器學習。通過訓練營後，這些員工可以帶著新的技能回到原工作崗位，或加入該公司的策略與人工智慧團隊。

2020 年，威訊通訊（Verizon）在員工學習與發展計畫上投入超過 2 億美元，提供了數據科學、5G 技術和人工智慧等訓練課程。到了 2021 年底，威訊通訊培訓了超過 10 萬名員工，讓他們學習各種數位技能，「以確保團隊成員能做好準備，跟上未來不斷變化的需求。」

透過與 Guild Education 的合作計畫，沃爾瑪（Walmart）的員工只需繳交 365 美金（或每天 1 美元，為期 1 年）就能到高中或大學唸書並取得學位。自 2020 年 4 月至 2021 年 4 月，沃爾瑪表示該計畫讓公司的高中和大學畢業生都增加了 93%。

值得關注的原因：

傳統的職涯發展面臨重塑，技能訓練與職場的重新培訓取代了以往的專業學位。

Images courtesy of Guild Education

游牧經濟崛起

隨著世界各地漸漸開放遠距工作，新的經濟型態正在崛起，以滿足數位遊牧民族的需求。

只在辦公室工作的日子看似已成為歷史。疫情導致的封城迫使世界各地的公司必須打破傳統的工作型態，使得遠距工作者大幅增加，其中有些人首次成為數位遊牧工作者，並選擇到新的城市、州別甚至新的國家工作。

不幸的是，對於數位遊牧民族來說，他們只能在母國享有健保等社會權益等保障，一旦到了不同的國家或轄區便失去了這些原有的權益。

隨著數位游牧人口不斷攀升，新的經濟型態開始出現，以滿足他們對於行政、財務和後勤的需求。

保險公司 SafetyWing 為遠距工作者提供保險，無論他們身在何處。該公司在 2020 年初首度推出數位遊牧保險，讓遠距工作者在面臨不可預料的健康狀況或旅遊意外時能有所保障。在 2021 年募集到 800 萬美元的資金後，SafetyWing 將推出新的服務，提供民眾遠距醫療與遠距工作者的退休金計畫。

位於美國的保險科技公司 Insured Nomads 也希望服務全球各地的遊牧工作者，為他們提供保障，承保範圍涵蓋了藥物、網路安全和遠距醫療門診等。Insured Nomads 在疫情爆發前成立，

> 新的經濟型態開始出現，以滿足數位游牧人口對於行政、財務和後勤的需求。

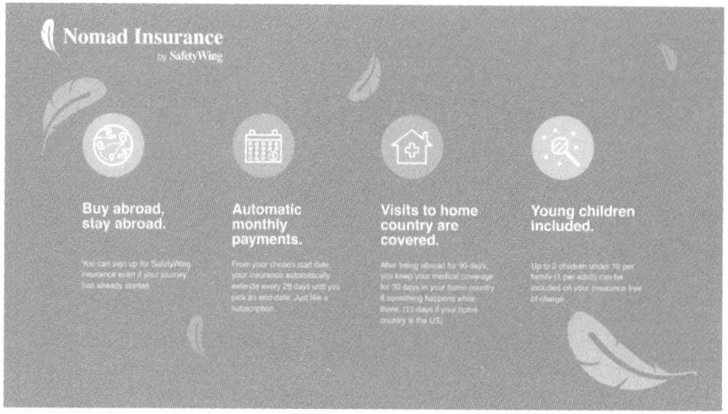

之後便持續推陳出新，希望能滿足全球勞工不斷變化的需求。2021 年 4 月，Insured Nomads 更推出新的心理健康諮詢服務以及全天候的急難救助等福利措施。

針對數位遊牧民族而設計的個人倉儲服務也不斷成長。Stuf 是 2020 年底成立的新創公司，致力將閒置的地下室和類似的空間改造為個人倉庫。與位在郊區的傳統倉庫設施不同，Stuf 認為遍布城市內的小型空間比較適合短期居住者，方便他們隨時取得個人物品。目前 Stuf 在洛杉磯、舊金山灣區、華盛頓特區和紐約四地推出了個人倉儲服務，預計在 2022 年擴展到 4,000 個地點。

值得關注的原因：

未來的工作型態將不受國界限制。隨著眼光銳利的公司逐漸排除遊牧生活的種種障礙，數位遊牧民族的人數與經濟影響力將持續成長。

Insurer SafetyWing offers coverage for remote workers

元宇宙徵才

從虛擬材料設計師到全面的創意人才，
企業開始打造元宇宙所需的人才。

元宇宙幾乎改變了生活的所有面向，就連徵才也不例外。「在未來數年，各式各樣的公司將重新調整為虛擬與實體並進的工作、生產、商務與溝通模式。」偉門智威的遊戲與電競主管 Grant Paterson 如此表示。「在虛擬世界裡，技術整合與新興消費者行為的雙重力量將使得『建立虛擬支柱』對企業而言更顯重要。」

Nike 在 2021 年 10 月申請了七項商標，包含「可下載的虛擬商品」（downloadable virtual goods）和「以虛擬商品為特色的零售服務」（retail store services featuring virtual goods）等。同月，該公司開始招募虛擬材料設計師加入旗下的數位產品創意團隊。招募公告中描述此職位將協助「打造 Nike 未來的製鞋材料」，並點燃「Nike 的數位與虛擬革命」。

2021 年 11 月，英國獨立電視台（ITV）在新的 Metavision 倡議下公開招募元宇宙創意人才，希望「結合遊戲、娛樂與廣告世界」。此職位將負責從發想至執行階段的元宇宙品牌活動。

「是時候該聘用一位元宇宙部門總監了嗎？」《Vogue Business》在 2021 年 10 月的文章中指出，擴增實境的零售服務、虛擬場所和數位財產正在崛起。與外部的科技與遊戲公司合作是過去一年的趨勢；如今品牌則自行招募人才，希望加速推出元宇宙相關的科技產品。

值得關注的原因：

還記得社群媒體躍為主流，公司爭相聘請社群媒體主管的時候嗎？現在公司紛紛展開徵才活動，以打造出元宇宙時代的商品，使得人才爭奪戰將再度上演，戰況甚至會更加激烈。

Nikeland on Roblox is the company's first step into the metaverse

關於偉門智威智庫（Wunderman Thompson Intelligence）

偉門智威智庫是智威湯遜面向未來思考的研究和創新單位，負責觀察剛興起的現象以及未來的全球趨勢、消費型態變化、創新發展模式，並在進一步解讀這些趨勢後，將其見解提供給品牌參考。本單位提供一系列諮詢服務，包含客製化研究、簡報、聯名品牌報告、工作坊，也勇於創新，與品牌合作，在品牌框架下引領未來趨勢，並執行新產品與概念。本單位由偉門智威智庫的全球總監 Emma Chiu 與 Marie Stafford 所帶領。

如欲瞭解更多資訊，請造訪：

wundermanthompson.com/expertise/intelligence

關於《改變未來的100件事》

這是由偉門智威智庫出版的年度預測報告，除了描繪未來一年的樣貌，也呈現了最受歡迎的趨勢，讓您能掌握潮流。這份報告紀錄了十大領域的 100 個趨勢，橫跨文化、科技與創新、旅遊與觀光、品牌與行銷、食品和飲品、美容、零售與商業、奢華、健康、工作領域。

WUNDERMAN THOMPSON

聯絡人

Emma Chiu
偉門智威智庫 | 全球總監
emma.chiu@wundermanthompson.com
台灣偉門智威
wt.taipei@wundermanthompson.com

總編輯

Emma Chiu

編輯

Emily Safian-Demers

撰稿人

Marie Stafford, Chen May Yee, Elizabeth Cherian, Sarah Tilley, Carla Calandra, Jamie Shackleton, Safa Arshadullah

副編輯

Hester Lacey, Katie Myers

中文版譯者

林庭如 Rye Lin

創意總監

Shazia Chaudhry

封面圖片

Raspberry Dream Labs

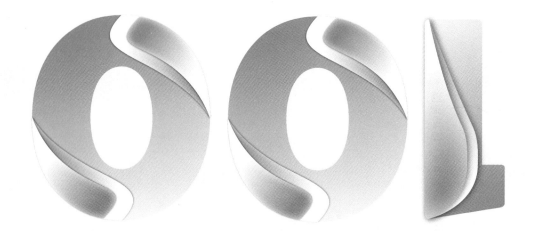

The future 100

WUNDERMAN THOMPSON

2022 The Future 100
Writer / Wunderman Thompson Intelligence

Editor-in-chief / Emma Chiu
Editor / Emily Safian-Demers
Writers / Marie Stafford, Elizabeth Cherian, Sarah Tilley, Carla Calandra, Jamie Shackleton, Safa Arshadullah
Sub editors / Hester Lacey, Katie Myers

Creative director / Shazia Chaudhry

Cover / Raspberry Dream Labs
Assistant editor / Jill Chang, Ophelia Lee, Jessica Chien, Dora Hsieh, Easy Tsai, Chia Huang, Bona Liu, Ann Chen, Cloud Kao, Kevin Huang, Joyce Lo, Vik Liu, Ai Hsiao, Pin Hsu

Chinese version contributor / Wunderman Thompson Taipei

Translator / Rye Lin Ting-Ru

Publisher / Wunderman Thompson Taipei
Address / 13F - 5, No.8, Sec. 7, Civic Boulevard, Nangang District, Taipei City, 115, Taiwan
Tel / (02) 3766-1000
Fax / (02) 2788-0260

Agent / China Times Publishing Company
Tel / (02) 2306-6842
Address / No.351, Sec.2, Wanshou Rd., Guisha District., Taoyuan City, 333, Taiwan

Retail price / NTD 500
ISBN / 9789869899222

First published in Taiwan by Wunderman Thompson in April 2022

Foreword

Join us on a journey into the near future, where daily life takes place in the metaverse and on a regenerative planet—and is packed with health-infused experiences, and, more importantly, is defined by an optimistic outlook. Welcome to "The Future 100: 2022."

As the world enters the third year of a pandemic, confidence in the end of COVID-19 in 2022 is expressed by the World Health Organization's chief, Dr Tedros Adhanom Ghebreyesu—providing everyone works together.

This year ushers in a resolute positivity that encourages playfulness and creativity—so much so that Pantone created a completely new color to define 2022 (see unbounded optimism, p13). Brands and marketers are eager to provide joy in people's lives by creating euphoric ads (p85) as they too ride the optimist wave.

Health and wellbeing remain prominent across sectors—from drinks that supercharge the immune system (see liquid immunity, p98) to dedicated spaces around the world offering an emotional outlet for those in need of a recharge (see emotional health, p199). The physical and emotional tax of the last two years is forging a holistic, sensitive and nuanced approach to wellbeing.

As lifestyles and businesses shift to become climate-friendly, being sustainable is not enough. Brands, governments and communities are working together for a regenerative planet and future. After all, 88% of global consumers believe companies and brands have a responsibility to take care of the planet and its people.

Finally, a new digital era is on the horizon as the metaverse evolves from a sci-fi concept into a reality. Virtual worlds where people can gather, create, buy and sell, socialize, live and work are becoming the new hangouts (see branded virtual worlds, p81). Technology that allows for advanced avatars (p36), virtual teleportation (p42) and NFT marketplaces (p154) is revolutionizing virtual engagement. And the rise of digital possessions and ownership brings about a new direct-to-avatar retail model (p137). The metaverse is also disrupting the physical world, forming liminal spaces (p18), and augmented reality is becoming the chosen medium for advertisers (see augmented ads, p93).

Dive into "The Future 100: 2022" and discover 100 bitesize trends to watch out for in the year ahead.

Emma Chiu
Global director, Wunderman Thompson Intelligence
wundermanthompson.com/expertise/intelligence

Foreword

Post-pandemic, metaverse, inflation, Russo-Ukrainian war compose an unpredictable year. "Unpredictable" has become our daily routine.

While we are learning to coexist with the Coronavirus and expecting the promising future of metaverse, we are forced to deal with economic issues caused by the inflation and the global crisis resulted from Russo-Ukrainian war. The future that we are facing is mixed with expectations and fears. Is there a time travel machine that can take us to the future and look back, so that we could have more confidence now and moving forward? The answer is "no," certainly.

Mark Twain once said,"History does not repeat itself, but it rhymes." And this is why we publish Future100 - 100 Events That Will Change the Future. Through the global research teams, Wunderman Thompson have compiled a list of 100 events happening around the world that could serve as a reference for future trends.

In this trend report, we find this pandemic has dramatically changed the way we live and work, and helped us reflect. With nearly two years of social isolation and interpersonal alienation, people have new expectations of intimacy. As extreme adventure and traditional travel are almost unattainable, jaunts and local trips hence become the alternatives in high demand. And digital technology has made virtual travel possible, allowing people to have immersive travel experience at their comfortable home.

Due to the panic caused by pandemic, happiness has become luxury ! So here come the prescriptions for happiness. Emotional charging stations star to appear in public spaces around the world. As the world gradually opens to remote work, digital nomads rise. A new economic model is emerging in response to the new way of working.

With Metaverse coming soon, people expect this world to be inclusive, ethical, and understandable to everyone. Remote working model makes meta-cosmetics developed as needed. The e-sports industry is showcasing both virtual makeup results with physical beauty products in games to enhance player involvement.

"People are no longer passive consumers, but more proactively expressing themselves with their virtual identities" in the digital world. From B2B ,DTC to DTA (direct-to-avatar),

the latest business model is to deliver digital goods directly to consumers' digital devices. The brand new concept of "headless brand" is surfaced in the virtual world.

Nevertheless, the issue of environmental protection never stops: the world started moving towards net zero emissions, and a new trend of de-carbonization technology emerged. In addition to carbon neutral websites, the concept of "less is more" has started to appear in social networks, and the physical world has started to adopt micro-dose maintenance guidelines.

The "Blue Zone" diet concept has risen, and the vegan diet now officially enters the upper class society. After artificial meat and seafood, coffee will be the next product from the laboratory. Spirits manufacturers are accelerating maturation to avoid waste through new environmentally sustainable methods.

In addition to "farm-to-table", environmental protection initiatives even have a whole new concept of "farm-to-closet." As companies continue to address ESG issues, here emerges a highly popular new position of Chief Impact Officer (CIO), whose task is to demonstrate the social influence of brands.

In this wave of environmental protection, even the advertising industry is being scolded. The so-called "Badvertising" campaign has accused the advertising industry of "polluting the brain." Besides, we also notice that digital currency may become one of the legitimate daily payment options.

Generations are changing and a new generation is emerging – Generation Alpha (born between 2010 and 2025), younger than Generation Z, is driving a new wave of retail trends. Chat commerce, the private domain commerce, is widely available on communication platforms. Brands are trying new ways to profit in the non-fungible token (NFT) space.

What's more interesting, technology start-ups plan to disrupt the manicure industry ecology with robots because they "won't make mistake, won't slow down and won't gossip." Some experts reckon that airships will lead to an aviation revolution in the next decade.

Do you see all these 100 events that are happening around the world?

Evan Teng
CEO, Wunderman Thompson Taipei

01

Culture

10

11

Tech & innovation

20

21

Travel & hospitality

30

31

Brands & marketing

40

41

Food & drink

50

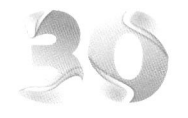

Beauty

Retail & commerce

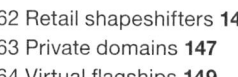

Luxury

Health

Work

91
Culture
10

01

Building the metaverse

The race is on as brands rush to stake their claim on the metaverse.

The metaverse dominated headlines, screens and boardrooms in the second half of 2021. Now brands and companies are rushing to prepare for this next iteration of digital engagement.

Big Tech brands are setting their sights on the metaverse. Facebook unveiled a massive brand pivot when it changed its company name to Meta in October 2021, after Mark Zuckerberg announced that the Meta's future lies in becoming a metaverse company. Microsoft CEO Satya Nadella said in August that year that Microsoft is working on building the "enterprise metaverse."

Gaming companies began seriously carving out space for the metaverse on their platforms in 2021. In April, Epic Games closed a $1 billion round of funding to support its "long-term vision for the metaverse." Niantic, the game developer behind *Pokémon Go*, raised $300 million in November to build what it describes as the "real-world metaverse." Nvidia jumpstarted its "metaverse for engineers" with the opening of Omniverse in August. Now, other companies are shelling out to buy up game developers. Most recently, *FarmVille* creator Zynga was purchased for $12.7 billion in January 2022, and Tencent purchased UK game developer Sumo Group for $1.7 billion in July 2021.

Even brands in industries that are not directly related to the creation of the metaverse, such as law and wealth management, started anticipating its growing value in 2021. In

March, the Metaverse Group announced plans to launch Metaverse REIT, a first-of-its-kind real estate investment trust for virtual assets. Law firm Reed Smith released a legal guide to the metaverse in May, covering legal issues ranging from intellectual property to privacy to competition in what the firm calls "the biggest-ever industrial revolution the world has ever seen." And in June, Roundhill Investments and Matthew Ball launched the Roundhill Ball Metaverse investment fund, which has holdings in companies including Nvidia, Tencent and Roblox.

Why it's interesting

Competition to create, define and own the metaverse has taken off. "There was a space race in the 1960s, and now there's a metaverse race in 2021," Krista Kim, digital artist and creator of the first NFT digital home, Mars House, tells Wunderman Thompson Intelligence. "People are really scurrying to build the new metaverse."

Left: Horizon Worlds. Image courtesy of Meta
Right: Nvidia Omniverse for AEC, showing Leeza Soho by Zaha Hadid Architects

02

Microforests

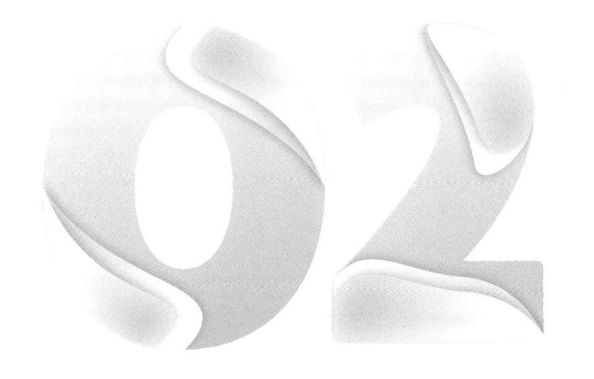

Mini forests are springing up in urban environments, offering inhabitants a new form of public space.

Heritage Forest. Image courtesy of Sugi

A rising focus on urban biodiversity sees communities around the world planting native forests in public spaces, uniting people to protect the planet, rewilding cities, and providing places for interaction.

Microforests popped up in LA's urban parks in October 2021 as part of the Park Forest Initiative by the Los Angeles Parks Foundation. Mature trees, including lush tipa and blue jacaranda, were strategically selected to provide cooling shade in urban neighborhoods including Lemon Grove Park, Mar Vista Recreation Center, Robert Burns Park, and Ross Snyder Recreation Area.

In the United Kingdom, a 240-square-meter "heritage" forest is being planted in London's Chelsea neighborhood to restore biodiversity and reconnect residents with nature. A range of 630 native trees and shrubs will fill the plot in a collaboration led by rewilding company Sugi, luxury fashion brand Louis Vuitton, and estate management company Cadogan. "The forest will be a green space for local neighbors to find quiet moments of respite and to take in the joys of nature in a vibrant and busy city," Sugi founder Elise Van Middelem told *Time Out*.

Also in London, Islington council announced plans to appoint a tree specialist for every housing estate at the end of October 2021. This initiative complements similar green-space projects led by Islington Together, including gardening collectives and park groups.

In January 2021, members of the Nelson Whakatu Microforest Initiative prepared 100 square feet of land for a microforest in New Zealand's Enner Glynn hills. It is part of a community push to

> *Cities are making room for microforests, allowing urban dwellers to reconnect with nature and wildlife.*

bring flora and fauna into urban areas to combat climate change.

Indian company Afforestt creates dense microforests in parking lots and backyards using the Miyawaki Method. This involves planting native species of trees close together, which can make the plants grow 10 times faster than usual.

Why it's interesting

Cities are making room for microforests, allowing urban dwellers to reconnect with nature and wildlife thanks to the seeding of new green public terrain.

WUNDERMAN THOMPSON SUGi Heritage Forest

03

The global K-wave effect

Korean culture is an increasingly potent global force, exerting influence on everything from film to fashion to food to fandoms.

In October 2021, *Billboard* launched its Hot Trending Songs chart, which ranks songs according to how much Twitter conversation they are driving. In an astonishing show of domination, 14 of the top 20 songs on the debut chart came from K-pop acts, including boy band legends BTS, rivals Enhypen and the Blackpink rapper Lisa. K-pop idols inspire fierce loyalty and their fandoms are a global cultural force on social media (see Mobilizing Fandoms, "Future 100: 2021"). The K-wave, also known as Hallyu, is taking the world by storm.

K-pop stars have graduated to the A-list, gathering brand endorsements by the dozen. Kai from Exo has partnered with Gucci and Blackpink's members can reel off a host of collaborations with brands including Chanel, Celine, Dior and Tiffany. Burberry has signed up girl band Itzy, while Blackpink singer Rosé and rapper CL were the first Korean female artists to be invited to the Met Gala in 2021.

K-pop is just one of several Korean cultural exports building a global audience. The international popularity of Korean food and beauty brands is at an all-time high, with the latter exceeding $6 billion in 2020 according to data from the South Korean government. Even the English language has

succumbed, with the Oxford English Dictionary adding over 20 Korean words for 2022, including *bulgogi* (a delicacy of thin slices of pork or beef) and *mukbang* (livestream broadcasts of people eating large amounts of food).

Perhaps most surprising is the seemingly meteoric success of Korean entertainment, or K-drama, from 2020's Oscar-winning film *Parasite* through to the Netflix phenomena *Squid Game* and *Hellbound*. The latter is already Netflix's most watched original show, topping the charts in 80 countries within 24 hours of its launch in November 2021. It has overtaken *Squid Game*, which previously held the record and whose lead female protagonist, HoYeon Jung, has been snapped up by Louis Vuitton for its stable of global brand ambassadors, alongside K-pop giants BTS. Netflix is giving the K-wave a major vote of confidence, investing $500 million in K-dramas in 2021, including *Bulgasal: Immortal Souls*, released in December.

Korea's rising star may seem to have come out of the blue but, as explained in a recent BBC Culture piece, it's the successful result of a long-term economic initiative by the South Korean government to invest in so-called "soft power." Now the rise of K-culture is being honored with a dedicated exhibition. From September 2022 to June 2023, London's Victoria and Albert Museum will host a celebration of Korea's cultural impact on the world. Hallyu! The Korean Wave is the first exhibition of its kind and has the backing of the Ministry of Culture, Sports and Tourism in Seoul.

Why it's interesting

The accessibility and freshness of Korean popular culture has taken the global stage, turning the nation's exports into powerhouses across music, fashion, entertainment and more. Brands can ride the K-wave, tapping into the currency of Hallyu stars that now transcends borders.

Top: Noh Juhan, creator of Netflix's Squid Game, with cast and crew
Bottom: Blackpink. Image courtesy of Spotify

Left: Korean musical artist Psy on Today 2012, New York. Courtesy of Jason Decrow, Invision, AP, Shutterstock Right: Tchai Kim Young-Jin Hanbok Collection 2015, modeled by Bae Yoon Young. Courtesy of YG Kplus

04

Unbounded optimism

Brands are projecting a progressive and positive outlook for 2022, encouraging playfulness and creativity.

Pantone created a completely new color inspired by and encouraging creativity for its Color of the Year 2022. Pantone 17-3938 Very Peri, a unique blend of blues, violets and reds, "displays a spritely, joyous attitude and dynamic presence that encourages courageous creativity and imaginative expression," the brand states.

British-Nigerian artist and designer Yinka Ilori and Lego unveiled a colorful installation celebrating play and community. "Launderette of Dreams" was an interactive and colorful presence in East London that encouraged children to create, play, and share ideas.

Adobe Stock's 2022 Creative Trends include "powerfully playful" themes for the year. "There is a primal need for play," Brenda Milis, Adobe's principal of consumer and creative insights, tells Wunderman Thompson Intelligence.

> 2022 is channeling a creative playfulness that symbolizes growth and freedom.

"A year ago you kept hearing the word 'resilience' but how do you remain resilient when the pandemic is so long term and everything is so uncertain?"

In anticipation of the next year, Milis says that "brands are using playfulness and optimism—there's an incredible consumer appetite for it. It has an underlying strength to it. There's a sense of awe, wonder, inspiration and creativity there—it really grounds it. The playfulness really comes from long-term consumer exhaustion—needing a touch of relief, a touch of entertainment."

Paint company Dulux announced Bright Skies as its Color of the Year for 2022. The airy and refreshing shade "perfectly captures the optimism and desire for a fresh start that is the mood of the moment."

Why it's interesting

After an unpredictable two years, 2022 is channeling a creative playfulness that symbolizes growth and freedom. Colors and design directions are solidifying this energizing spirit that will undoubtedly trickle into ads and marketing.

Powerfully Playful image by Stocksy. Adobe Stock

Yinka Ilori and Lego's "Launderette of Dreams."

05

Virtual genuinfluencers

A new class of influencer is emerging.

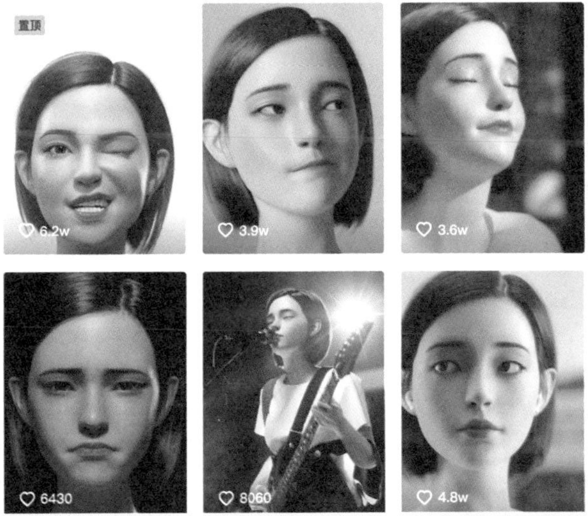

Meet the genuinfluencer—a term first coined by *WGSN*—who garners followers by being relatable rather than aspirational.

Angie, a virtual influencer on Douyin created by Jesse Zhang, is setting new beauty standards in China by celebrating her "imperfections." Unlike other virtual influencers, whose skin has been smoothed to perfection and whose faces are perfectly symmetrical, Angie's skin is sometimes dry or flushed, she gets acne and acne scars, her makeup creases and her teeth aren't perfectly aligned. Instead of posing in designer clothes, she wears simple white T-shirts and athletic shorts. "The reason I like Angie is that she is more realistic

WUNDERMAN THOMPSON

Douyin's virtual influencer Angie, created by Jesse Zhang

Douyin's virtual influencer Angie, created by Jesse Zhang

than many people who are actually real," Xiao Qi, a millennial living in the southwestern Chinese city of Chongqing and one of Angie's nearly 300,000 followers, as of December 2021, told *CNN*.

Yoox, an online luxury marketplace owned by Yoox Net-a-Porter Group, first launched its virtual influencer Daisy in 2018 and is now shifting its strategy. Yoox's priority for Daisy in 2021 was to make her more relatable, Yoox brand and communication director Manuela Strippoli told *Vogue*. "We're moving away from her initial image where she always seemed flawless and we're humanizing her by giving her likes and dislikes as well as flaws." This includes developing her voice, and having her engage more in social issues. "She has a point of view, whether it's on fashion or social causes. It's important that she's not neutral," added Strippoli.

Gen Z's approach to brands is likely a significant contributor to this shift—the vast majority prefer a brand that they can relate to and that shares their values. In the United States, 73% of gen Zers want a brand that understands them and 76% want a brand that is accepting of a range of identities and experiences, according to October 2020 findings from Wunderman Thompson Data.

Why it's interesting

Influence is shifting. "Being too aspirational is repellent now," the *Guardian* reported in August 2021. This is also filtering into the virtual realm, where brands have an opportunity to craft their avatar influencers around core values and relatability.

06

Liminal spaces

Virtual venues and physical space are melding together, giving way to new event locales.

WUNDERMAN THOMPSON

Holiday Space augmented reality artwork by Kaws, 2020
Image courtesy Kaws and Acute Art

Alongside the rise of fully virtual venues and spaces, extended reality is informing physical spaces, elevating events to limitless interactions and experiences.

Independent host Surreal launched in March 2021: a platform for hybrid events that combines virtual experiences in physical spaces. Built with Epic Games' Unreal Engine, the platform offers endless possibilities. Acting as a "digital twin" to the physical environment, Surreal allows hosts and audiences to reimagine experiences by integrating liminal interactions, and incorporate hyper-realistic 3D avatars through a partnership with DNABlock.

In New York City, High Line Art and westside cultural institution The Shed collaborated to create The Looking Glass, an augmented reality installation of virtual sculptures located in the High Line park in July and August 2021. Visitors could use the Acute Art app to view hidden interactive artwork.

Captivating locals and international travelers, TeamLab's Borderless exhibition in Tokyo is the most visited single-artist museum in the world, setting a Guinness World Record in July 2021. Borderless, also located in San Francisco, features music and mirrored walls that are reminiscent of a kaleidoscopic box and are "ultimately closer to entertainment than art," according to the *Wall Street Journal*.

For socialites looking to mingle between realities, digital platform *Dezeen* opened a virtual social club in April 2021—leading creatives met in the virtual rooftop bar for a panel discussion themed around the metaverse and design.

The Royal Shakespeare Company used Unreal Engine to present *Dream*, an interactive performance of live actors that brings the audience into the production for an almost game-like experience.

Why it's interesting

Liminal spaces, which blend virtual and physical experiences, present brands with an opportunity to reinvent how physical experiences and bricks-and-mortar spaces can look.

Left: Surreal conference. Image courtesy of Meta
Right: Dream by the Royal Shakespeare Company

07

Sportsvolution

Female athletes are uprooting outdated federation rules and challenging cultural norms in sports.

In 2021, a slew of female athletes pushed back on inherent sexism in sport, rejecting expectations that they should wear revealing clothing to compete.

Team GB pole-vaulter Holly Bradshaw was so dismayed by her official uniform kit for the Tokyo 2020 Olympics—effectively a crop top and bikini bottoms—that she negotiated the right to wear a modified Adidas rowing unitard instead. Similarly, German gymnast Sarah Voss competed in a full bodysuit instead of a leotard at the European Championships. Two of the German's teammates, Kim Bui and Elisabeth Seitz, later joined her in long leotards, taking a stand together against sexualization in gymnastics.

Many women who participate in sports suffer objectification from fans, commentators, and even coaches. Sexist uniform rules that put women in unnecessarily revealing kit are now triggering widespread outrage and an influx of global support. In July 2021 American singer-songwriter Pink posted a tweet offering to pay an "improper clothing" fine imposed on the Norwegian women's handball team. The team was fined €1,500 after wearing shorts like their male counterparts instead of bikini bottoms. In November 2021, the International Handball Federation updated its rules around women's uniforms.

Why it's interesting

Gender divisions still deeply bifurcate sport but female athletes are now pushing back against inequality. Brands can help support and elevate their fight to break down problematic gender barriers, seizing the opportunity to redefine cultural norms and, in doing so, boost women's participation in sport.

08

Social media-tainment

Plots that develop entirely on profiles, dramas that unfold in feeds, and fictional characters who chat with their followers. Is this the next big thing in entertainment?

FourFront is "revolutionizing TV through TikTok," *Fast Company* reported. FourFront, which secured $1.5 million in seed funding in October 2021, is a new kind of content studio. It produces scripted narratives on social media that have the look and feel of regular posts, featuring fictional characters who have their own storylines, social media pages, and interact with followers organically. As of October 2021, FourFront had reportedly garnered 1.9 million followers and 281 million views across its characters' TikTok accounts. "We're blurring the line between reality and storytelling," Ilan Benjamin, FourFront cofounder and CEO, told *Fast Company*.

This could point to a new kind of social media-based interactive entertainment format. "Not only have we been creating this universe of characters on TikTok, we've also been iterating with a new interactive format," Benjamin said. "There's an evolution in entertainment happening from motion pictures, where audiences can engage in what we call living pictures with characters who feel alive, who live in our world, who are on social media, and react in real time to audience engagements. That fourth wall is completely broken."

Invisible Universe is another startup scripting entertainment specifically for social media. CEO Tricia Biggio, a former senior VP of unscripted television at MGM, calls it "the Pixar of the internet." With the mission of creating what the company calls "the next 100-year animated franchise," Invisible Universe develops original animated characters on social media in partnership with high-profile celebrities, influencers and brands. Founded in August 2021 by former Snap executive John Brennan and launched with $8 million in funding, Invisible Universe has since released characters in partnership with Jennifer Aniston and Serena Williams.

Why it's interesting

Storytelling is evolving, with emerging formats that are tailored for social media feeds. As movie theaters struggle and TV viewership declines, the entertainment industry is rethinking how it reaches and serves audiences.

Above: FourFront, courtesy of TikTok
Right: Invisible Universe

09

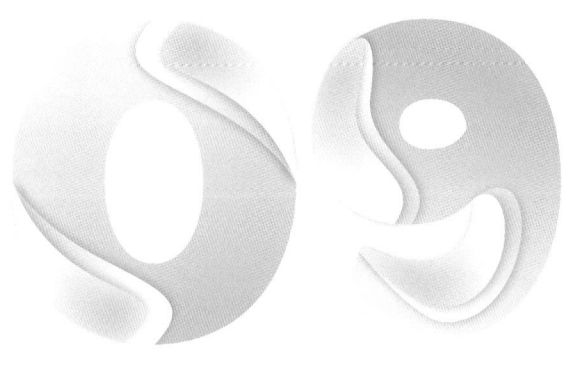

Renewed intimacy

After nearly two years of distance and isolation, a renewed desire for intimacy is shaking up dating culture.

Intentional dating is on the rise, according to Match. In its November 2021 “Singles in America” study, 62% of American singles said they are looking for meaningful, committed relationships, while only 11% are dating “casually.” According to an April 2021 report from the Kinsey Institute for Research in Sex, Gender, and Reproduction, 44% of Americans say that commitment is more important to them post-pandemic. Even younger consumers are looking for committed relationships—81% of gen Zers want to be in a relationship within the next year, Match findings revealed.

New apps and platforms are helping facilitate deeper intimacy. Elate, an “anti-ghosting” app, launched at the end of 2020 to encourage slower dating and stronger emotional connections. In place of endless swiping, Elate users are served 10 recommended profiles per day and are only

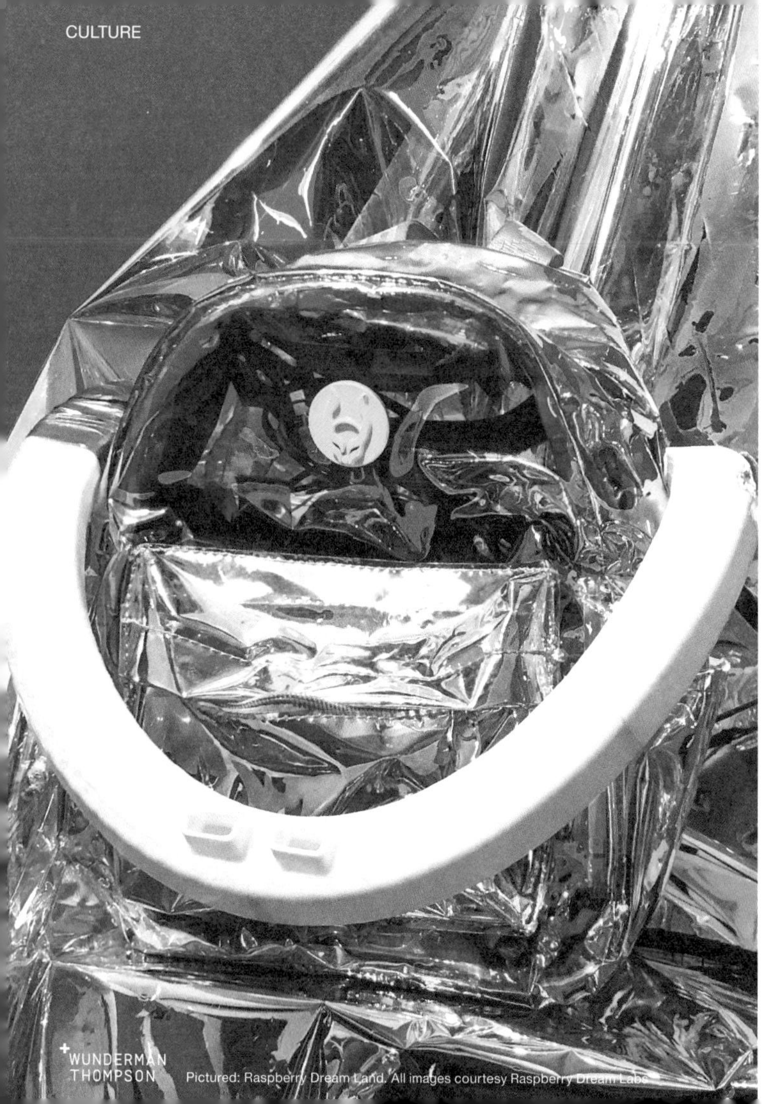

WUNDERMAN THOMPSON Pictured: Raspberry Dream Land. All images courtesy Raspberry Dream Labs

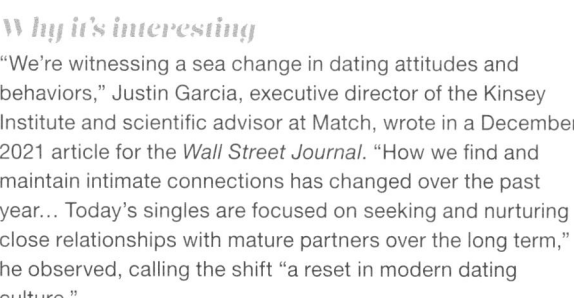

allowed to chat with three people at a time.

Raspberry Dream Labs is reframing cybersex experiences to form meaningful connections. Its first project, Sensory Seduction, uses extended reality (XR) to allow users to feel haptic pulses on their bodies, mimicking the sensation of being touched. The experience is designed to offer an opportunity to "explore your sensuality and engage your sexual accelerators through the sensory stimulation." The company has released a beta version of Raspberry Dream Land, an XR social event platform offering a virtual space for "radical self-expression, progressive arts and entertainment, social interactions and virtual relationships."

Why it's interesting

"We're witnessing a sea change in dating attitudes and behaviors," Justin Garcia, executive director of the Kinsey Institute and scientific advisor at Match, wrote in a December 2021 article for the *Wall Street Journal*. "How we find and maintain intimate connections has changed over the past year... Today's singles are focused on seeking and nurturing close relationships with mature partners over the long term," he observed, calling the shift "a reset in modern dating culture."

10

Metasocieties

A digital reality that reflects the values and standards of our physical lives—or better versions—is in the making.

The metaverse is offering a chance to create a world that is inclusive, ethical and accessible. "Think about creating a new online society but doing it right from day one," Daren Tsui, CEO of Together Labs, tells Wunderman Thompson Intelligence. Tsui is describing IMVU, the company's 3D avatar-based friendship discovery social network. The platform is designed to foster social presence and authentic connections.

The evolution of tech points to a positive future for the metaverse: 88% of global consumers believe tech can make the world a better place, and 78% agree it can help create a more equitable society, according to a July 2021 survey by Wunderman Thompson Data published in the "Into the Metaverse" report.

IMVU. Image courtesy of Together Labs

WUNDERMAN THOMPSON

Top: Nowhere's Networking at Crane Gallery; exhibit by The Most Famous Artist
Bottom: Microsoft Mesh
Right: Meta's Horizon Worlds

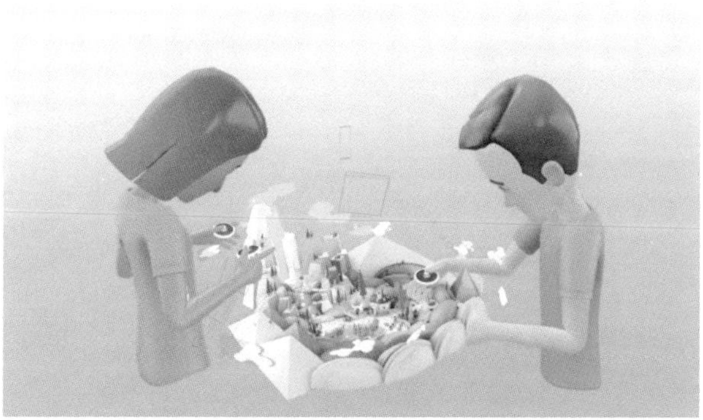

The race to create virtual worlds that nurture connections, collaboration and discovery is on. Nowhere is a new social networking platform that places people in 3D environments ranging from forests to an island in the sky. Jon Morris, CEO of Nowhere, describes the platform as "the first online event space where you can truly be present, whether feeling the raw energy of a virtual performance or serendipitously vibing with a stranger you just met."

Meta's Horizon Worlds aims to be a "VR social experience" where explorers play, build and create together. And Microsoft Mesh uses mixed reality to create interconnected worlds that allow people in different physical locations to be together in real-time via holographic experiences.

Why it's interesting

The metaverse is still in its infancy and the window of opportunity to build virtual worlds and societies from the ground up is opening now.

11
Tech & innovation
20

11

3D audio

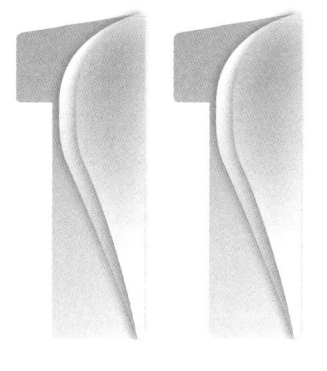

Immersive listening ushers in the next generation of audio experiences

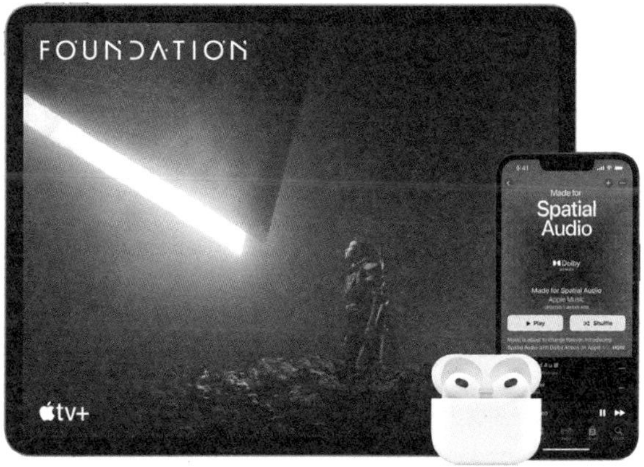

Across its product line, Apple is rolling out new spatial audio features, which create immersive, multidimensional sound that mimics surround sound. At its October 2021 Unleashed event, Apple announced that its new AirPods 3 and MacBook Pro laptops will be equipped for spatial audio, after first unveiling the functionality, powered by Dolby Atmos, for Apple Music in June 2021. "Apple Music is making its biggest advancement ever in sound quality," says Oliver Schusser, vice president of Apple Music and Beats.

Sony introduced two new home speaker systems in 2021 with 360-degree spatial sound mapping technology for an immersive listening experience.

Apple AirPods: third-generation spatial audio

Audio company Spatial unveiled its first suite of products in March 2021. The new startup creates immersive, interactive soundscapes for public spaces, including lobbies, retail stores, offices and even hospitals. The bespoke soundscapes are designed to have a specific emotional impact on listeners—from encouraging relaxation and focus to destressing. Companies are "fundamentally rethinking the future of work in this hybrid environment," Spatial co-founder and CEO Calin Pacurariu told *Fast Company*. "And they see sound as a competitive advantage."

In November 2021, Cartier brought its immersive audio experience, The Great Animal Orchestra, to the Peabody

Essex Museum in Salem, Massachusetts, for its North American debut. The exhibition, which first launched in Paris in 2016, features soundscapes of biodiversity across North America, Latin America, Kenya, Rwanda and Zimbabwe, recorded by soundscape ecologist Bernie Krause. *Elle* described it as "an exploration of sound: how we digest it, the ways in which animals express it."

Why it's interesting

Social media platforms such as Instagram have driven a hyper-focus on visual elements over the past decade. Now, especially as digital platforms mature and engagement evolves, focus is shifting to multisensory elements—audio, in particular—for a truly immersive experience.

Left: The Spatial experience
Right: The Spatial concept

12

Rise of the super apps

China exports its super-app formula to eager neighbors.

WUNDERMAN THOMPSON

Top: GrabPay's QR-scan service
Bottom: GrabTaxi

Even as China's super apps come under a government anti-trust crackdown, their progeny abroad are going from strength to strength. Super apps offer multiple functions on a single seamless platform, from messaging to ecommerce to ride-hailing to payments and financial services.

Indonesia's Gojek started as a motorbike ride-hailing service to help people cut through Jakarta traffic and now delivers everything from food to medicine to masseurs. In 2021, in a deal valued at $18 billion, it announced it was merging with Tokopedia, the country's largest online marketplace, which also offers fintech and logistics services. The combined entity, aptly named GoTo, has more than 100 million active users, 11 million merchants, two million drivers and revenue that represents 2% of Indonesia's $1 trillion economy.

It's not the only super app in the region. Singapore-headquartered Grab, which calls itself the "Everyday Everything app," started with ride-hailing around Southeast Asia and swiftly added delivery, payments and financial services, landing a digital bank license with partner SingTel in 2020. Grab went public on the Nasdaq via the world's largest special-purpose acquisition company deal, raising $4.5 billion, at the end of 2021.

GoTo and Grab boast marquee investors, including Chinese tech giants Alibaba, Tencent, Meituan and Didi Chuxing, as well as Facebook, Google, Sequoia, SoftBank, Google, and Singapore government fund Temasek.

In 2020, online commerce in Southeast Asia grew faster than in any other region, according to Forrester. Online sales expanded 53% to $50 billion, led by grocery commerce, which registered growth of 97%. Total online sales are expected to keep growing by double digits annually, to hit $143 billion in 2025.

WUNDERMAN THOMPSON Gojek and Tokopedia's GoTo GoCar

Why it's interesting

Chinese tech giants invested early in Southeast Asian platforms and exported many of the super-app concepts pioneered back home to their neighbors. As Chinese tech firms face increasing regulation, they are likely to look abroad more than ever for growth opportunities.

Indeed, consumers in many Southeast Asian countries appear readier than elsewhere for super apps that stitch together a plethora of services. According to Wunderman Thompson's Future Shopper Survey 2021, eight out of ten consumers in Thailand and Indonesia agree with the statement "I wish brands communicated with me seamlessly across different channels."

13

Carbon neutral browsing

Brands are redesigning their online experiences to be less damaging to the environment.

According to Cleanfox's February 2021 report on email pollution, "if the internet were a country, it would be the sixth biggest polluter in the world." The report also revealed that promotional emails are responsible for two million tons of carbon dioxide (CO_2) emissions annually in the United Kingdom.

In response, brands are overhauling their websites to lower the carbon footprint of their online activity.

Amsterdam-based design studio Formafantasma redesigned its website in February 2021 to be more energy efficient, with small images, basic typefaces, and a logo created from standard Unicode symbols. The simple visuals decrease the energy needed to load the site, reducing carbon emissions.

Volkswagen reconstructed its Canadian website for a more sustainable browsing experience in February 2021. The Carbon-Neutral Net online redesign shrinks the brand's digital carbon footprint by removing all color and replacing photographs with mosaics created from low-data text characters. The project has significantly lowered the amount of CO_2 generated by browsing. The site produces an average of only 0.022 grams of CO_2 per page view, compared to the average website, which produces 1.76 grams of CO_2 per page view, according to an assessment by digital carbon emissions calculator Website Carbon.

Why it's interesting

Last year we noted how the acceleration of digital habits has driven a heightened awareness of data sustainability. Since then, brands have already begun rethinking their digital touchpoints to align with consumers' values. Now, especially as the metaverse looms, sustainable practices in the virtual realm will be more important than ever.

Volkswagen Canada's Carbon-Neutral Net online redesign

14

Finite social networks

Social networks are channeling the concept of less is more.

Social media has a bad rap, from promoting addictive behaviors and sleep deprivation to causing anxiety and depression. And yet globally, in 2021, there are billions of monthly active users on Facebook and Instagram, over 300 million monthly active users on Twitter, and, according to a September report from the company, one billion monthly active users on TikTok.

A number of apps such as Social Fever, Offtime and Freedom aim to pry eyeballs away from social media by limiting usage. But what if social platforms had fewer, more curated posts instead? This is where Minus comes in. The platform, created by Ben Grosser to challenge existing social network models, only allows users to have 100 posts for life. Self-dubbed a "finite social network," the platform aims to raise the quality of content through limitations.

Similarly, Thursday is a dating app that is only live on one day of the week. Launched in May 2021, the company was created to counter online dating fatigue. The app hopes to boost matches, conversations and dating opportunities by limiting its usage to one day a week. Prior to launch, over 100,000 curious singles had already signed up.

Why it's interesting

Companies are seeking to cut through the noise and endless stream of online content by installing restrictive parameters that prompt new behaviors—thus promoting a healthier and more mindful approach to the future of social networking.

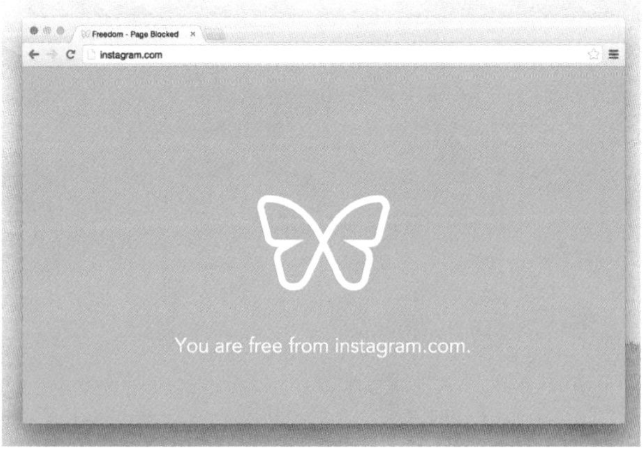

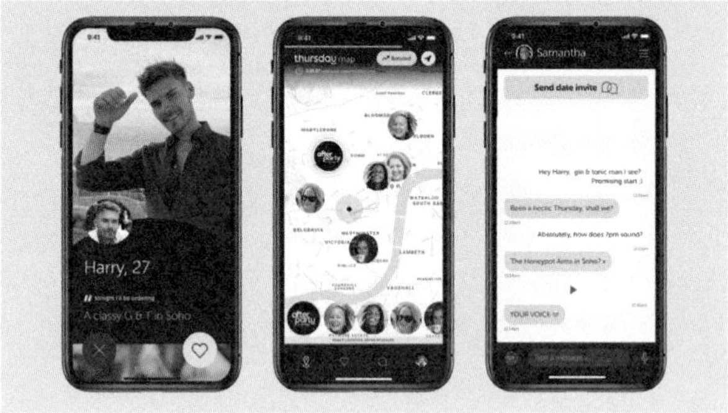

"Companies are seeking to cut through the noise and endless stream of online content by installing restrictive parameters that prompt new behaviors."

Top: Freedom app blocked site screen
Bottom: Thursday dating app

15

Advanced avatars

Photorealistic digital humans are moving from our screens to the real world—make way for the next-generation avatars.

MetaHuman Creator by Unreal Engine. Image courtesy of Epic Games

Nvidia is preparing for a future where 3D avatars with conversational artificial intelligence (AI) will operate in both the virtual and physical world. In a November 2021 demo, the company announced the Omniverse Avatar platform. "The dawn of intelligent virtual assistants has arrived," said Jensen Huang, founder and CEO of Nvidia. "Omniverse Avatar combines Nvidia's foundational graphics, simulation and AI technologies to make some of the most complex real-time applications ever created."

Epic Games' Unreal Engine believes "digital humans are the future." In April 2021, Unreal Engine started offering early access to the MetaHuman Creator, which allows real-time creation of photorealistic avatars in minutes. The cloud-based app can replicate intricate details of a person's features, from complexion and wrinkles to broken capillaries and scars. In September 2021, California-based avatar-generating startup DNABlock raised $1.2 million in seed funding to make

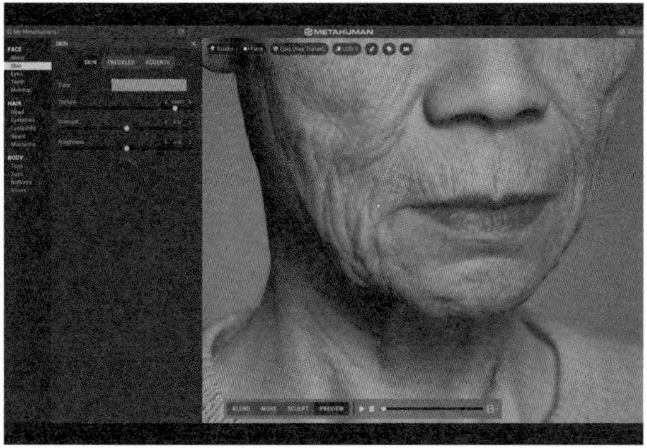

the metaverse more diverse and inclusive. "The metaverse needs to represent everyone," Anthony Kelani, CEO and co-founder of DNABlock, told *Protocol*. "This needs to represent the world. And with avatars, specifically, you should be able to generate an avatar that looks like you or like someone of color."

Why it's interesting

Forget the blue avatars that took over our screens in 2009. In 2022, new-age avatars will not only seem hyper-realistic, but also reflect the world's diversity.

Left: MetaHuman Creator by Unreal Engine. Image courtesy of Epic Games
Right: Omniverse Avatar by Nvidia

China's tech crackdown

A crackdown on technology is reshaping China's economy and society.

Since late 2020, China has investigated and/or fined affiliates of its biggest tech companies Alibaba, Tencent, JD.com, Meituan and Didi Chuxing for monopolistic practices. A mega-IPO for Alibaba's Ant Financial was halted at the eleventh hour. In April 2021, Alibaba incurred a record fine of $2.8 billion for imposing "forced exclusivity" rules on merchants.

The magnitude of the crackdown is unsurprising, considering that China is the world's most digitized country. Chinese tech companies play an outsized role in almost every faces of citizens' lives, collecting vast tracts of consumer data along the way.

Some 70% of China's population—989 million people— were online at the end of 2020, almost all via their mobile phones. Of these, almost 80% were shopping online, 86% were using

mobile payments, and 94% were consuming online video, according to the China Internet Network Information Center. Initially focused on antitrust, data security and cybersecurity issues, the crackdown has spread to societal concerns, from too much homework for young kids (solution: banning for-profit online tutors) to excessive gaming (solution: strict time limits for minors) to obsessive fandoms.

"I think the issues that regulators in China are trying to address are clearly not unique," Vey-Sern Ling, managing director of Union Bancaire Privée in Singapore and an expert on China's Internet economy, tells Wunderman Thompson Intelligence. "But there is a lot more autonomy in China, much less time spent on discussion/ consultation, and implementation is heavy-handed."

The US government and the European Union are also trying to curb the reach of Big Tech by suing the likes of Facebook, Amazon and Google for anti-trust issues, though these efforts will take longer to wind their way through courts.

Why it's interesting

For Chinese consumers as well as the brands that sell to them, the changes could mean more choice as rival tech ecosystems are forced to work with each other. For example, shoppers on Alibaba's ecommerce platforms previously could not use WeChat Pay—owned by rival Tencent—for purchases. Similarly, shoppers on JD.com and Pinduoduo—part-owned by Tencent—could not use Alipay. These walled gardens are coming down.

Left: JD.com services
Right: Alibaba's ecommerce platforms

17

Carbontech futures

The world shift toward net zero ushers in a new boom in carbontech.

WUNDERMAN THOMPSON

Climeworks Orca facility in Iceland

In the transition to net zero, the world urgently needs carbon-reduction strategies. As innovations in carbon capture start to become less expensive, a carbontech boom could be on the way.

Tech will be crucial for tackling emissions, as Jan Wurzbacher, founder of the Swiss carbon capture company Climeworks, told *Wired* in October 2021: "We have to mitigate, but that will not be enough; we will have biological solutions, they won't be enough, and so we need technical solutions."

In September 2021, Climeworks opened its biggest facility yet in Iceland. The plant uses modular carbon dioxide collector units to filter carbon out of the air and turn it into a liquid. Working with Icelandic company Carbfix, it then pumps the liquid underground, where it reacts with Iceland's native rock, turning the carbon dioxide into stone. Although the technology currently only sucks a small percentage of carbon out of the air, the modular nature of the system means the solution can be easily and economically scaled.

Looking to the skies, Israeli startup High Hopes Labs is betting on large balloons to trap carbon dioxide high up in the atmosphere where it freezes almost solid, making it easier to gather. Having tested its cryodistillation process with small balloons, the company is hoping to scale up its operation within the next two years, capturing the same amount of carbon dioxide at a lower cost than many on-the-ground solutions available today.

> "As innovations in carbon capture start to become less expensive, a carbontech boom could be on the way.

Once carbon has been captured, other brands are stepping in to use it in their products, turning waste into valuable resources. Chicago-based Aether uses carbon dioxide to create diamonds, while Canadian sportswear brand Lululemon joined forces with biotech company LanzaTech in July 2021 to create fabric made from waste carbon dioxide.

Why it's interesting

While carbon capture on a grand scale remains expensive, new projects are proving that costs can come down—and a nascent economy is emerging to capitalize on waste carbon. "Has the carbontech revolution begun?" asked the *New York Times* in June 2021. As the drive toward net zero becomes the new normal, the appetite for these solutions is only set to grow.

18

Virtual teleportation

Technologists are opening up digital portals—making virtual teleportation a plausible reality.

Transforming communication and collaboration is at the heart of Varjo Teleport VR. The headset, launched in October 2021 by Helsinki-based tech manufacturer Varjo, uses the Varjo Reality Cloud platform, which allows for photorealistic virtual teleportation.

Meta is also betting big on virtual reality (VR). "By 2030, the new generations of Oculus will allow users to teleport from one place to another without moving from their couch," Mark Zuckerberg told *The Information*'s *411* podcast.

Microsoft Mesh uses mixed reality (MR) to create interconnected worlds where the physical and digital come together. The selling point with Microsoft's new platform is that people in different physical locations are able to collaborate and work in real time on the same project via holographic experiences across different devices. "You can actually feel like you're in the same place with someone sharing content or you can teleport from different mixed reality devices and be present with people even when you're not physically together," said Alex Kipman, Microsoft's technical fellow.

London-based design practice Space Popular proposes an even more ambitious concept—a civic infrastructure that allows for virtual teleportation. The idea was delivered in November 2021 at Dezeen 15 online festival, with the two cofounders envisaging a "threaded network of virtual textiles that our virtual selves pull aside to move between virtual environments."

Why it's interesting

Distance is becoming less of an obstacle. As people spend more time working, socializing and collaborating online, technology is paving the way for teleportation into a new virtual dimension that offers more intimate, close-to-reality in-person interactions.

Left: Alex Kipman and John Hanke. Images courtesy of Microsoft Mesh
Right: Varjo Teleport VR

19

Cryptonomics

Is cryptocurrency finally on the path to legitimacy?

Cryptocurrency has seen its share of ups and downs, but recent moves from major financial and political players may be sanctioning the digital currency as a legitimate and accessible payment option.

PayPal launched its cryptocurrency service in the United Kingdom in August 2021, letting British users buy, hold and sell digital currencies on the popular epayments app. The UK launch marks the first international expansion for PayPal's cryptocurrency product since it launched in the United States at the end of 2020. "The tokens and coins have been around for a while," Jose Fernandez da Ponte, PayPal's general manager for blockchain, crypto and digital currencies, told CNBC, "but you had to be a relatively sophisticated user to be able to access that. Having that on a platform like ours makes a really good entry point."

Eric Adams, the mayor-elect for New York City, announced in November 2021 that he wants to be paid in Bitcoin. Taking to social media, Adams signaled his intention to make New York the "center of the cryptocurrency industry," starting by taking

his first three paychecks in the digital currency.
Several countries are experimenting with nationally regulated digital currencies. China is currently piloting a digital yuan, with plans to eventually roll out the electronic currency for mass public use. Over the past year, the People's Bank of China has distributed several million dollars' worth of the digital currency via an app connected to six major state-owned banks, according to CNBC. Major cities including Beijing, Chengdu and Shenzhen have joined the pilot program in recent months, as have Tencent-backed WeBank and Alibaba's Ant Group-backed MYbank. China may even test the digital currency with foreign visitors at the 2022 Beijing Winter Olympics, CNBC revealed in April 2021.

In April 2021, the Bank of Japan (BOJ) kicked off its first phase of digital currency testing, and this initial exploratory step will continue through March 2022. The BOJ will focus on testing the technical feasibility of issuing, distributing and redeeming a central bank digital currency.

Also in April 2021, the UK finance minister Rishi Sunak told a fintech industry conference that the UK Treasury and Bank of England had launched a joint task force "to coordinate exploratory work on a potential central bank digital currency."

Why it's interesting

The wild west of cryptocurrency is slowly being regulated and legitimized, opening the door to a future of digital economies.

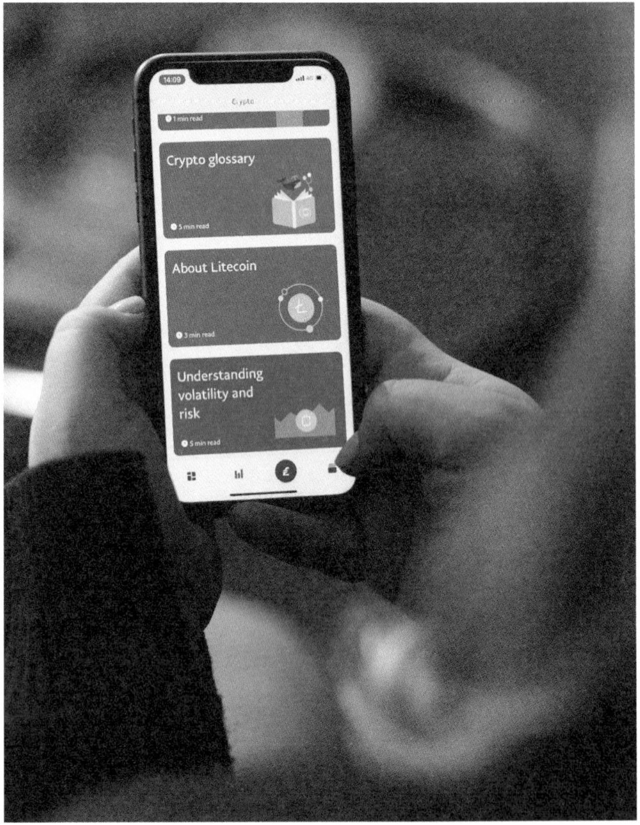

PayPal cryptocurrency service in the UK

20

Purification tech

Innovative purifying technology is battling greenhouse gases in public spaces.

AirBubble, presented at the COP26 United Nations Climate Change Conference in 2021. Image by Naaro

AirBubble playground by EcoLogicStudio. Photography by Maja Wirkus

A new wave of technological innovations are using biotechnology to purify air spaces. As this tech develops, its functionality is being tested in public spaces, aiming to mitigate the effects of air pollution.

Architecture and innovation firm EcoLogicStudio has revealed a project that removes pollutants from the air. The AirBubble air-purifying eco-machine is currently in use at a children's play pavilion in Warsaw, Poland. It uses solar-powered bioreactors and algae to remove pollutants and carbon dioxide from the air, drawing on natural photosynthesis. The playscape's surrounding bioreactors ultimately keep its pollution levels within the World Health Organization's guidelines. EcoLogicStudio also presented the AirBubble at the Glasgow COP26 United Nations Climate Change Conference in 2021.

A 3D-printed "intelligence forest" created by two Spanish studios, External Reference and Onionlab, debuted at Expo 2020 in Dubai. The artificial forest is made up of sustainable bioplastic polymer trees, composed of sugar and pure.tech, a mineral compound that captures and breaks down greenhouse gases. Microalgae designed for the exhibition produces oxygen through photosynthesis, increasing its levels and decreasing levels of the surrounding greenhouse gases, with the ultimate goal of reducing the effects of global warming. The idea is that the artificial forest, implemented in a city setting, could produce more oxygen than native flora and can be used to produce biofuels and protein-rich food.

Why it's interesting

Heightened focus on air quality is opening the door to new technology and devices, ensuring clean breathing in public spaces.

Left: AirBubble playground by EcoLogicStudio. Photography by Maja Wirkus
Right: AirBubble presented at COP26. Image by Naaro

21
Travel & hospitality
30
BRITAIR
F-HMLA

21

Microadventures

Avid travelers are finding local adventures a satisfying fix for the travel bug.

Travelers are finding unique ways to engage with nature locally for smaller, shorter excursions, and some studies indicate that these microadventures are as impactful on mental and emotional health as traditional getaways.

A study by the Greater Good Science Center at the University of California, Berkeley, and the University of California, San Francisco, found that participants who embarked on 15-minute walks each week "reported greater joy" and even smiled more than those in the control group. The results, which are part of a larger study, indicate that taking a long trip isn't necessary to inspire awe: short, simple excursions still have a positive effect on our mental health.

French travel brand Chilowé offers microadventures exclusively, encouraging travelers to travel locally and in small groups. The company's concept emphasizes the travel possibilities that are close to home for French natives, offering sustainable and less expensive travel options.

In the United Kingdom, a one-night adventure company offers mini stays in remote locations. Much Better Adventures' short excursions are designed for people with busy lifestyles and a thirst for adventure. Hotel and resort chain Best Western is promoting microadventures in the United Kingdom, advertising unique getaways that last a maximum of 48 hours.

Where there is adventure, there is gear for explorers. US clothing brand M22 has expanded its lifestyle range to develop experiences for adventurous locals near Lake Michigan. The brand offers microadventures curated to help travelers escape everyday life and personalized to fit any mood. From surfing and kayaking to hiking and nature walks, COO Nick Madrick wants the destination's branded escapades to "get people outside in the natural environment to reconnect with nature and experience the local community," as he told *Travel and Leisure*.

Why it's interesting

When extreme adventure and traditional travel aren't possible, microadventures are proving popular, satisfying swaps for an outdoor escape. Brands are finding ways to introduce this travel habit to consumers looking to satisfy their wanderlust.

Left: M22. Image by Andy Noel
Right: Much Better Adventures

22

Travelportation

The digital world is offering immersive travel experiences from the comfort of home..

WUNDERMAN THOMPSON Microsoft Flight Simulator. Images courtesy of Xbox

> **Immersive technology gives travel the potential to be less cost prohibitive, more accessible and more imaginative.**

True teleportation may be a sci-fi fantasy (for now), but the sensorial experiences of travelportation make it possible for travelers to immerse themselves in a physical destination without actually going there.

Japanese airline group ANA Holdings and JP Games launched the Sky Whale digital platform in May 2021. The platform hosts multiple digital worlds that consumers can travel between and shop in with friends and family, supporting an interactive, cultural travel experience. The platform features a Sky Park, Sky Village and Sky Mall, and is partnering with companies in countries including Australia, Austria, Canada, Hawaii, the Philippines and Singapore to connect users from around the world.

Microsoft Flight Simulator, already compatible with Xbox Series X and S, now offers a TCA Yoke Boeing Edition controller for the ultimate virtual flight experience. Players can control the pitch of their virtual aircraft with this one-to-one replica of the control yoke of a Boeing 787, with additional Xbox buttons and an audio jack for a seamless adjustment to the new console. Pre-orders were available from November 2021, with consumers scheduled to receive their stainless steel controllers the following month.

Why it's interesting

This immersive technology gives travel the potential to be less cost-prohibitive, more accessible and more imaginative.

Microsoft Flight Simulator. Images courtesy of Xbox

23

Mycological retreats

All-inclusive resorts are offering an unexpected draw: guided psychedelic trips.

At Soltara Healing Center, an all-inclusive resort in Costa Rica, stays are built around ayahuasca, a psychoactive tea, used under the guidance of native Shipibo healers. Silo Wellness in Jamaica offers psilocybin-assisted ceremonies that are individually tailored to the group or individual. And at psilocybin wellness retreat MycoMeditations in Jamaica, guests can enjoy a luxurious week-long trip with options for guided psychedelic ceremonies for $10,500. MycoMeditations expanded its packages in June 2021 to include Companions Retreats for friends and family, to "improve their mental, emotional and spiritual health as a unit," says Justin Townsend, MycoMeditation's CEO and lead facilitator.

The practice is even making its way into mainstream pop culture. Gwyneth Paltrow famously participated in a psychedelic retreat in the first episode of her Netflix show, *The Goop Lab*. More recently, it was also the basis of Hulu's show *Nine Perfect Strangers*.

Douglas Gordon, CEO of Silo Wellness, told Bloomberg that his company's retreats reflect the changing notions of luxury. "Real luxury is being able to wear flip-flops to dinner," he said. "It's not necessarily black tie, you know? It's about an authentic experience. That's the type of person we want to attract, someone who puts value into experiences."

Why it's interesting

Wellness tourism and luxury travel continue to overlap as luxury travelers seek not just physical escape and creature comforts, but also a deep mental and psychological reset.

Soltara Healing Center

24

Green mapping

Conscious consumers have new eco priorities when planning trips and journeys.

In October 2021, Google announced the launch of three new environmentally conscious options in Google Maps. Eco-friendly routing allows drivers to see the most fuel-efficient routes rather than just the fastest, while lite navigation is aimed at cyclists who don't want turn-by-turn instructions to distract them from the road. In the third initiative, Google has extended bike and scooter-share information to over 300 cities globally, helping riders more easily find the micro-mobility options available to them. Beyond Maps, 2021 has been a busy year for Google's sustainable travel-information offer. Worldwide flight searches now come with emissions estimates, while hotel listings now feature sustainability credentials and eco-certifications.

For upscale travelers, US-based Wild Nectar Immersive Travel Collection launched in autumn 2021 with the goal of providing environmentally positive, luxurious trips. It has created a unique Eco Score to aid destination decision-making based on factors such as conservation, emissions, and betterment of local communities.

In a similar vein, Small Luxury Hotels of the World launched its new Considerate Collection in October 2021. Working with the Global Sustainable Tourism Council, the brand has selected the hotels in the collection for their exceptional commitment to sustainability, such as increasing local

biodiversity or improving the wellbeing of local communities. Transportation accounts for 24% of direct global CO_2 emissions from fuel combustion, according to the International Energy Agency's "Tracking Transport 2020" report. Though lockdowns in 2020 and 2021 reduced these emissions, the rebound has been significant enough for the International Transport Forum to predict in 2021 that CO_2 emissions from the sector will increase by 16% by 2050, versus 2015 levels. Growing awareness of this impact is leading transport apps and travel companies to redesign their offerings, giving travelers more planet-first options.

Why it's interesting

Not wanting to forgo travel altogether, travelers are looking to brands to help them make more sustainable plans. Not only do services like this speak to value-driven consumers but they also help to reduce choice fatigue. According to Wunderman Thompson Data, 79% of global consumers say they are interested in tips and advice from brands on how to live more sustainably.

WUNDERMAN THOMPSON

Bhutan Spirit Sanctuary in Shaba, Bhutan, one of the Small Luxury Hotels of the World's Considerate Collection destinations

Arctic Bath in Harads, Sweden, one of the Small Luxury Hotels of the World's Considerate Collection destinations

25

Top three destinations

The top three hot-to-trot destinations for 2022 offer something for everyone: sustainable tourism, COVID-19 assurance for long-term stays and ecological marvels.

Ljubljana, Slovenia. Photography by Martino Pietropoli, courtesy of Unsplash

Ljubljana, Slovenia

For eco-conscious travelers, the capital of Slovenia is the place to go as Ljubljana was ranked European Best Green Capital for 2022 by European Best Destinations. The city boasts more than 542 square meters of public green space per capita and more than 200 kilometers of bike paths, which locals and visitors alike can take advantage of thanks to a free-to-use bike-share scheme. Slovenia is globally recognized for its sustainable tourism industry and is the most-awarded destination by the European Commission for its sustainable travel options.

Valletta, Malta

For anyone looking for COVID-19 reassurance when traveling, Valletta, the capital of Malta, is a good bet. The country boasts one of the world's highest vaccination rates—and the highest anywhere in Europe—with 81% of residents fully vaccinated, as reported by the BBC in November 2021. In May 2021, Reuters reported that the country had achieved herd immunity.

The Nomad Residence Permit, launched in June 2021, makes it a great option for a long stay. The permit allows remote workers to live and work in Malta for up to one year, with the option to renew.

Left: Ljubljana, Slovenia. Photography by Greenvalley Pictures, courtesy of Unsplash
Right: Valletta, Malta. Photography by Mike Nahlii, courtesy of Unsplash

> “Xishuangbanna boasts the most intact tropical ecosystem in China, featuring dense tropical rainforests and waterfalls, and is home to a quarter of the country's animal species.

Xishuangbanna, China

Xishuangbanna, located in Southwest China's Yunnan province, was ranked one of the top three regions to visit in 2022 by *Lonely Planet*. Each destination was chosen for its “topicality, unique experiences, ‘wow’ factor and its ongoing commitment to sustainable tourism practices,” *Lonely Planet* states. Xishuangbanna's unique environment and “wow” factor are due in large part to its botanical and ecological variety. Xishuangbanna boasts the most intact tropical ecosystem in China, featuring dense tropical rainforests and giant waterfalls, and is home to a quarter of the country's animal species and one sixth of plants.

Xishuangbanna, China. Image courtesy of Unsplash

26

Meditative travel

Meditative integrations are making every journey a mindful one.

Travel and navigation brands are incorporating apps for meditative practice to soothe consumers during their travels.

Waze and Headspace are collaborating to make commuting less stressful. Drive with Headspace, launched in October 2021, incorporates the meditative, relaxing Headspace experience into the navigation app with five mood selections: Aware, Bright, Joyful, Hopeful and Open. Users can change their in-app icons and car image to reflect their mood, change the navigation narrator to Headspace's director of meditation, Eve Lewis Prieto, and listen to meditative music curated by Headspace on Spotify. Available in four languages, the integration is meant to help drivers "find more joy and meaning on the road," according to Waze.

The Avanti West Coast train operator in the United Kingdom will offer app-based hypnotherapy for its passengers, to help them when feeling overwhelmed, tired and more. Announced in October 2021, the 20-minute sessions will guide listeners with tips for power napping, guidance for improving productivity, and tools for confidence building. The hypnotherapy app Clementine is free to riders on the West Coast Main Line services, because the "onboard journey experience is as important as getting to the destination itself," according to an Avanti West Coast representative.

Delta Airlines will soon offer custom Peloton relaxation, meditation and stretching classes on planes with seatback screens. Announced in November 2021, the partnership aims to help passengers relax on their flights, with sessions lasting five to 20 minutes taught by some of the fitness app's popular instructors.

Why it's interesting

Meditative apps for wellness are finding new space in the travel sector, giving stressed and anxious travelers access to therapeutic sessions to ease their minds during their journey.

Left: Waze and Headspace
Right: Clementine and Avanti West Coast

27

Academic adventures

NASA scientists and culture connoisseurs are leading off-the-beaten-path excursions for the ultra-curious traveler.

WUNDERMAN THOMPSON

Adero Scottsdale's Dark Sky Zone at the SkyTop Lounge

Adero Scottsdale's Dark Sky Zone at the SkyTop Lounge

Expert-led experiences are popular travel offerings that hospitality groups and informational brands are embracing, providing guests with unique and one-of-a-kind experiences.

In August 2021, the NPR media organization launched NPR Travels, offering immersive, educational trips for fans of the public radio service and those with a taste for history, music, astronomy and more. Starting in 2022, expert-led trips to destinations from Iceland to South America will host up to 24 people at a time, featuring curated reading, listening, and recommendations from NPR journalists. "These guided tours are an opportunity to connect with like-minded people over their love of travel and NPR," says Jane Scott, director of consumer products.

Guests at the Adero Scottsdale can sip cocktails while stargazing from the hotel's SkyTop Lounge. Adero's Dark Sky Zone experts, known as Star Dudes, guide guests through the constellations via binoculars and high-powered telescopes while guests indulge in "astro-cocktails." Telescopes are also provided to allow stargazing from individual rooms.

During 2021, guests at the Hyatt Regency Maui Resort and Spa had the opportunity to learn about any of the 80 constellations viewable from the hotel in sessions led by NASA ambassador Edward Mahoney. NASA is stepping into the hospitality company's exclusive education space as part of the hotel's broader Stay, Learn and Play experience package—an out-of-this-world experience.

Why it's interesting

The hospitality industry is expanding its offerings, catering to academic adventurers and turning to scientific and cultural experts to curate elite, one-of-a-kind escapades.

28

In flight rejuvenation

Air travel channels spa-like comforts and wellness recharges for travelers.

Airlines are updating accommodations in the air, creating spaces of comfort and rejuvenation for travelers to enjoy throughout their journey.

Singapore Airlines announced a new partnership with Golden Door, bringing the top spa resort's wellness retreat experiences to the skies. From January 2022, fliers aboard the Los Angeles to Singapore route can view relaxing in-flight meditation videos, take exercise courses, choose from new gourmet menus, and even participate in sleep education courses during their 17-hour direct flight. Golden Door's goal, according to COO Kathy Van Ness, "is to affect every single person inside that plane in a positive way."

Superbusiness minisuites, with doors for privacy and reclining chairs for ultimate comfort, are gradually replacing traditional first-class seating. Qatar Airways has offered Qsuites with closed-off spaces since 2017, and now Delta, China Eastern, JetBlue, British Airways, Shanghai Airlines and Air China will offer similar facilities.

Why it's interesting

The journey is as important as the destination, and airlines are betting on travelers' thirst for comfort every step of the way with revolutionary luxury offerings.

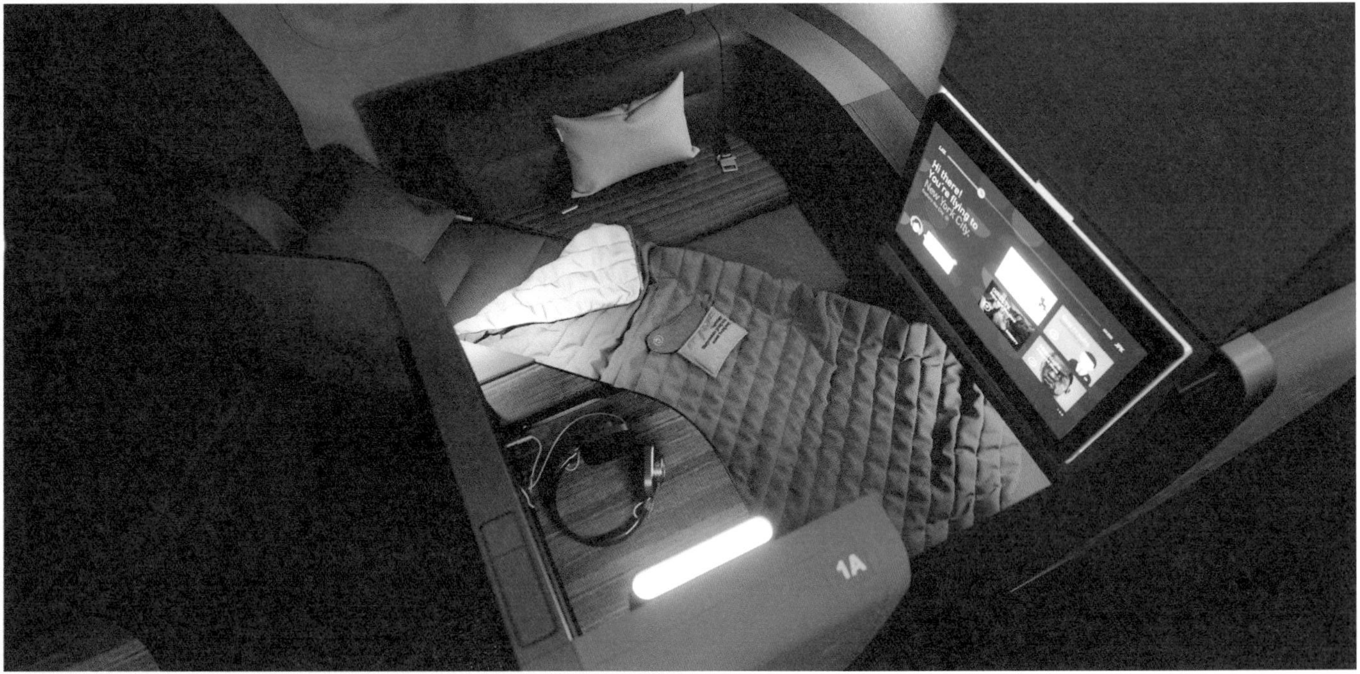

 JetBlue Mint suite

29

Boosting China's travel economy

China's travel industry gears up for a post-pandemic future with new mega-airports, theme parks, and expanded duty-free shopping.

China's outbound travel market was once the world's biggest, peaking at 169 million trips in 2019. Chinese tourists were so ubiquitous that hotels in Hawaii hired Mandarin speakers and London's Marylebone train station debuted platform announcements in Mandarin. Then COVID-19 hit and national borders clanged shut. But China's travel economy hasn't exactly stalled. It's just turned more domestic—for now.

Despite periodic local lockdowns, the total number of domestic trips taken between January and September 2021 rose 39% year-on-year to 2.69 billion trips, the Ministry of Culture and Tourism reported.

Three things China is doing to boost its travel economy:

Premiumizing airports

Beijing's starfish-shaped Daxing International Airport, the capital's second international flight hub, opened in September 2019. Designed by Zaha Hadid Architects, it cost over $11 billion, features a central courtyard inspired by traditional Chinese architecture and skylights for intuitive navigation, and is expected to eventually serve over 100 million passengers a year, rivaling Hartsfield-Atlanta International Airport, the world's busiest.

In China's southwest, Chengdu Tianfu International Airport opened in June 2021, with capacity of 60 million passengers a year, offering a second international gateway to Sichuan province's giant pandas and signature spicy cuisine.

WUNDERMAN THOMPSON

Enhancing duty-free shopping

Unable to fly to Paris, New York or Milan to buy the latest designer bag, luxury shoppers are instead flying to the duty-free zone of Hainan island, known as China's Hawaii.

In July 2020, China tripled duty-free shopping limits and expanded eligible categories in Hainan. In the year since, duty-free sales jumped 226% to $7.2 billion, according to Hainan Customs.

LVMH, Kering, Shiseido, L'Oréal and other global brands have all opened stores here, and Hainan has become a test bed for stitching together physical stores with elements of social commerce and livestreaming.

Hainan's success in catering to pent-up demand for foreign luxury brands has since inspired five metropolises—Beijing, Shanghai, Guangzhou, Tianjin and Chongqing—to also start developing their duty-free offerings as "international consumer centre cities."

Encouraging a boom in theme parks

Just as international retail is rushing into China, so too are Western-style theme parks.

Five years after Disneyland opened in Shanghai, Universal Studios opened in Beijing in September 2021. The Beijing theme park, Universal's fifth and largest globally, has seven themed lands, including the first Kung Fu Panda Land of Awesomeness.

The UK's Merlin Entertainments is building three Legoland theme parks in China. The 2023 Sichuan opening will feature local cultural elements, including a panda-themed area, while the Shenzhen and Shanghai parks will open in 2024 and focus on China's high-tech digital experiences and ancient water town architecture respectively.

Why it's interesting

As national borders shut down, China's travel economy has turned toward the domestic market. That has pulled significant investment into travel retail and entertainment within China, by both international and domestic partners, who are betting on a long-term boost to domestic tourism as well as the return of foreign visitors when borders finally re-open.

> **"As national borders shut down, China's travel economy has turned toward the domestic market.**

30

New age nautics

Eco-conscious travelers are taking to the seas.

Since teen climate activist Greta Thunberg sailed across the Atlantic in 2019 to avoid flying on a greenhouse-gas emitting airplane, a growing cohort of individuals and organizations have likewise turned to wind for a more climate-friendly mode of transportation.

In collaboration with the Swedish government and research organizations, Swedish shipbuilder Wallenius Marine is designing a transatlantic car carrier that will be entirely wind-powered, in an effort to help clean up the automotive trade industry. The Oceanbird carrier will have five steel wind sails and the capacity to carry over 7,000 vehicles.

TransOceanic Wind Transport, a cargo company founded in France, aims to build and operate solely wind-powered cargo vessels. The company is in the process of building four such vessels for global trade routes, with the ability to carry 1,100 tonnes of cargo and reduce emissions by 90%.

A new sporting challenge will help to accelerate the transition

The Oceanbird by Wallenius Marine and Alfa Laval

to cleaner water technologies by promoting electric solutions. The E1 Series is the world's first electric powerboat racing championship, set to take place at a series of coastal locations around the world in 2022. Teams will compete in the Racebird, an electric foiling boat that is inspired by nature. Alongside thrilling races, the Series' biggest impact will be its sustainable legacy. Organizers will leave behind electric charging infrastructure in every city marina, as well as hosting week-long festivals promoting sustainability.

E1 Series cofounder and CEO Rodi Basso tells Wunderman Thompson Intelligence, "Just as the automotive sector is shifting towards electrification and clean technologies, so must the marine industry, to prevent potentially irrevocable damage being caused to such an important ecosystem for our planet."

For individuals, a new crop of organizations is making sailing more accessible. Sailcoop is a French company that is setting up a sailboat cooperative; customers can book trips from January 2022. By creating networks of nautical professionals, passengers and shipowners, Sailcoop provides the opportunity to travel locally or internationally by water, guided by private sailors.

Why it's interesting

Land and air travel no longer have the same sheen, as carbon emissions and climate consequences grow by the day. Thoughtful electric- and wind-powered nautical designs are making carbon-neutral transportation more feasible for everyone, from businesses to competitive athletes to individuals who don't own their own boats.

Top: Sailcoop
Bottom: Oceanways, the world's first zero-emisson submarine conceptv

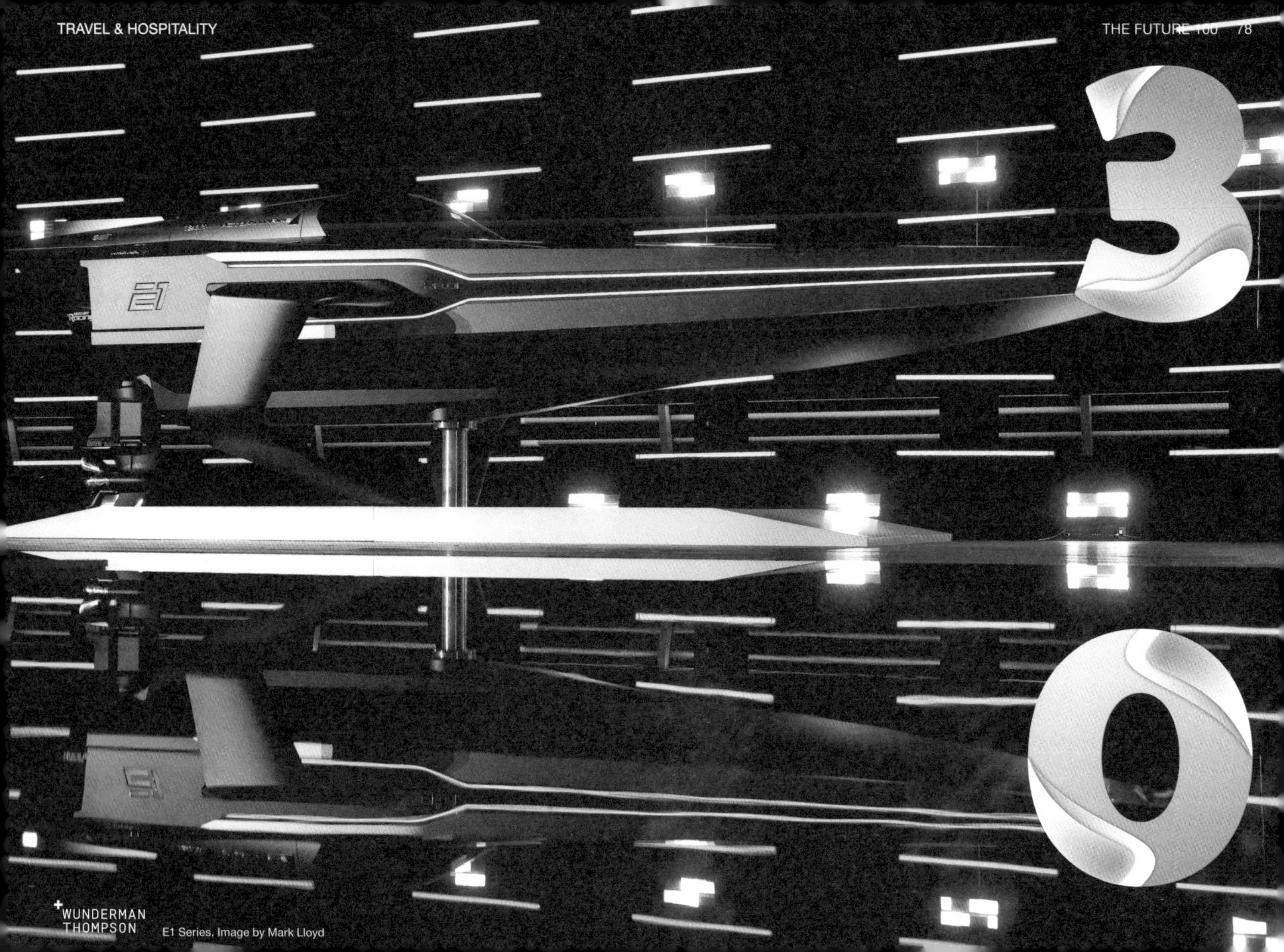

WUNDERMAN THOMPSON

E1 Series. Image by Mark Lloyd

31 Brands & marketing 4.0

31

Brandalism

Vandalism for good hijacks ad space—
exposing brands and demanding they do better.

Climate activists are expanding their targets from the world's biggest corporate polluters to those who enable them, from governments to banks and ad agencies.

Groups including Brandalism, Badvertising and Adfree Cities launched organized, guerilla-style efforts in the United Kingdom around COP26, the global climate conference hosted in Glasgow in November 2021.

In October, the anonymous Brandalism network also plastered more than 100 posters onto billboards and bus stops in 20 UK towns and cities, accusing ad agencies Ogilvy, MediaCom and VCCP of helping to "greenwash" high-carbon clients such as Shell, BP and British Airways, the *Drum* reported. Brandalism had earlier criticized banks such as Barclays and HSBC for providing financing to clients in the fossil-fuel business.

Ford poster by Brandalism

The New Weather Institute think tank has created "Badvertising," a campaign that labels the ad industry as "brain pollution" and calls for the government to control high-carbon advertising.

"For too long, the advertising industry has escaped scrutiny for its role in the climate crisis," Robbie Gillett of Adfree Cities was quoted as saying in the *Drum*. "Whether it's using the best creative talent to promote high-carbon products, providing misleading greenwash for big oil companies or filling our public spaces with energy-intensive ad screens, the juggernaut of polluting PR needs to end."

Another common complaint is that ad agencies promote unsustainable lifestyles through conspicuous consumption during shopping festivals.

Local governments have not been spared. The European Citizens' Initiative Ban Fossil Fuel Advertising and Sponsorships is urging local councils to follow Amsterdam in banning advertising and sponsorship for cars, airlines and fossil-fuel companies.

Why it's interesting

The ad industry itself has made serious efforts in recent years to reach carbon net zero in its own operations. Activists say this isn't enough and efforts pale in comparison to the carbon footprints of some ad agencies' biggest clients.

Posters by Brandalism

32

Co creative platforms

The next generation of digital platforms is putting creative power in the hands of the user.

IMVU social network. Image courtesy of Together Labs

IMVU calls creativity "the new status symbol" for the next digital era.

Creativity is increasingly informed and powered by technology, setting the stage for the next era of digital platforms and creative influence. Digital tools have "activated an entirely new world" of creativity—one where "creations can transcend physical limitations," Helena Dong, creative technologist and digital designer, tells Wunderman Thompson Intelligence.

72% of gen Z and millennials in the United States, the United Kingdom and China believe that creativity today is dependent on technology, and 92% believe that technology opens up a whole new world of creation, according to Wunderman Thompson Intelligence's research for "Into the Metaverse," conducted by Wunderman Thompson Data in July 2021.

"For generation alpha and generation Z, customization and creation are intricate parts of their gaming experience," Keith Stuart, games editor at the *Guardian*, tells Wunderman Thompson Intelligence. "For them, customization and the play element are part of the same thing—self-expression and exploration."

Snapchat believes that creativity is the driving force propelling the future of digital engagement. As a user, "you're not creating content that people consume, you're creating content that people then create with," Carolina Arguelles Navas, group product marketing manager at Snap Inc, tells Wunderman Thompson Intelligence. "That's really powerful. You're putting out a piece of content that everyone personalizes and has a personal experience with."

This momentum is spurred on by what she refers to as the snowball effect of digital creativity. "The biggest opportunity with augmented reality (AR) is that it is a catalyst for other people to now create content with that AR experience you've developed; then they are sharing it with their group of friends

IMVU social network. Image courtesy of Together Labs

IMVU social network. Image courtesy of Together Labs

and their group of friends are unlocking that and sharing. You've created a catalyst where you're scaling creation on your behalf."

IMVU is a "next-generation social network" that revolves around creativity, Daren Tsui, CEO of the social app and its parent company Together Labs, tells Wunderman Thompson Intelligence. "There are over 200,000 creators on our platform. Over the years we've amassed 15 million items in our catalog," almost all of which are user-driven, Tsui says. "We create 0.001%; everything else is done by creators." IMVU calls creativity "the new status symbol" for the next digital era—dethroning influence and income. When users come onto the platform, "making money is not the most important thing for them. It's about being recognized for their creations," Tsui explains.

Why it's interesting

Online habits are evolving. As stated by digital fashion house The Fabricant, in the digital world "people are not passive consumers, but creative agents crafting their self-expression and curating their virtual identity."

33

Superfollowers

Digital creators are making money from their content with new in-app subscriptions on social platforms.

Social media apps are allowing users to monetize their content without using third-party apps, creating new tiers within their creator communities.

Twitter launched Super Follows in September 2021—a new feature that allows paying Tweeters to view subscriber-only content. It allows content creators to tweet out exclusively to their Super Followers and at the time of writing is limited to Twitter iOS app users in the United States who elected to test the feature. Super Follows users can charge from $2.99 to $9.99 a month through payment app Stripe, and can earn up to 97% of their subscription revenue after third-party fees until they reach earnings of $50,000 across all Twitter monetization products. After that, they can earn up to 80% of their revenue after third-party fees.

Twitter is also testing Professional Profiles for businesses. Since April 2021, businesses with Twitter accounts have unique setups to display specific information about their brand or company directly on their profile. The additions include a verification badge, business category, and a section for broader business information, such as hours or location.

Tumblr also launched a new subscription feature in September 2021, open to all users in the United States. Its Post Plus offering allows creators to post only to subscribed followers, similar to Twitter's Super Follows. Tumblr posters can charge from $1.99 to $9.99 a month, and can paywall existing content, not only new posts.

Why it's interesting

Social platforms are evolving to offer more than entertainment in multimedia content. Boosted features and incentives to attract, gain and maintain a significant following are driving creativity and enhancing conversations for creators and consumers on social media.

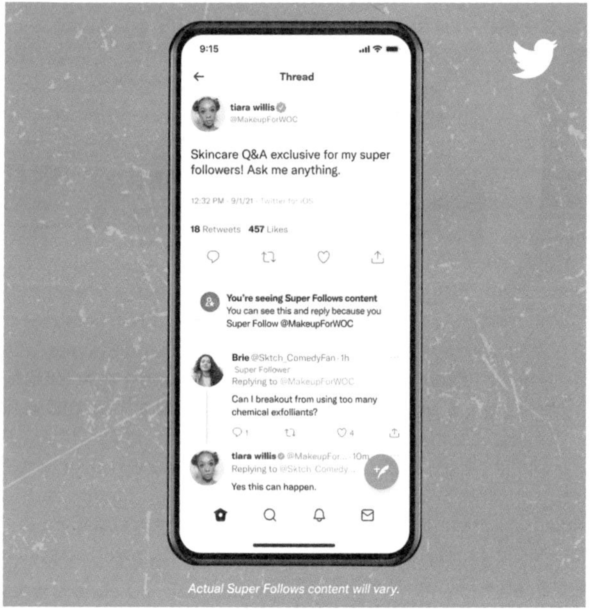

WUNDERMAN THOMPSON

Left: Twitter Super Follows feature
Right: Tumblr Post Plus

34

Branded virtual worlds

Does the future of advertising and marketing lie in gaming?

WUNDERMAN THOMPSON

Top: Ralph Lauren Winter Escape on Roblox
Bottom: Nikeland on Roblox

With the in-game advertising market set to grow by $3.54 billion between 2021 and 2025, according to a 2021 report by Technavio, brands are diving headfirst into gaming with branded virtual worlds.

Many brands are turning to established gaming platforms such as Roblox, creating novel in-game branded experiences in the hope of engaging the platform's 46 million daily active users.

Ralph Lauren announced the launch of its Winter Escape on Roblox in December 2021. The holiday-themed virtual destination includes activities like ice skating, toasting marshmallows, scavenger hunts, and shopping the Ralph Lauren Digital Collection, available for purchase exclusively on Roblox. Nike unveiled *Nikeland* on Roblox in November 2021. The virtual world lets users dress their avatars in virtual Nike gear and explore *Nikeland*'s arenas, fields and buildings that are host to various mini-games. *Vans World*, launched in September 2021, is a virtual skatepark on Roblox where players can practice skateboarding tricks, design their own Vans shoes and skateboards, and try on virtual gear. Also in

WUNDERMAN THOMPSON BMW's Joytopia virtual world

September on Roblox, Hyundai launched its *Hyundai Mobility Adventure*. The space contains five "parks" where users can race, play games, learn about Hyundai's technologies, and take part in festivals.

Other brands are creating branded virtual worlds on their own platforms. For CES 2022, Procter and Gamble invited visitors into a virtual world where they could learn about the company's full portfolio of products, play games, learn about the company's sustainability initiatives and more. BMW launched its virtual world *Joytopia* in September 2021 as part of BMW's participation in the IAA Mobility 2021 international motor show. As well as being the backdrop for BMW to present its vision for the future of mobility, *Joytopia* offered festival-esque elements including an exclusive Coldplay concert. Japanese beauty brand SK-II launched a virtual city in May 2021. Visitors can navigate a virtual rendering of SK-II City to shop, learn about products, and even catch a movie in the SK-II cinema.

"There's something unique about the growth of gaming as a marketing platform," Grant Paterson, head of gaming and esports at Wunderman Thompson, tells Wunderman Thompson Intelligence. "We talk about gaming as being the nexus of a new consumer paradigm."

Why it's interesting

For younger generations especially, gaming is replacing advertising channels such as print and television. "A lot of the traditional ways of marketing to young people are gone forever," Keith Stuart, games editor at the *Guardian*, tells Wunderman Thompson Intelligence. "Gaming is where they are." Expect to see more branded virtual worlds as companies and marketers tap into this growing space.

35

Headless brands

A new wave of consumer creators, powered and incentivized by decentralized organizations, are taking the reins of brand storytelling.

Decentralized technology and finance are paving the way for headless brands, built by communities who collectively decide on products, assets and messaging. Members who buy into these communities, often by acquiring crypto tokens, earn the right to participate in brand decision-making and can even take a share in financial success.

The term headless brand was first coined in a 2019 paper authored by the strategy and research firm Other Internet, which describes these brands as "self-enforcing, self-incentivized, contagious narratives that emerge and evolve in ways that are unexpected and irrepressible." The paper identified Bitcoin as the first iteration of a headless brand as it has no central authority, operating and evolving in line with the decisions of a multitude of stakeholders. "A headless brand is a meme," say the paper's authors, Toby Shorin, Laura Lotti and Sam Hart. "It belongs to no one, and can be remixed by anyone."

More recently, NFT-based marketplaces have emerged that formalize the trend uniting culture, community and crypto. Metafactory, a self-described "factory for headless brands" launched in 2020, aims to bring artists, consumers and brands together in a partnership to create community-run fashion brands. Artists (including Italian digital artist Van and Indonesian cryptoartist Twisted Vacancy) submit their designs and members have a say, voting for their favorites to be produced centrally by Metafactory. Brand members and investors then share in the profits as well as enjoying exclusive NFT drops and promotions.

The Bored Ape Yacht Club, which launched in April 2021, is a

WUNDERMAN THOMPSON Metafactory

community of owners of ape character NFTs. Crucially, owners are assigned the rights to their ape character, allowing them to creatively commercialize their asset. Many owners have already done so, spawning everything from branded craft beer and skateboards to an animated YouTube series. As the New Yorker's Kyle Chayka explains, these "cultural creations can expand organically through the efforts of many users while remaining recognizable, resulting in a kind of user-generated mythology."

Why it's interesting

"Are the Bored Apes a silly collectible or are they a decentralized competitor to Supreme?" mused Twitter user @punk6529 in October 2021. It's likely the latter, if press reports that suggest the Bored Apes ecosystem is already worth $1 billion are accurate. For now, headless startups are perhaps most potent in culture-led categories such as streetwear and music, but brands across the board should keep a watchful eye on this trend that will see consumers grow their stake in brand narratives.

36

Euphoric ads

Moments of joy are keeping spirits high in brand advertising and engagement.

Brands are filling their ads with uplifting and heartwarming moments, inviting audiences to join them in joy and jubilation.

Crowded with dance videos, funny pranks and stunt trends, TikTok is a solid source of joy—and a source of opportunity for brands seeking lighthearted, authentic connections with their audience. According to a study by the Flamingo Group, 73% of TikTok users said they felt happier after logging into the app. Associating those positive emotions with a brand continues to be a top strategy among marketers, as brands hone their marketing into positive spaces and platforms.

Emotional intelligence was at the forefront of a Lexus campaign in October 2021. The ad, promoting the Lexus ES Self-Charging Hybrid, uses facial recognition technology to read and adapt the ad to the consumer's emotions. The goal of the "Feel Your Best" campaign is to leave viewers feeling more positive after their personalized experience.

Gap's "All Together Now" 2021 holiday campaign focused on love, kindness, and "modern American optimism"—one of the brand's core philosophies. The campaign starred Katy Perry and ran to the tune of "All You Need is Love" by the Beatles. Themes of unity, love and joy are consistent with the brand's optimistic marketing motif.

Target's 2021 holiday update of its "What We Value Most Shouldn't Cost More" campaign featured a rendition of "Best of My Love" by The Emotions, performed by the Black Pumas and Sofia Reyes. "This year's holiday campaign provides an opportunity for Target to connect with all of our guests while helping them discover the joy that's within reach every day throughout the season," said chief marketing and digital officer Cara Sylvester.

Why it's interesting

Consumers are seeking authentic, uplifting content, and brands are meeting them on positive platforms, aiming to generate joy in their marketing strategies. Themes of optimism and unity are important to consumers, and brands that focus on those communal aspects are generating positive reactions from customers and increasing engagement within their branded communities.

WUNDERMAN THOMPSON The Lexus ES "Feel Your Best" campaign

> *Brands are filling their ads with uplifting and heartwarming moments, inviting audiences to join them in joy and jubilation.*

37

Regenerative brands

Across industries, more brands are stepping up to commit to regenerative practices, supercharging their sustainability goals.

PepsiCo regenerative farming

Regeneration goes beyond doing less harm to the planet, aiming to reverse negative impacts by restoring and renewing resources—84% of global respondents believe that we need businesses to drive regeneration, or it will not happen, according to Wunderman Thompson Intelligence's 2021 report "Regeneration Rising." In response, brands across categories are pledging to become regenerative.

Looking to grow its farm-to-closet model, in September 2021 Californian sustainable fashion label Christy Dawn launched The Land Stewardship, a new program that focuses on regenerative agriculture. Via the initiative, customers can invest $200, helping to convert a plot of land from conventional cotton farming to farming using regenerative practices. When the cotton is harvested, they are reimbursed in store credit based on the yield of the cotton on the plot they invested in. Christy Dawn customers thus have a real stake in making the company truly regenerative.

Big-name fashion brands are also investing in regenerative agriculture. In October 2021, Ralph Lauren announced it was partnering with the Soil Health Institute to launch the US Regenerative Cotton Fund. This followed the appointment by Conservation International and global luxury group Kering of the first seven grantees under their Regenerative Fund for Nature initiative, getting their mission to transition one million hectares of land to regenerative practices over the next five years under way.

Retailers are also getting on board with regeneration. Morrisons, the UK grocery store chain, announced a partnership with McDonald's, Harper Adams University, and the National Farmers' Union in October 2021. The collaborators have launched the United Kingdom's first school of sustainable food and farming, ultimately aiming to transform the country's farming practices. This follows Walmart's September 2020 pledge to become a regenerative company, which includes a commitment to restore at least 50 million acres of land by 2030.

Over the past few years Big Food has set the pace on regenerative farming, with multinationals Danone, Nestlé and General Mills all revealing plans to help some of their suppliers adopt regenerative techniques. In April 2021, PepsiCo announced an ambitious goal to scale such techniques across seven million acres of land—equal to its entire agricultural footprint—by 2030.

Why it's interesting

Brands are acknowledging that doing less harm to the planet is no longer enough. Regenerating the world's resources and repairing the damage accrued over centuries is now the ultimate sustainability stretch goal.

WUNDERMAN THOMPSON PepsiCo regenerative farming

37

WUNDERMAN THOMPSON The US Regenerative Cotton Fund, a Soil Health Institute partnership with Ralph Lauren

38

New company manifestos

Companies are updating their internal brand messaging to stay culturally relevant and connect with the modern-day employee.

Amazon wants to be the world's best employer for its 1.3 million employees around the world. In an update to its list of Leadership Principles, bringing the total to 16, the company added two new entries in July 2021. The first, "strive to be Earth's best employer," says that Amazon leaders work to "create a safer, more productive, higher performing, more diverse, and more just work environment." The second, focused on scaling sensibly and responsibly, notes "we are big, we impact the world, and we are far from perfect." Andy Jassy, who took over as CEO after Jeff Bezos stepped down, hopes to bring about a new employee-first and responsible future for Amazon.

In response to the continued proliferation of work-from-home set-ups, which triggered frustrations and lack of work-life balance for some, Google released a wellbeing manifesto that includes relatable sentiments such as "It's OK to put your family before your work" and "It's OK to say you're not OK."

Why it's interesting

Companies are going through a rebrand—one that looks to update internal policies to meet today's needs and put employees first. The shift signals a new respect for employee wellbeing and happiness that demands a new level of understanding and empathy from employers.

39

Dreamvertising

Brands and advertisers are looking to guide our dreams.

The commercial exploitation of dreams is becoming a reality, but not without eliciting concern from the scientific community. Calls for regulation are placing early adopters of dream incubation advertising in the spotlight. While possibilities still run wild, the next wave of subliminal marketing is uncertain.

Dream incubation or targeted dream incubation (TDI) is a modern field of science with ancient roots where sensory cues like sound are used to shape or "prime" people's dreams. In a clinical setting, TDI can be used to change negative behaviors, like smoking. In marketing, it is being used to inspire brand affinity.

Anheuser Busch has exclusivity to Super Bowl advertising sewn up, so in January 2021 Molson Coors found a very different way to target Super Bowl fans. Using TDI advertising reminiscent of Microsoft's Xbox "Made From Dreams" campaign, Molson Coors collaborated with dream psychologist Deirdre Barrett of Harvard University to produce the Coors Big Game Dream film and soundscape, designed to cause viewers to have pleasant dreams set in mountain scenes—that just happen to sway people toward Molson Coors products. The press release reads: "Coors Light and Coors Seltzer want to ensure you'll have a refreshing dream using the science of guiding dreams."

Sounds pleasant enough in context, but Massachusetts Institute of Technology neuroscientist Adam Haar believes these practices in a marketing context are scary. While they are known to interfere with our natural nocturnal memory processing, they also could pave the way to more sinister

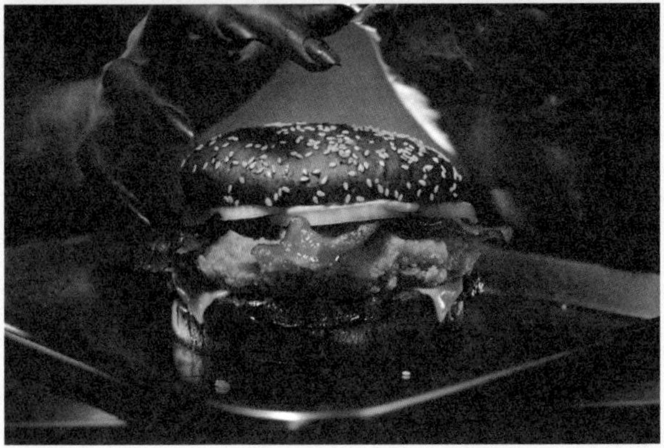

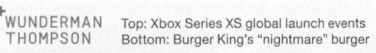

Top: Xbox Series XS global launch events
Bottom: Burger King's "nightmare" burger

> "77% of US marketers say they plan to use dreamtech for advertising purposes in the next three years.

ends. For example, back in 2018 Burger King had more devilish plans. Its "nightmare" burger for Halloween was "clinically proven" to induce nightmares. Supported by 40 professional signatories from diverse fields of academia, Haar cowrote an opinion piece for DXE, published in June 2021, that cautioned: "proactive action and new protective policies are urgently needed to keep advertisers from manipulating one of the last refuges of our already beleaguered conscious and unconscious minds: Our dreams."

Why it's interesting

There is a growing appetite from brands to experiment with dream influencing technology and techniques: a 2021 study by the American Marketing Association found that 77% of US marketers say they plan to use dreamtech for advertising purposes in the next three years. While there are no prohibitive regulations in place, some consumers could perceive such techniques as dystopian. Until we have a deeper scientific understanding, it's perhaps best that brands approach "dreamvertising" with caution.

40

Augmented ads

Brands are leveling up digital advertising with augmented reality.

Augmented reality (AR) is hitting the mainstream, and consumers are showing a growing appetite for AR brand engagement. Currently, there are 1.5 billion frequent users of AR, and this is forecast to hit 4.3 billion by 2025, according to August 2021 research from Statista. And, notably, 70% of consumers say they want to see more AR ads, according to a July 2021 survey from Ericsson.

Brands are embracing AR to engage digital consumer bases. In November 2021, Volkswagen launched AR ads embedded on Amazon boxes. By scanning a QR code printed on the Amazon box, users can learn about Volkswagen's new 2022 Taos SUV through an AR driving experience.

AR Labs WPP partnership with Snap

In September 2021, Snap and ad giant WPP launched an AR partnership, AR Labs, to deliver augmented marketing solutions for brands. AR Labs will also develop a custom scorecard for WPP clients, which will be used to generate more effective campaigns. In October 2021, Snap also launched a new creative studio, Arcadia, to create AR ads and help brands develop AR advertising and experiences—on Snapchat as well as other digital platforms. The studio has already partnered with companies like Shake Shack, P&G Beauty and Verizon.

Malls will soon have floating augmented ads. In July 2021, Brookfield Properties partnered with The Aria Network to open up air space in malls to augmented advertisements. The new deal will give Aria exclusive rights to the virtual air space of Brookfield Properties, which encompasses over 150 million square feet in 100 different locations. Aria will use the square feet from the deal to create the ability for brands to advertise through augmented reality, which consumers can access through their phones.

"AR has a major role to play in the future of marketing and commerce," says Sanja Partalo, executive vice president of strategic development and partnerships at WPP.

Why it's interesting

The advent of AR ads is teeing up the next era of digital marketing and advertising—for ads that consumers want to engage with.

> **"AR has a major role to play in the future of marketing and commerce.**

41

Food & drink

50

41

Foraged cocktails

Sustainable cocktail offerings are taking inspiration from the natural world.

WUNDERMAN THOMPSON

Visit Sweden's elderflower vinegar. Photography by Martin Vallin

Locally foraged ingredients are being used to create one-of-a-kind craft cocktails and offer consumers a greater range of sustainable drink options.

In September 2021, national tourism organization Visit Sweden announced it was expanding its rewilded tourism offering to the United Kingdom, the United States and Germany. Building on Visit Sweden's Drinkable Country program, the new "Taste of Swedish Summer" campaign highlights 22 natural ingredients that can be found in Sweden during the sunniest months, from spruce buds to wild flowers, alongside food preservation methods such as pickling and fermentation, and innovative recipes. In collaboration with Forsman & Bodenfors and Mindshare, the promotion centers on local produce. Drinkable Country encourages visitors to explore Sweden's countryside as the "world's largest outdoor bar," with local guides on hand at 14 nationwide locations to help guests collect berries and greens to mix into their custom beverages.

Spirits company Hangar 1 has used damaged merlot and malbec grapes from the 2020 Glass Fire in Napa Valley to make vodka. Distilled from fruit unsuitable for wine, the 80-proof Smoke Point Vodka has a hint of anise and vanilla for a different take on the spirit. The company is donating all proceeds from sales to the California Fire Foundation.

Why it's interesting

Whether rewilded or repurposed, foraged craft cocktails are lifting spirits. Local, self-sustained cuisine is minimizing waste and reforming menus as contemporary innovators incorporate local flora into their craft.

 Visit Sweden. Image by Niklas Nyman

42

Liquid immunity

Wellness aficionados are quenching their thirst while supercharging their immune systems.

In October 2021, LA-based children's snack brand Bitsy's launched Swish, an immunity-boosting drink mix for children. Containing electrolytes, vitamin C and zinc, the mixes are designed to be added to kids' water bottles for a quick immunity hit on the go.

Harnessing the power of the microalgae spirulina, Netherlands-based Ful Foods launched its range of Ful Revive vitamin-rich drinks in the United Kingdom in autumn 2021. The drinks' distinctive blue color comes from the phycocyanin natural antioxidant found in spirulina, which is renowned for its immune-boosting properties. Alongside their health benefits, the brand also claims the drinks are "climate active" thanks to the microalgae's ability to absorb one and a half to two times their weight in carbon and photosynthesize it, releasing oxygen.

US food and drinks brand Ocean Spray is also looking to health-first options. In November 2020 the company launched the B1U functional-beverage brand, which includes a lemon and chamomile-infused water called I Need Immunity. Going beyond beverages, the brand followed up in March 2021 with Ocean Spray Fruit Medley, a new line of dried-fruit blends with key benefits. The Immunity Blend contains beta glucan, which has been shown to improve immune defense.

As continued focus on illness prevention drives growth in the global immunity-boosting food market—set to grow at a CAGR of 8.2% from 2021 to 2028, according to Stratagem Market Insights—immunity-assisting drinks are a new focus for innovation.

Why it's interesting

With six in 10 global consumers looking to food and drink items to help their immune system, according to Innova's Consumer Survey 2020, brands have good reason to create products that support overall health.

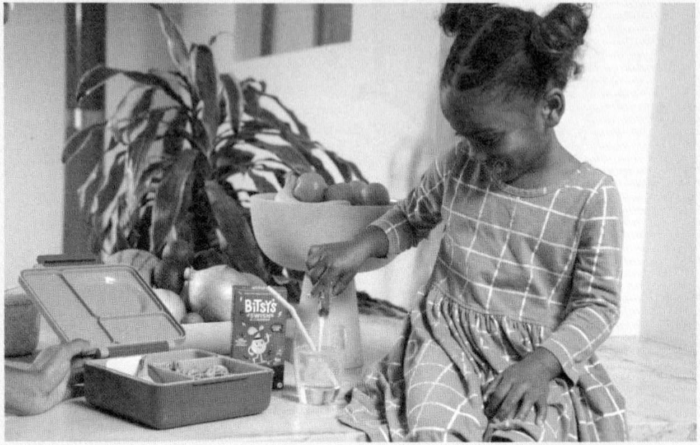

WUNDERMAN THOMPSON

Left: Ocean Spray's B1U functional-beverage brand
Right: Bitsy's Swish is an immunity-boosting drink for kids

43

Haute veganism

Vegan dining evolves from earthy-crunchy to exclusive.

A swath of Michelin-starred restaurants and top chefs are going vegan, giving vegetables the rarefied and gourmet status once bestowed on meat.

Previously renowned for its duck, lobster and foie gras dishes, the three-Michelin-starred Eleven Madison Park reopened in June 2021 after lockdown with a fully plant-based menu. "The future for me is plant-based," said head chef and owner Daniel Humm.

Geranium, a three-star-Michelin restaurant in Denmark, announced in November 2021 that it would remove meat from its menu. Voted the second-best restaurant in the world in October, the restaurant is refocusing on plant-based and pescatarian dishes. "I feel like we need a clean slate,"

Mushroom dish at Eleven Madison Park. Photography by Evan Sung

head chef and co-owner Rasmus Kofoed told *Berlingske*. “We are waving goodbye to our signature dishes and I think that is a big step.”

In June, Michelin-starred Gauthier Soho in London reopened with an all-vegan menu. ONA, which stands for origine non-animale (animal-free origin), became the first all-vegan restaurant in France to earn a Michelin star in January 2021. And the three-Michelin-starred team behind SingleThread in California announced plans in May 2021 to open a casual meatless restaurant.

Why it's interesting

Acclaimed chefs and restaurateurs are elevating vegan cuisine to a highbrow fine-dining experience.

Left: Tonburi dish at Eleven Madison Park. Photography by Evan Sung
Right: Geranium. Photography by Claes Bech-Poulsen

44

Cell cultured coffee

Following meat and seafood, coffee could be the next item grown in a lab.

In September 2021, VTT Technical Research Centre of Finland said it had produced a brew that smelled and tasted like regular coffee—all without growing a single coffee plant. The coffee was lab-grown from cell cultures in a bioreactor, with steel vessels filled with a nutrient-rich broth.

"The experience of drinking the very first cup was exciting," VTT research team leader Dr Heiko Rischer says. "I estimate we are only four years away from ramping up production and having regulatory approval in place."

The impetus for an alternative way to make coffee is similar to that for meat and seafood: growing world demand that's taxing the earth's productive resources. The global coffee

Coffee produced in a bioreactor through cellular agriculture by VTT Research

market was worth over $102 billion in 2020, according to Mordor Intelligence. The market—from whole bean and ground and instant coffee to pods and capsules—is marked by fierce competition and innovation.

Rising coffee production and consumption worldwide have sparked concerns about deforestation as well as river pollution from processing run-offs. Traditionally coffee plants were grown under the shade of trees but, as demand skyrocketed, coffee farmers began cutting down trees to create rows of higher-yield coffee. Scientists warn that in the future climate change could also lead to shrinking areas for coffee cultivation, particularly for high-end varieties in countries like Ethiopia. Hence the search for an alternative cup of java.

Rischer says that more research on processing and formulation lies ahead, as well as regulatory approval. "That said," he adds, "we have now proved that lab-grown coffee can be a reality."

Why it's interesting

Scientists already know they can grow animal and plant biomass in labs. But the process tends to be laborious and expensive, and still tends to evoke a "Frankenfood" vibe among consumers. The first lab-grown meat—chicken nuggets made by Silicon Valley company Eat Just—was approved for sale at the end of 2020 in Singapore and hasn't really taken off anywhere else since. Coffee won't have that baggage. The big test will be whether the brands that commercialize lab-grown coffee can eventually meet a price point consumers can swallow—on a daily basis.

Coffee produced in a bioreactor through cellular agriculture by VTT Research

45

Net zero alcohol

Global distilleries are addressing climate change by going carbon neutral.

Alcoholic brands are reinventing their processes to be more sustainable and less wasteful to combat climate change. In addition to new carbon-neutral distilleries such as Air Company and Bespoken Spirits, traditional spirits brands are promising to do better for the planet with reformed operations.

Diageo opened its first carbon-neutral distillery in North America in September 2021. The operation will use 100% renewable electricity, zero fossil fuels for production, and virtual metering technology by 2030. It will also support the local community with 30 full-time jobs and even source 100% non-GMO corn locally. The spirits giant announced plans in 2020 to achieve net-zero carbon emissions by 2030 as part of its Society 2030: Spirit of Progress initiative. Some of its distilleries, such as Oban and Royal Lochnagar, are already carbon neutral.

Air Company manufactures its alcohol from recaptured carbon dioxide (CO_2) and takes an extra pound of carbon from the air in the process. After launching in 2020, the company won first place in the NASA CO_2 Conversion Challenge in August 2021.

Absolut Vodka announced in May 2021 that all production is on track to function fully without fossil fuels by 2025. Declared carbon neutral back in 2013, it is ahead of the game, boasting 85% renewable energy, sending zero waste to landfills, and repurposing by-products either for fuel or food for farm animals.

Why it's interesting

As prominent spirits distilleries join the fight against climate change, the food and beverage industry is lowering its production waste and carbon emissions.

Air Company's recaptured CO_2 vodka

46

Blue Zones diets

Brands and communities are embracing Blue Zones lifestyles in the pursuit of health and wellness.

Blue Zones residents live longer and healthier lives compared to those in other parts of the world, and signs collectively point to holistic, integrated wellness habits as the main cause. Ikaria in Greece, Okinawa in Japan, the Ogliastra region of Sardinia, Loma Linda in California, and the Nicoya Peninsula, Costa Rica, have all been identified as Blue Zones. Research shows that people living here are part of communities that focus on collective care, food in moderation, and sustainable habits. Outsiders can now adopt the meals and practices that make Blue Zones residents so healthy.

Bush's Beans introduced a new Blue Zones line of organic plant-based toppings for meals and soups in October 2021. Beans, which are considered a "longevity food all-star" by the Blue Zones organization, are at the center of the collaborative offering. Bush's senior vice president of marketing, Stephen Palacios, said this new product line "makes it easy for anyone, anywhere to eat more like the longest-living cultures in the world."

A neighborhood in Tucson, Arizona, has repurposed an abandoned school as a community food hub, inspired by the collaborative nature of Blue Zones communities. The Midtown Farm, a small-scale group, plants seeds and harvests affordable food for the local community, which is predominantly Latino and Indigenous. Using rainwater harvesting systems and collective workshops to involve the community, the initiative is checking multiple boxes when it comes to Blue Zones lifestyle habits.

Why it's interesting

Living life intentionally, with moderation and community in mind, has brought Blue Zones lifestyles into the mainstream, as many around the world attempt to adopt more holistic wellness habits. Due to heightened focus on health, consumers are looking for healthy habits of collective care, and Blue Zones diets offer a formula for that.

> **Bush's Beans' new product line "makes it easy for anyone, anywhere to eat more like the longest-living cultures in the world."**

Bush's Beans Blue Zones Zesty Black Bean organic plant-based meal toppings

47

Three hot new ingredients

The latest ingredients hitting pantries in 2022 are good for the body and the planet.

Kernza

This climate-friendly grain, a sustainable, domesticated form of wheatgrass developed and trademarked by the Land Institute, is making its way into everything from beer to cereal. Unlike traditional wheat, which yields a single harvest and needs to be replanted every year, Kernza is perennial—meaning that a single seed will provide grain for years. It also nourishes the soil, reducing the need for fertilizer for surrounding plants, and is a natural carbon capturer.

In September 2021, Patagonia Provisions released its third beer made with Kernza, in partnership with the Hopworks Urban Brewery based in Portland, Oregon. And General Mills-owned Cascadian Farm uses Kernza in its honey toasted Kernza cereal.

Kernza. Image courtesy of the Land Institute

Peruvian gooseberry
Aguaymanto, also known as the Cape gooseberry or goldenberry, is a berry native to the Andes with a bittersweet flavor. The fruit is gaining popularity for its health benefits, which include a high content of antioxidants, vitamins A and C, and minerals. Most recently, the berry has made its way onto the menu at the Freehand hotel's newest Latin American restaurant, Comodo, which opened in New York City in October 2021.

Tea seed oil
Tea seed oil, which has been cultivated and used for centuries in Asia, is the latest cooking oil to hit Western shelves. It is known as "the olive oil of the East" thanks to its neutral flavor profile and high smoke point. Made from the seeds of Camellia oleifera, a flowering plant native to East Asia, tea seed oil is packed with antioxidants, omega-3s, minerals, and vitamins E, A, & B. Yóu Yóu, a new brand launched in October 2021, is bringing the oil to the United States—while preserving its heritage. Cofounder Anthony Chen told *Well & Good* that it takes eight years to make one bottle of Yóu Yóu tea seed oil. "We're working with producers in the Hunan region who have literally been doing this for generations."

Left: Comodo at the Freehand. Photography by Gentl and Hyers
Right: Yóu Yóu tea seed oil

48

Accelerated maturation

Why wait years to sample aged liquor when it is possible in a matter of days?

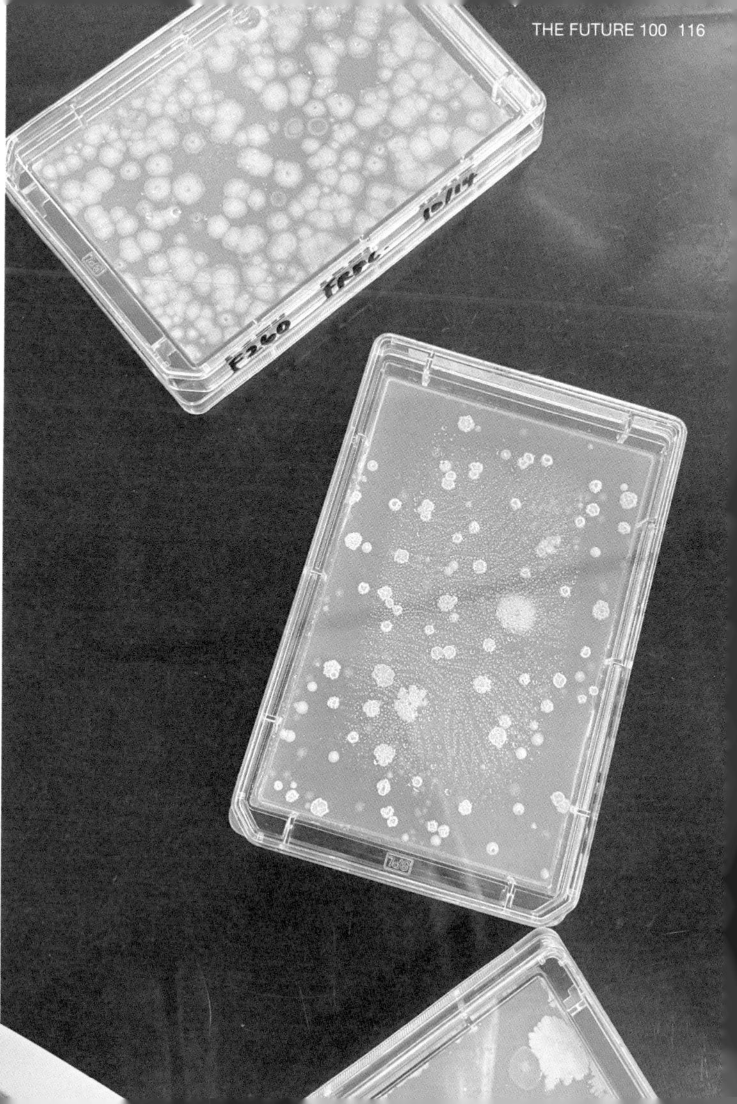

WUNDERMAN THOMPSON

Kingdom Supercultures

Bespoken Spirits aims to upend the slow, wasteful and antiquated spirits industry with a sustainable new maturation process. Leveraging modern technology, material science and data analytics, the Californian company meticulously tailors the aroma, color and taste of craft spirits in under a week—the traditional whiskey maturation process takes years.

The accelerated process has over 20 billion different recipes and is shaking up the global spirits market, which is expected to grow in value from just over $143 billion in 2020 to nearly $209 billion in 2025, according to Research & Markets. "From day one it was about disrupting the industry, but it was about disrupting it for the better," Stu Aaron, who cofounded Bespoken Spirits with Martin Janousek, tells Wunderman Thompson Intelligence.

WUNDERMAN THOMPSON Bespoken Spirits

"From day one it was about disrupting the industry, but it was about disrupting it for the better."

New York-based biodesign company Kingdom Supercultures aims to use science to speed up the fermentation process in plant-based food, beverages, and natural consumer goods. Founded in 2020 by Kendall Dabaghi and Ravi Sheth, the startup has already created new flavors of sauce that have been snapped up by Michelin-starred restaurants including Eleven Madison Park and Gramercy Tavern, and in October 2021 the company received $25 million in Series A funding.

Why it's interesting

Time-consuming processes such as alcohol maturation and food fermentation are being upended by startups with ambitions to economize on time and output, as well as explore new taste frontiers.

49

The new terroir

Climate change is having a seismic impact on global agriculture, making previously fertile places untenable while also creating new northern growth areas for crops.

The Morettino family's Sicilan-grown coffee, served in antique Arabian coffeeware

While climate change wreaks havoc on global agriculture, some brands are seeing an upside to higher temperatures in traditionally colder climes.

Wine has seen strong growth in more northerly geographies, which are increasingly able to grow highly esteemed grape varieties due to temperature rises. Across Canada, new wineries are springing up, with production increasing over 75% in the last 20 years according to figures drawn from the Food and Agriculture Organization of the United Nations cited by *Wine Industry Advisor*. In 2019, British Columbia-based CheckMate Artisanal Winery received a perfect score from wine writer, sommelier and author John Schreiner for its 2015 Little Pawn Chardonnay—a Canadian first. The establishment of the winery was due to the effects of climate change in the region, which have made it possible to grow old-world grape varieties to a high standard.

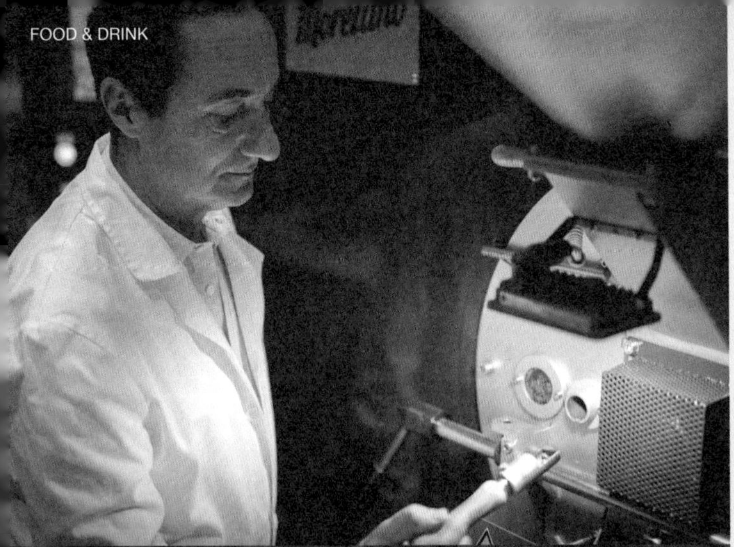

Other crops are also travelling northwards. In December 2020, the *New York Times Magazine* and ProPublica described changes in Russia, as warmer temperatures turn previously barren eastern parts of the country into fertile land for farming. Given that the country is now able to sustain crops such as soybeans, wheat and corn in more areas, it is looking to become a top food producer for the world.

Although not traditionally considered a cold climate, Italy is seeing new produce pop up too. Sicilian farmer Andrea Passanisi is growing avocados on his grandfather's land, which was previously used to grow grapes. As the weather has become too hot for grape vines, the land now provides the perfect environment for fruit such as avocados, lychees and passion fruit. Committed to sustainable practices at Sicilia Avocado, Passanisi is carrying on the tradition of farming by working with the changing climate. In 2021, another Sicilian crop finally began to bear fruit: coffee beans. The Morettino family had their first successful harvest of coffee beans after 30 years of trying. The family's ultimate dream is to create a zero-km Italian coffee brand.

Why it's interesting

Climate change is forcing farmers and agricultural entrepreneurs to adapt and embrace new crops that would have been impossible for them to grow even 10 years ago. New terroirs could forever change the way we think of the heritage and provenance of food.

Top: Alberto Morettino
Bottom: Coffee plant in Palermo. Images courtesy of the Morettino family

50

Edible escapism

In search of outlets for their wanderlust, travelers are now turning to the kitchen.

Counter of Joy invited diners to "travel through your taste buds from the mountains of China to the coastlines of West Africa, city bakeries of Turkey, and country pastures of the British Isles." From November 11 through December 18, 2021, London diners could book the seven-course tasting experience for a culinary trip around the world, prepared by Michelin-starred chefs as part of the Great Feast festival at the Old Selfridges Hotel.

Londoners looking for a more approachable entry point into foreign food can stop in at one of the American candy shops taking over the city. On London's famous Oxford Street, there are now nine mega candy stores specializing in American sweets in less than a square mile, NBC News reports, with names like American Candy Land and Candy Surprise, which opened in early 2021.

The *Colombiana: A Rediscovery of Recipes and Rituals from the Soul of Columbia* cookbook, released in June 2021, transports readers and home chefs to the South American country. Alongside traditional Colombian recipes, the cookbook includes hosting tips, photography highlighting leading artists—from ceramicists to textile makers to fashion and jewelry designers—and short profiles of Colombia's female food heroes for a truly transportive look into Colombian culture and dining.

Why it's interesting

With travel still not possible or appealing for many, people are opting to take their taste buds for a trip, driving a wave of globally inspired eating experiences.

+WUNDERMAN THOMPSON The Great Feast by Counter of Joy

51
Beauty
60

51

New beauty labels

Beauty brands are rethinking labeling to offer transparency about their products' environmental impact.

An increasing number of beauty brands are using packaging to clearly display the sustainability of their production methods, to better align with consumer expectations of environmental impact transparency.

In September 2021, a group of prominent beauty brands collaborated to develop a system for tracking the environmental impact or sustainability of their products. The brand-agnostic approach will give consumers a clear view of the impact of the product they're buying, with a labelling system that compares items from companies opting into the initiative. Ultimately the brands—Unilever, Henkel, L'Oréal, Natura & Co and LVMH—aim to support sustainability practices and invite others to join the project to achieve full transparency across the beauty sector.

Skincare and beauty brand Tata Harper has earned the Sustainable Forestry Initiative label for several of its products, which indicates that its packing comes from sustainable and responsible sources. The packaging is also recyclable—a clear indicator and perhaps a purchasing incentive for the sustainability-focused consumer.

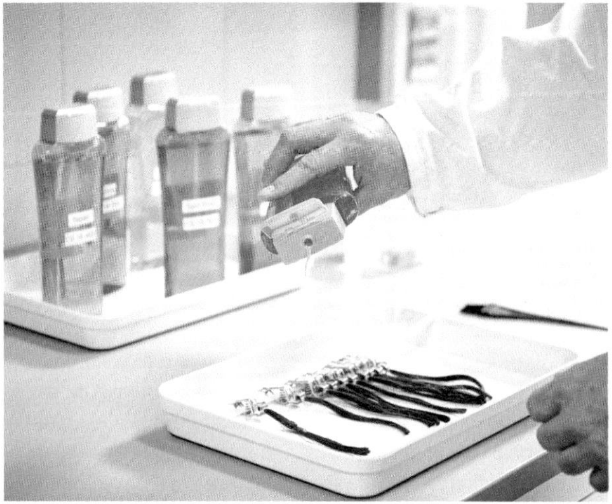

Skincare brand Cocokind also focused on creating transparency with its packaging in 2021. It has introduced a fact panel on each product's label to break down details of the item's sustainability and carbon footprint so that consumers can easily visualize the environmental impact.

Why it's interesting

More beauty brands are displaying the environmental impact of their products on packaging labels, opting for transparency in their sustainability practices. Consumers are paying attention, indicating that these initiatives are important to the market.

> Beauty brands are displaying the environmental impact of their products on packaging labels.

WUNDERMAN THOMPSON

Left: The Henkel brand collaborated in the development of a brand-agnostic system to track the environmental impact of beauty products. Right: Image courtesy of Unilever

52

Mineral skincare

Skincare gets elemental—brands are now taking inspiration from ancient Indo-Asian beauty rituals by adding precious metals to their formulas.

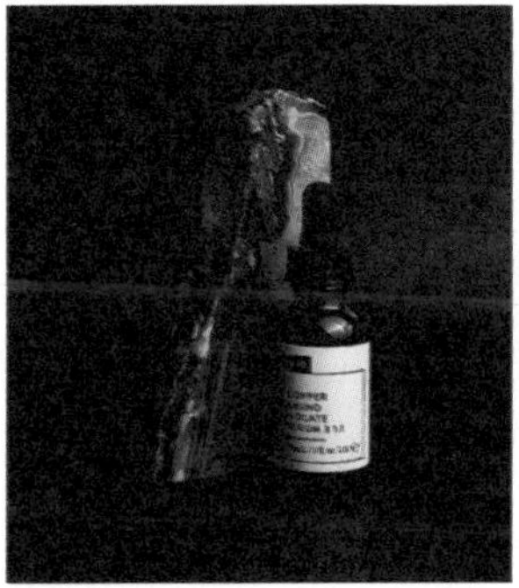

Niod, sister brand to The Ordinary, launched a skin serum with copper peptides in September 2021. Copper peptides have wound-healing and anti-inflammatory properties, play an essential role in skin growth, and also stimulate collagen and elastin, alongside other benefits, making them a potent ingredient in skincare formulas.

Cult Polish pharmacy skincare brand Tolpa launched a face mask with silver microparticles in July 2021. The mask is exfoliating, antibacterial, and helps lighten hyperpigmentation. African Botanics released its Silver Rescue Cream with colloidal silver—known for its antimicrobial and healing properties—in May 2021.

Why it's interesting

After a tumultuous two years, consumers are looking for extra indulgence in their self-care rituals and turning to mineral skincare for a dose of luxurious pampering.

WUNDERMAN THOMPSON

Left: Copper peptide serum by Niod
Right: Silver face mask by Tolpa

53

The demise of "normal" beauty

Brands are radically redefining the beauty industry, one word at a time.

In March 2021, Unilever announced it was removing the word "normal" from packaging and advertising across its beauty and personal care brands, in a dedicated effort to become more inclusive. The move is an acknowledgment of Unilever's global influence and a reflection of evolving consumer values.

"With one billion people using our beauty and personal care products every day, and even more seeing our advertising, our brands have the power to make a real difference to people's lives," says Sunny Jain, president of beauty and personal care at Unilever. "We are committed to tackling harmful norms and stereotypes, and shaping a broader, far more inclusive definition of beauty." In addition to removing the word "normal," the company also stated it would not use excessive editing of models used in its advertisements.

Harry Styles, known for his gender-fluid aesthetic, launched new beauty brand Pleasing in November 2021 with four nail polishes, a dual roller ball lip and eye serum, and a facial serum. The brand, which features both men and women in its advertisements, celebrates "the multitude of unique identities in our community," and is working to "dispel the myth of a binary existence," Styles says.

Neutrogena unveiled its "For People With Skin" campaign in April 2021. Founded in 1930, the beauty brand now aims to focus on combating inequality in skincare, in relation to socioeconomic status, race, ethnicity, and access to health care. "We want to be there for all skin, and all people," Kerry Sullivan, then general manager of Neutrogena, told *WWD*.

Why it's interesting

A new inclusive lexicon is redefining the beauty industry, making room for more individualized and accepting expressions and interpretations of beauty. The concept of a one-size-fits-all beauty ideal has been thrown out the window—and there's no going back.

Images courtesy of Pleasing

54

Absurdist makeovers

Beauty as self-expression is getting experimental.

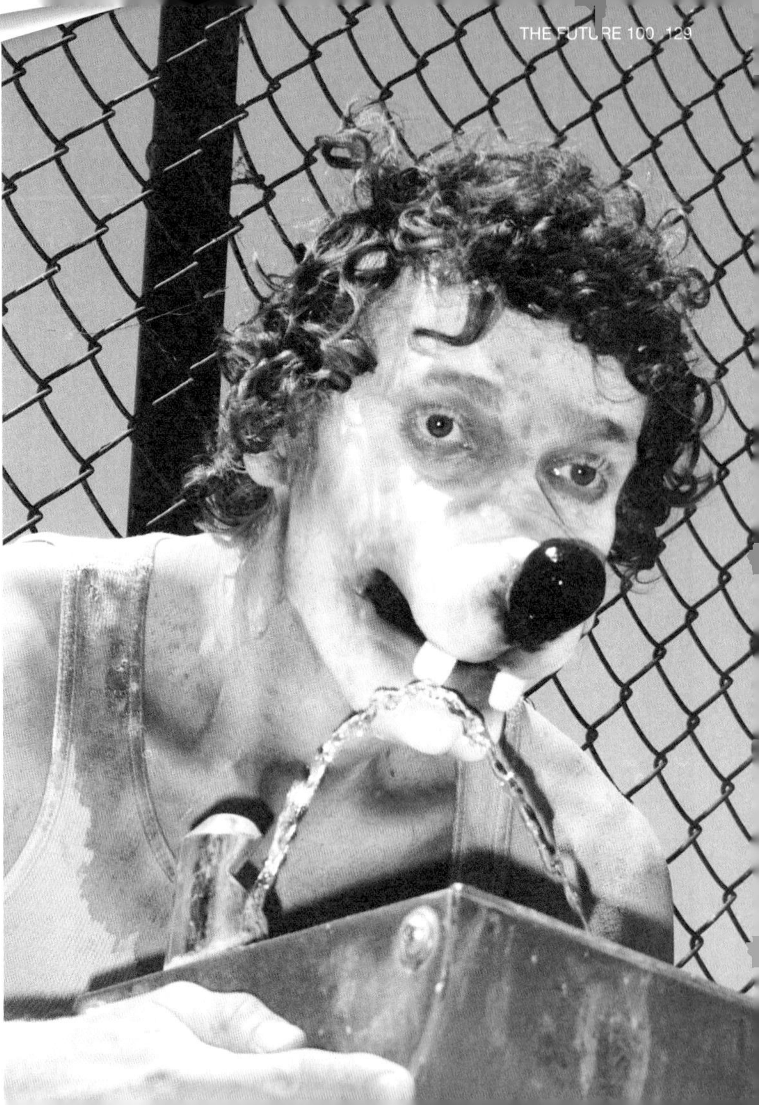

Image from the first issue of Jackson Bowley's Circus magazine

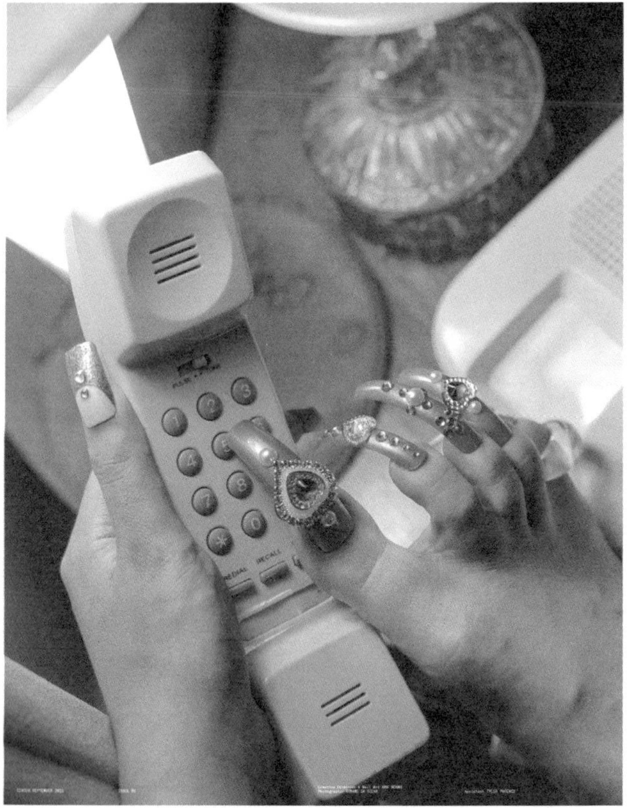

After a difficult few years for many, beauty consumers are seeking out opportunities to play and experiment. *Circus* is a new kind of beauty publication that is "not to be taken too seriously." Announced in September 2021, it celebrates the absurdity and playfulness of beauty. *Dazed Beauty* called it an "unserious beauty platform for total weirdos." It features avant-garde looks, from the wacky, such as bedazzled teeth, to the silly, like acrylic toenail art, to the clownish.

"Everything at the minute seems super serious," *Circus* creator and editor-in-chief Jackson Bowley told *i-D*. "I just wanted to create a publication that was fun, simple and loud. That, and I wanted to create a beauty magazine that really pushes how we see and what we can do with beauty imagery."

The beauty looks in Schiaparelli's 2022 spring/summer collection digital presentation were "suitably surreal," *Vogue* reported. Models wore elongated gold-plated nail accessories, umbrella hats, and handbags embellished with faces.

Why it's interesting

Consumers are approaching beauty with a newly liberated attitude of uninhibited self-expression—picking up their makeup brushes not necessarily to look "good" but to have fun, experiment, and test the boundaries of their creativity.

Image from the first issue of Jackson Bowley's Circus magazine

55

Metabeauty

Gaming systems are introducing virtual beauty and real-world cosmetics to their realms, heightening user engagement and opportunities for beauty brands and creatives.

Gamers are customizing their avatars using virtual cosmetics, bringing new forms of creativity and personality to gaming. Even in violent or action-centered games such as *Grand Theft Auto* or *Fortnite*, players are turning to digital high-fashion clothes and hair and makeup options for enhanced self-expression and immersion. "By dressing your character how you want, it pushes the imagination a little further," Jo-Ashley Robert, *Dead by Daylight*'s associate producer, told *Vogue*. "It's only getting more popular."

Traditional beauty brands including Nars Cosmetics and Gucci are creating virtual makeup for players to use. Nars Cosmetics added 30 virtual products to the Drest app in October 2021, displayed using virtual model avatars. Also in October, Gucci Beauty added 29 virtual makeup products to Drest's Beauty Mode feature, with more than 40 potential combinations and links for users to purchase the physical products in the app.

The *Sims 4 Spa Day Game Pack* got a beauty upgrade in September 2021. Players can now add a High Maintenance trait, do yoga, meditate, and get facials, pedicures and manicures with new nail designs. At least 100 new skin-tone swatches, hairstyles, and makeup options were included in the update.

> *Players are turning to digital high fashion clothes and hair and makeup options for enhanced self expression.*

3D digital artist Nathalie Nguyen photoshops alien-inspired digital beauty effects and 3D nail art into her self-portraits, blurring the viewer's sense of reality. Using real objects and digitally rendered 3D makeup, Nguyen's beauty concept redefines what is real and highlights how we portray ourselves online versus in real life.

Why it's interesting

Adaptation of digital beauty has evolved from CGI model Perl's AI makeup line, which we identified as an early indication of this trend in "The Future 100: 2019," to brands restaging their physical products for digital platforms. As gamers continue to engage with metabeauty, brands will find opportunities to sell and promote their beauty offerings in the metaverse.

Gucci Beauty added 29 virtual products to Drest's Beauty Mode feature

56

Acidic care

Skincare brands are homing in on the benefits of these top three acidic ingredients.

Acidic skincare is taking over beauty shelves, so we're focusing on three acid-based ingredients taking center stage for 2022.

Tranexamic acid

My Topicals skincare debuted its Faded brightening and clearing serum in 2021. Faded relies on tranexamic acid to benefit sun-damaged or scarred skin; the acid prevents excess pigmentation spots and melasma, toning skin for an even glow.

My Topicals Faded serum with tranexamic acid

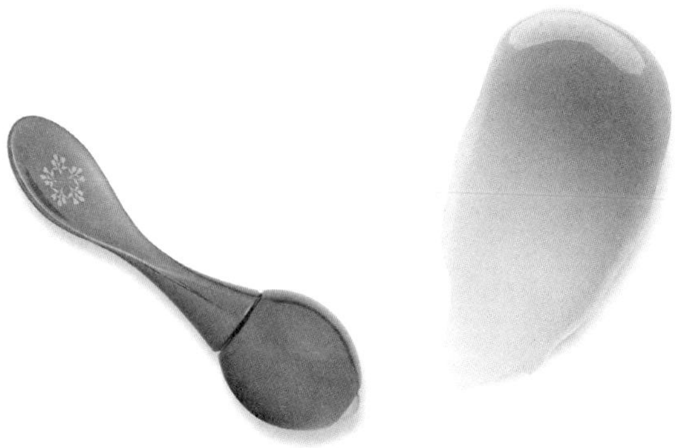

Azelaic acid
In October 2021, the Bloomeffects beauty brand launched its Black Tulip Skincare collection, which highlights azelaic acid as a key ingredient in the range's eye treatment gel. Azelaic acid helps to improve skin's firmness, and reduces dark circles, puffiness and crow's feet.

Polyhydroxy acids
A new skincare line from Juvia's Place, launched in September 2021, features polyhydroxy acids in its exfoliating facial pads, which clarify the skin and add glow. Johnson & Johnson released research in April that year highlighting that the acid supports skin hydration, exfoliation and pigmentation control, even for those with sensitive skin.

Why it's interesting

Acidic ingredients are the latest buzzword for skincare benefits and are already popular additions to the beauty aisle.

Black Tulip Eye Treatment with azelaic acid by Bloomeffects

57

Adaptive packaging

Beauty packaging is being accessibly redesigned for a wider range of users.

The beauty and wellness industries are rebranding to better accommodate users with disabilities or limited mobility, making their product packing more accessible.

Procter & Gamble unveiled an easy-open lid on several Olay Regenerist moisturizers in November 2021, to assist consumers who had previously found its products hard to access. The container lid now features winged sides and a raised top, textured for better grip, labels with higher color contrast for ease of reading, and braille text that reads "face cream." Olay has shared the design with the wider beauty industry, encouraging others to adapt the concept and improve their own accessibility efforts across products.

Unilever designed the world's first adaptive deodorant package in March 2021. The Degree deodorant brand collaborated with people with disabilities to develop a genuinely accessible product concept. The design, which can

Easy Open Lid by Olay

be used one-handed, includes a hook for storage, a magnetic cap for easy replacement and braille labels. Christina Mallon, global head of inclusive design and digital accessibility at Wunderman Thompson, spearheaded the design concept. She tells Wunderman Thompson Intelligence: "Every consumer will experience disability at multiple times in their lives but most product designs don't consider the needs of the disabled consumer."

Also in March 2021, bath and body care brand Cleanlogic rebranded its packaging to include braille across its entire product offering. A portion of all Cleanlogic sales revenue is donated to organizations supporting the visually impaired, including the American Foundation for the Blind.

Why it's interesting

"Brands must think about adaptive packaging in order to be truly customer-centric," Mallon says. Consumers are requesting more accessible packaging across the beauty industry, and brands are consulting consumers and rethinking product packaging to better serve users with disabilities.

> **Brands are rethinking product packaging to better serve users with disabilities.**

Wunderman Thompson: Degree Inclusive

58

Microdose skin regimes

Skincare experts are taking advantage of effective ingredients at the microlevel with a new less-is-more approach.

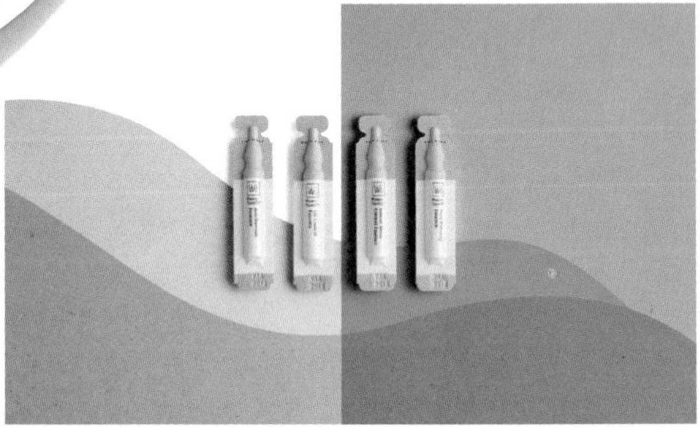

Microdosing has made its way into skincare. Beauty aficionados are gravitating towards this popular new approach, applying smaller amounts or concentrations of ingredients to the skin for long-term results without harsh side effects.

The Wǒ skincare brand, for example, is built upon a range of products packaged in what the brand calls "mono-dosed" amounts. The blister packs contain enough product for just one application, allowing buyers to tailor their routine to their skin's day-to-day needs and only purchase as much as they anticipate needing to use.

Subscription skincare brand Skin & Me connects consumers with dermatologists who prescribe custom approaches at low dosage or percentages as necessary. This makes microdosing approachable and easy, and includes professional input.

Wǒ packages its skincare products in single-application blister packs

WUNDERMAN THOMPSON Spectacle Skincare's Performance Crème comes in a microdosed formulation

Spectacle Skincare's Performance Crème delivers retinaldehyde, polyhydroxy acids and vitamin C in a microdosed formulation. These small amounts don't sensitize the skin, thus maximizing their effects over time, even with consistent use. Andre Condit, formulator and cofounder of Spectacle Skincare, tells Wunderman Thompson Intelligence that beauty product users "need to think of this more as a marathon, not a race. The skincare journey should be a slow, steady pace over a lifetime."

Skincare "boosters," which have increased in popularity recently, are also an applicable and popular form of microdosing. These lower-percentage concentrations can be gradually added to everyday products such as moisturizers, making them effective additions to basic routines. La Roche-Posay offers a low-dose retinol serum at 0.3%, and Paula's Choice offers a vitamin C booster that can be added to moisturizers drop by drop.

Why it's interesting

Andre Condit says that the concept of microdosing skincare is being revisited as the "best therapeutic way to deliver key nutrients, communicators and cellular activators in a daily dose that is most bioavailable, best tolerated in all skin types and least reactive." Low-dose applications that achieve beneficial results in the long term are attracting consumers seeking low-risk, high-reward solutions to their skin concerns.

59

Inclusive haircare

Care for textured hair types, often excluded from mainstream hair branding, is taking up more shelf space and selling fast.

The Pressed Roots hair salon in Dallas, Texas

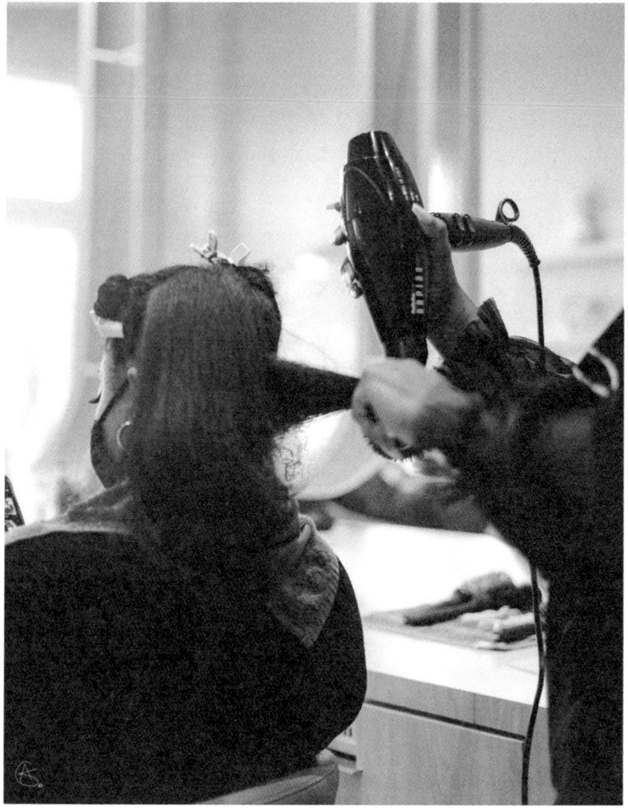

Hair stylists and celebrities are embarking on an inclusive journey to make haircare for all hair types effective and accessible. In a market that often excludes textured hair needs, women of color are creating new space for Afro-centric hair, introducing consumers to dedicated salons and curated new product lines.

Pressed Roots in Dallas, Texas, which opened in October 2021 after a previous incarnation in pop-up form, is dedicated to delivering professional blowouts and hair treatments for customers with highly textured hair. Founder Piersten Gaines, a graduate of Harvard Business School, launched the service for a largely underserved market and told *Wallpaper** that she is "challenging the broader beauty and haircare industries that have excluded ethnic hair textures for decades."

Tracee Ellis Ross's Pattern Beauty haircare line launched at Sephora in September 2021, making it widely available. Pattern's success challenges the attitude "that Black haircare is a niche market," Ross told *InStyle*.

Gabrielle Union's Flawless products are now accessibly stocked by both Walmart and Amazon. Flawless, developed with celebrity hairstylist Larry Sims, comprises 12 nourishing, luxurious products designed for afro-textured hairtypes and includes shampoos, conditioners, serums and more.

Why it's interesting

As brand narratives continue to focus on diversity and inclusion, new labels are stepping up, creating space for authentic products curated by and for Black entrepreneurs. Stores are stocking up on inclusive haircare products and original new services are blossoming, ushering in inclusive care for textured hair.

The Pressed Roots hair salon in Dallas, Texas

WUNDERMAN THOMPSON The Pressed Roots hair salon in Dallas, Texas

60

Robomanicures

Tech startups are disrupting the nail salon by deploying robot manicurists.

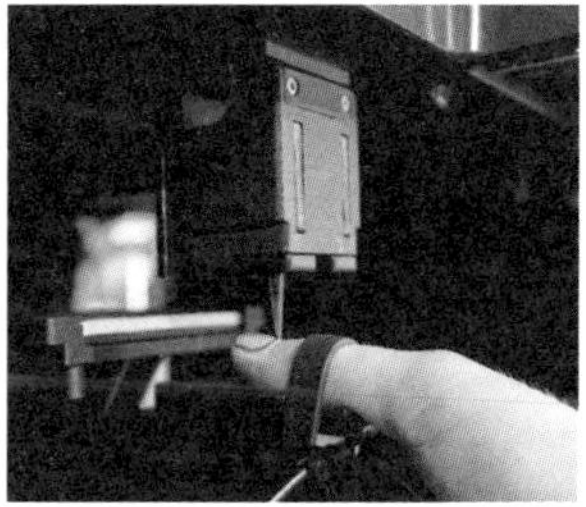

Clockwork in San Francisco offers robot manicures

"No slip ups. No slow down. No small talk," promises Clockwork, a San-Francisco-based company that claims to offer the first robot manicure. Launched in March 2021, the nail tech startup also set up shop in New York's Rockefeller Center in fall the same year. Convenience and precision are at the heart of Clockwork—in under 10 minutes, painted nails are complete. "Think of us as a fast-casual restaurant and a nail salon like a sit-down restaurant," Renuka Apte, founder of Clockwork, told *Allure*. "They each have their own place in people's lives."

Nimble is an at-home nail-painting machine slated to go to market at the end of 2021. The company's Kickstarter campaign aimed to raise $25,000, and had received over $1.8 million as of November 2021. Like Clockwork, Nimble's machine only takes 10 minutes to paint and polish the nails.

Why it's interesting

The express manicure option will soon be diverted to robots as tech startups identify a growing appetite for salon and at-home convenience. As for the business rationale, the global nailcare market is expected to reach a value of $11.6 billion by 2027, according to figures published by Reportlinker in April 2021.

61
Retail & commerce
70

61

Direct to avatar

From B2B and DTC to DTA—the latest business model sees brands releasing digital products direct to screens.

Adidas and Karlie Kloss collaboration. Image courtesy of The Fabricant

In addition to business-to-business (B2B) and direct-to-consumer (DTC) models, various fashion brands introduced direct-to-avatar (DTA) shopping in 2021. In December 2021, Nike acquired virtual sneaker marketplace RTFKT. Three months earlier, Balenciaga released a collection of in-game clothing in *Fortnite*. In the summer, Ralph Lauren launched a 50-piece digital wardrobe, available to buy in social networking app Zepeto, and American Eagle debuted its DTA apparel for Bitmojis. Gucci and The North Face started the year with a collaboration on avatarwear for *Pokémon Go*. And digital fashion house The Fabricant has partnered with brands such as Adidas, Puma and Tommy Hilfiger to virtualize their clothes.

Luxury auto brands are also driving the trend. Maserati, Aston Martin and Tesla launched virtual models of their cars in Tencent's *Game for Peace*—the Chinese mobile version of PlayerUnknown's *Battlegrounds*—between 2020 and 2021. And Rolls-Royce unveiled its first virtual vehicle in 2020 for Tencent's *QQ Speed* mobile game.

Why it's interesting

The future of consumerism lies in virtual products, Kerry Murphy, founder and CEO of The Fabricant, predicts. "People are going to start seeing value in digital items," he tells Wunderman Thompson Intelligence, "and realize that they'd rather interact with a digital item, or have an infinite wardrobe of digital fashion items but a very limited wardrobe of physical items."

Puma, featured with digital fashion house The Fabricant

Puma. Image courtesy of The Fabricant

62

Retail shapeshifters

Long-term challenges are forcing retailers to rethink their core offers, with some diversifying into novel areas.

Few sectors have had a more turbulent couple of years than retail. The story of 2020 was one of deserted high streets, shuttered shops and plummeting sales. Fast-forward to today, and retailers are burdened by disrupted supply chains and labor shortages. These crises are hastening a realignment.

In times of uncertainty, adaptability is key. Enterprising retailers are shifting gears, finding creative ways to diversify that go beyond the borders of their business.

In July 2021, John Lewis Partnership—British parent company of retail brands John Lewis & Partners and Waitrose & Partners—revealed plans to become a private landlord. With the company posting the first full-year loss since it was founded in 1864, for the period to January 2021, diversification is a crucial plank in its turnaround strategy. A survey of its land portfolio identified excess space that could be used for at least 7,000 homes. The properties, ranging from studio

flats to four-bedroom houses, will be built on the partnership's sites, meaning householders could soon be living above a Waitrose supermarket or next to a distribution center. By 2030, John Lewis Partnership aims to have 40% of its profits coming from non-retail lines, principally financial services, housing and outdoor living.

As part of its move to be climate-positive, Swedish furniture retailer Ikea is also branching out, by selling renewable energy to households. In a swing away from flat-pack furniture, the retailer is aiming to build the world's biggest renewable energy movement, making electricity from sustainable sources universally accessible and affordable.

Why it's interesting

In the new retail era, consumers no longer see brands as serving one core purpose. People want deeper experiences with the brands they trust, so there are opportunities to capture new revenue streams. Diversification could be key to the bricks-and-mortar retail recovery.

Left: John Lewis & Partners
Right: Ikea Strömma sells renewable energy to households

63

Private domains

Messaging platforms are becoming the next battleground for brands and loyalty.

Chat commerce (ccommerce, c-commerce or cCommerce) is sprouting on messaging platforms. It is also known as private domain commerce, to differentiate it from the public domain of brand websites or marketplaces such as TMall or Amazon.

In China, WeChat—which has 1.2 billion monthly users—has been especially successful in building relationships with luxury brands through livestreaming and private messaging. Consumers spend an annual average of RMB 170,000 ($26,550) via WeChat, according to a 2020 report by Boston Consulting Group and Tencent Marketing Insight.

Guangzhou-based direct-to-consumer color cosmetics brand Perfect Diary combines savvy cultural partnerships and a premium look with low prices. It is present everywhere its target gen Z audience plays, from the social media and ecommerce platform Xiaohongshu (or Little Red Book) to short-video platform Bilibili to Douyin (as TikTok is known in China).

Perfect Diary also invites consumers who buy on marketplaces to join its official WeChat account or that of its virtual influencer Xiao Wanzi. This recruits followers in groups of several thousand to offer them sneak peeks of launches, and plays the role of a personal shopping assistant.

"Not only does Xiao Wanzi let you preview new products and deals, but you get inspiration from the conversations of the entire chat group," says Joyce Ling, chief strategy officer of Wunderman Thompson China. "Even though it appears a little 'fake' and like a show, it is literally a condensed version of the consumer journey from awareness to purchase to loyalty."
Chat commerce is expanding beyond China. Vietnam and

WUNDERMAN THOMPSON

Thailand lead the world in using Facebook's chat functions for online retail, measured by the volume of messages between merchants and customers, as reported in *Nikkei Asia* in June 2021. In Thailand, global brands including Burberry, Louis Vuitton and Chanel have launched official accounts on messaging app Line, engaging consumers with custom stickers, livestreamed fashion shows and digital ads. Line Shopping, the commerce arm of the chat platform, boasts over seven million users in Thailand alone, Lertad Supadhiloke, head of e-commerce at Line Thailand, told the *Bangkok Post* in July 2021.

Why it's interesting

As people increasingly converse on WeChat, WhatsApp and Line, brands are also jumping on these chat platforms to build smaller but more intimate, personalized relationships with groups of consumers.

"Brands are jumping on these chat platforms to build smaller but more intimate, personalized relationships with groups of consumers.

AI bot Xiao Wanzi chats with consumers about Perfect Diary cosmetics on WeChat

64

Virtual flagships

Digital flagship stores are taking over ecommerce storefronts.

Today, 81% of global consumers agree that a brand's digital presence is as important as its in-store presence, a July 2021 Wunderman Thompson Data survey found. This is prompting brands to enhance their ecommerce storefront prominence and create virtual flagship stores.

Samsung opened a virtual replica of its flagship New York City store in Decentraland in January 2022. In July 2021, luxury brand Fendi opened a 360-degree digital flagship based on its 57th Street store in New York City, offering visitors virtual tours and access to its latest collections. Hermès has rolled out digital flagships in Singapore, the United Arab Emirates and Thailand.

Beauty brands are also upping their digital storefront impact. Lancôme debuted its first temporary virtual flagship in Singapore, in summer 2020. The Lancôme Advanced Génifique #LiveYourStrength virtual flagship offered 3D shopping experiences, consultations and educational events, and included a "discover zone" where visitors could take a personality test, designed by psychologist Perpetua Neo, to find their strength. The L'Oréal-owned skincare brand has since introduced virtual pop-ups for Australia, Korea and the United States. In April 2021, Nars opened a digital flagship store, immersing visitors in a 3D shopping experience.

Why it's interesting

According to predictions from *eMarketer*, the global ecommerce market will grow from $4.89 trillion in 2021 to $5.42 trillion in 2022. Virtual flagships are becoming the new storefront to entice shoppers and enhance a brand's overall digital experience.

Fendi's 360-degree digital flagship on 57th Street in New York City

65

Gen Alpha retail

Three ways in which generation alpha are driving the next era of retail.

Born between 2010 and 2025, generation alpha—gen Z's younger siblings—are already making waves in the retail world.

Genderless shopping

Brands and retailers are eschewing traditional gender categories in favor of gender-neutral products and lines. PacSun launched a new gender-neutral children's clothing brand, PacSun Kids, in June 2021, followed by its own gender-neutral label, Colour Range, in September and its first gender-free kids' clothing store two months later. In October 2021, California became the first US state to enforce genderless retail, thanks to a new law requiring large stores to have gender-neutral sections for toys and childcare. "The segregation of toys by a social construct of what is appropriate for which gender is the antithesis of modern thinking," says Democrat assembly member and the law's co-author Evan Low.

PacSun Kids gender-neutral clothing. Photography by Chris Martin

Inclusive aisles

Brands and retailers are also widening their offerings to be more inclusive of a range of physical and mental abilities. JCPenney launched children's clothing with adaptive features in July 2021, and partnered with adaptive fashion marketplace Patti & Ricky to expand its range of adaptive accessories for kids. In June 2021, Headspace, *Sesame Street* and Penguin Random House joined forces to launch *Monster Meditation*, a six-book series to "help children learn the fundamentals of mindfulness, meditation, and social and emotional learning."

WUNDERMAN THOMPSON Patti & Ricky collaborated with JCPenney to make children's clothing with adaptive features. Photography by Alexis Buatti-Ramos/Hyphen Photography

Sustainable play

Toy brands are leaning heavily into sustainability to appeal to younger generations. In May 2021, Mattel launched a program that lets families give back their old Mattel products so the materials can be reused to make new ones. And Lego unveiled its first prototype brick made from recycled plastic in June 2021.

Why it's interesting

Following in their older siblings' footsteps, gen alphas are cementing the key retail ethics that gen Zers pioneered.

Department stores reformatted

Retailers are rethinking the traditional department store model.

The latest department stores are more town squares than retailers, reflecting a shift in the retail landscape from big-box luxury to community microcosm.

Beales, which closed all of its UK stores in 2020, has reopened three locations under new ownership—and is looking beyond retail. The top floors of the Poole branch will be turned into a "health village" run by the National Health Service, with dermatology, orthopedics, ophthalmology, and breast cancer screening departments, as well as counselling rooms for those suffering from long COVID.

A new concept department store is reinventing a location formerly occupied by legacy British retailer Debenhams. Called Bobby's, the new store opened in the UK town of Bournemouth in September 2021 and houses a beauty hall, an art gallery and ice-cream and coffee parlor, alongside shopping and local artisans, in place of floors filled with clothing, accessories and homeware. Future plans include a hairdressing salon, dental services, a microbrewery, and even a smokery.

"I don't ever see a big department store chain emerging again," Beales' CEO Tony Brown told the *Guardian*. "We will see small local chains popping up with eight or 10 stores. The model will change dramatically over the next couple of years. People want something more localized."

Why it's interesting

It's clear that the traditional department store format is no longer working. We reported the death of the luxury department store in "The Future 100: 2020," following a string of closures and bankruptcies among big, long-established names. Now, the next generation of department stores are having to rethink and adapt.

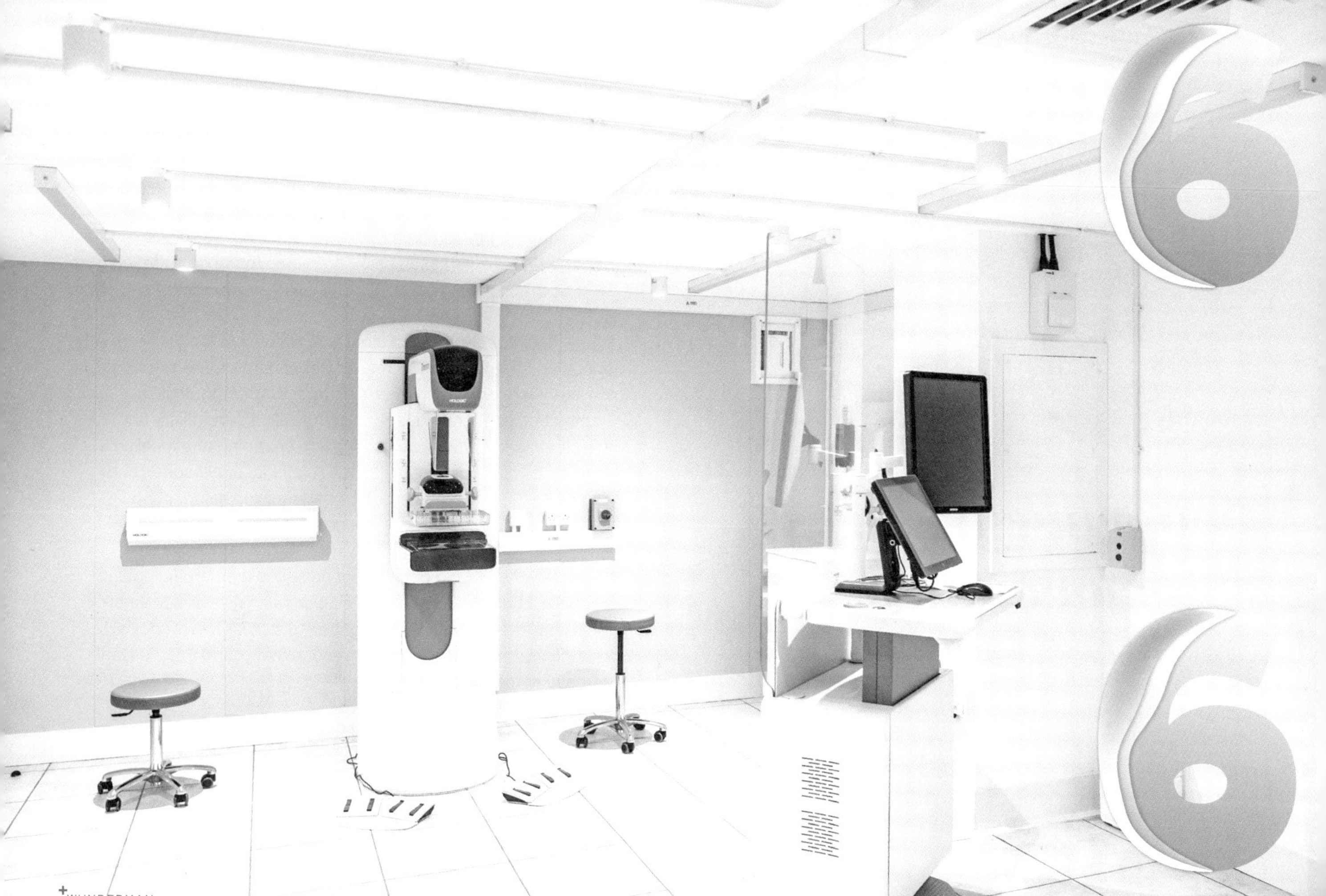

Beales department stores in the UK repurposed the Poole storefront as a "health village" for the National Health Service

67

Digital twins

Retail stores and factories are being cloned for the virtual world, to promote familiarity and efficiency.

BMW and Nvidia are partnering to create a digital twin of the carmaker's factory in Regensburg, Germany

"In the future, every single factory and every single building will have a digital twin that will simulate and track the physical version of it," Jensen Huang, CEO of Nvidia, told *Time* in April 2021. Huang's vision of the metaverse is "ultimately about the fusion of the virtual and the physical worlds." Currently, Nvidia and BMW are partnering on a digital twin of the carmaker's factory in Regensburg, Germany, allowing the teams to virtually plan and play out new workflow logistics before implementing these changes at BMW's physical facility.

Tech companies are making it easier to create digital twins. In November 2021, Amazon unveiled the AWS IoT TwinMaker, a service that conveniently and speedily generates digital duplicates of real-world systems for businesses. Microsoft's Azure Digital Twins allows for the creation of buildings, infrastructure, and even entire cities, with the aim of driving "better products, optimized operations, reduced costs, and breakthrough customer experiences."

Retailers are also opening digital twins of existing stores to promote familiarity and more natural navigation for shoppers. In March 2021, Burberry launched a digital replica of its flagship store in Ginza, Tokyo. And Coach collaborated with virtual store developer Obsess to clone its New York Fifth Avenue flagship store. "The digital showroom enables wholesale buyers to experience our new collections each season without having to fly in to see products in person, reducing the carbon footprint of our business and speeding the buying process," explains Giovanni Zaccariello, senior vice president of global visual experience at Coach.

Why it's interesting

Digital twin stores are innovating the retail sector, with the promise to solve logistical issues for the real-world and replicate the in-person shopping experience.

WUNDERMAN THOMPSON

Left: Burberry Ginza virtual store in collaboration with Elle Digital
Right: Coach cloned its New York Fifth Avenue flagship store with Obsess

68

Big Tech bricks and mortars

Tech giants are moving off screens in their latest consumer push.

Amazon plans to open department stores, as reported by the *Wall Street Journal* in August 2021. The intent marks a continued foray into physical retail, following the opening of its first cashierless grocery store in 2020, the launch of its first Amazon 4-Star store in 2018, and the purchase of Whole Foods in 2017. The stores will expand the retailer's footprint, reportedly feature Amazon-owned clothing brands and household items, and function as return and customer service centers.

Google turned heads in June 2021 when it opened the doors to its first ever physical store, located in New York City. More showroom than traditional retail outlet, the store sells all of Google's products, from Nest to Fitbit, and includes a "workshop space" reserved for sub-brand events such as photography lessons with Pixel, cooking demos with Nest, YouTube concerts and more.

Apple is also banking on physical stores, expanding its retail operations in the United States, as Deirdre O'Brien, senior vice president of retail and people, told *Reuters* in June 2021. Part of this strategy will include doubling down on its pre-pandemic strategy of in-store events and experiences beyond shopping.

Why it's interesting

Big Tech has its sights set on physical retail, which could further cement the growing crossover between IRL and URL shopping.

Google's first physical store in New York City

69

NFT marketplaces

Brands are finding new revenue streams in the evolving non-fungible-token sector.

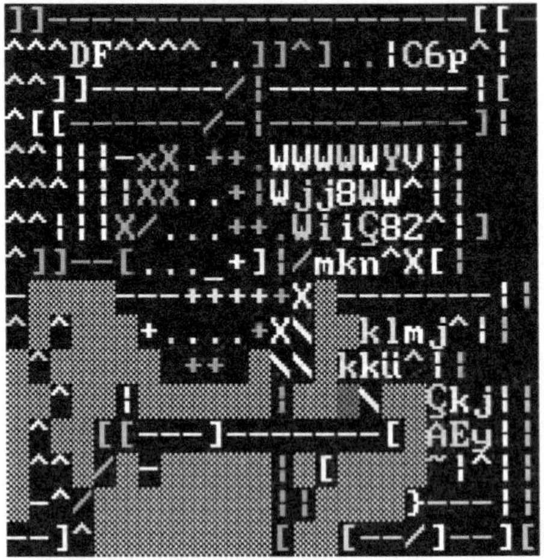

Companies are growing their revenue in this new digital frontier. Where consumers are looking to collect and trade, artists and brands are ready to create and mint non-fungible tokens (NFTs)—and all parties are meeting in emerging forums in the metaverse.

Sotheby's is the first auction house to launch a marketplace dedicated to NFTs. Announced in October 2021, its Metaverse is backed by celebrities and supports numerous digital artists that it has worked with during the past year. Managing director Sebastian Fahey told *Hypebeast* that Sotheby's plans to use its "expertise and curation to the burgeoning world of art for the digitally native generation."

Series 4 Glitchbox from Sotheby's Natively Digital NFT collection

In the same month, cryptocurrency exchange Coinbase announced it was launching an NFT marketplace, and opened an early access waitlist for interested investors. The Coinbase NFT platform will include "social features" supportive of the "creator economy"—people who make money from creating videos and online content.

Why it's interesting

As major brands and industries continue to invest in NFTs and participate in their trade, the metaverse is evolving in its potential for revenue and opportunities. Brands who take advantage of this uncharted territory may find new dividends in these developing marketplaces.

> "As major brands and industries continue to invest in NFTs and participate in their trade, the metaverse is evolving in its potential for revenue and opportunities.

Left: MoonCat from Sotheby's Natively Digital NFT collection
Right: Yuga Labs' Bored Ape Yacht Club from Sotheby's Natively Digital NFT collection

70

Retro retail

The latest high-design stores are turning back the hands of time with nostalgic interiors.

Superette's Sip 'n' Smoke cannabis dispensary. Photography by Alex Lysakowski

Superette's newest cannabis dispensary in Toronto was designed to resemble a retro grocery store. Its vibrant colors, punchy graphics, and what *Dezeen* called "pop art aesthetic" are evocative of mid-century retail branding and design. In August 2021, the company opened Sip 'n' Smoke, an express kiosk with a similar look inspired by old-school cafeterias.

The interior of Los Angeles grocery Wine & Eggs, opened in 2021, was partially inspired by public schools. Saturated hues of blue and yellow feature throughout the space and branding, complemented by bright green. Rounded wood shelving and displays call to mind building blocks, and the blue-and-green checkered floor is made from commercial-grade vinyl composition tile (VCT). "I love VCT because it actually feels both playful and reminiscent of our childhood in public schools," Adi Goodrich, who created the interior, told *Dezeen*.

Creative agency Saint of Athens designed a jewelry store, opened in August 2021 in Mykonos, Greece, that nods to the splendor of luxury swimming pools in a bygone era. The interior is decked in light-blue tiles with red-and-white striped accents. "Soft blue, a color reminiscent of urban pool luxury of the '60s, furniture made from metal, vintage elements and custom blue terrazzo displays constitute a retro yet modern, Wes Anderson kind of universe," agency founder Nikos Paleologos told *Dezeen*.

Why it's interesting

The past two years saw people turning to nature-inspired design to create a sense of comfort and stability. Now, the latest store designs are opting for kitschy, playful interiors that offer a nostalgic escape.

Superette's Sip 'n' Smoke cannabis dispensary. Photography by Alex Lysakowski

71
OCEANSKY
CRUISES
Luxury
80

71

Hypnotherapy

Healing hospitality is awakening to the potential of hypnosis.

Luxury hotels are expanding their wellness treatments from thermal body mapping and sleep coaches to hypnotherapy.

The Mandarin Oriental Hong Kong appointed hypnotherapist Christine Deschemin in June 2021, rolling out workshops for relaxation and to improve eating habits, and offering a bespoke service of tailored hypnotherapy sessions. In spring 2021, the Belmond Cadogan Hotel in London introduced a complimentary sleep concierge service in partnership with hypnotherapist Malminder Gill. The hotel provides its rooms with a meditative recording by Gill designed to send guests to sleep, and a motivational recording to get the mornings going. One-to-one consultations and focused hypnotherapy sessions are also available.

The Spa at the Four Seasons New York Downtown launched its Resident Healer Program in 2018, noting that guests are seeking spiritual wellness, not just a traditional spa experience. Residents appointed in previous years include sonic alchemist Michelle Pirret and crystal healer Rashia Bell.

In December 2020, Nicole Hernandez, also known as the Traveling Hypnotist, joined as resident healer, offering unique hypnotic journeys that can help relieve anxiety and overcome fears and phobias. Hernandez's unique Time Traveler program can even delve into past life regression to enhance present life.

Why it's interesting

Hotel wellness programs are deepening their spiritual healing offering, graduating from crystals and tarot card readings to hypnotic journeys that claim to improve health, habits and mindfulness.

> Hotel wellness programs are deepening their spiritual healing offering.

Left: The Spa at the Four Seasons New York Downtown Resident Healer Program
Right: Mandarin Oriental Hong Kong

72

Austere luxe

Luxury brands are recalibrating in the face of China's "common prosperity" policy.

During China's 2021 National Day holiday, a market in Shanghai became the center of a social media frenzy. Thousands descended on the Wuzhong wet market in the former French Concession to buy fruit, vegetables and eggs—but these basic foodstuffs were encased in Prada-branded wrapping and carrier bags.

The high-low pop-up celebrated the launch of Prada's fall/winter 2021 campaign "Feels Like Prada." This could be seen as a successful marketing campaign—selfies abounded and stallholders ran out of bags and wrap—or a sign of gentrification, or, as Zhu Tianhua, an assistant researcher at Shanghai Academy of Social Sciences, told *Sixth Tone*, "a kind of consumerism of daily life." However it is viewed, the campaign struck an appropriately austere chord at a time when the world continues to grapple with crises from COVID-19 to climate change to yawning economic inequity.

In mid-2021, Chinese President Xi Jinping, after a months-long crackdown on the country's biggest technology firms, announced a new "common prosperity" policy, urging businesses and entrepreneurs to narrow the country's wealth gap.

The government pledged to lift more workers into the middle class and make basics such as schooling, housing and health care more affordable. Some of China's biggest billionaires have since agreed to donate billions of dollars to charity.

Outside China, there are also signs of a bling backlash. In November 2021, a Vietnamese minister was pilloried on social media after a video showed him being hand-fed gold-plated steak in London at the Knightsbridge restaurant of Nusret Gokce, a celebrity chef also known as Salt Bae.

Kim Kardashian, the queen of conspicuous consumption, appeared at the Met Gala 2021 not in customary glitter and gloss but fully encased, face and all, in a clingy black sheath.

Why it's interesting

The personal luxury goods market rebounded in 2021 to €283 billion, up 29% from the trough of 2020, according to Bain & Company's "Luxury Study 2021." That rebound was driven by China, which now makes up 21% of the global market. But the pandemic has provoked a reassessment of what luxury means. "The emergence from the COVID crisis comes as a renaissance for luxury brands," says Claudia D'Arpizio, lead author of the Bain study. "Where once it was all about status, logos and exclusivity, luxury brands are now actors in social conversations, driven by a renewed sense of purpose and responsibility."

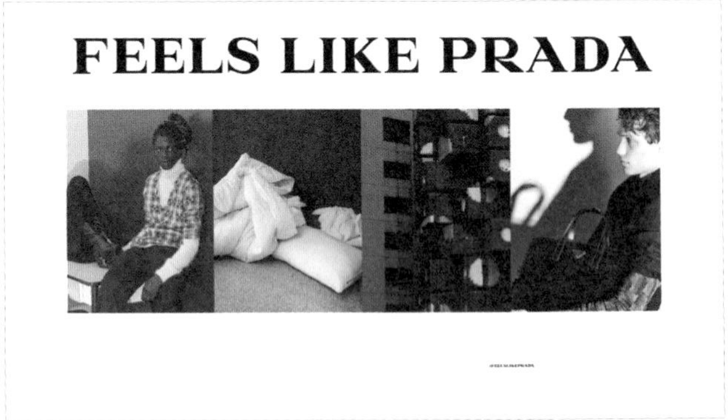

Prada's "Feels Like Prada" fall/winter 2021 campaign. Photography by David Sims

73

Crypto elites

There's a new way to signal your social status with the emergence of desirable and, crucially, ownable digital assets in the shape of NFT characters.

WUNDERMAN THOMPSON

Gutter Cat Gang Pigeon avatar

From star athletes to rappers to tech entrepreneurs, the rich and famous are snapping up NFT characters. NBA star Steph Curry paid $180,000 for Bored Ape Yacht Club character #7990. Former boxing champ Mike Tyson has a Cool Cat, while tech entrepreneur Alexis Ohanian owns a Pudgy Penguin. Ohanian also invested in a $280,000 CryptoPunk for his wife, tennis legend Serena Williams. Not bad for a CryptoPunk—in 2021, rare versions have sold at Christie's and Sotheby's for upwards of $7 million. Even finance giant Visa is getting in on the action, acquiring a mohawked CryptoPunk for $150,000. Once acquired, it is of course de rigueur to use your NFT as your social media avatar.

The market for NFTs exploded in 2021, and these communities of limited-edition character avatars have proliferated in tandem. The avatars, which feature animated character headshots in profile, are usually generated by algorithms to a theme, with different colors, hairstyles, clothing or accessories—some of which may be rare or even unique. Alongside apes, punks and penguins, prospective buyers can also choose from cats (Gutter Cat Gang), dogs (The Doge Pound), ducks (Sup Ducks), aliens (Lonely Alien Space Club) and all kinds of "ladies" (Fame Lady Squad).

While NFT avatars at their most basic are a "flippable" asset with genuine market value, they are also a way to underline both wealth and status, marking any owner as a paid-up member of the crypto-elite. Alongside their asset, investors gain access to valuable social and networking opportunities with their fellow owners via memberships to exclusive Discord or Telegram channels. So intense is the urge to get behind the virtual velvet rope, there are already rental and fractional ownership models for those who can't afford to own their own character.

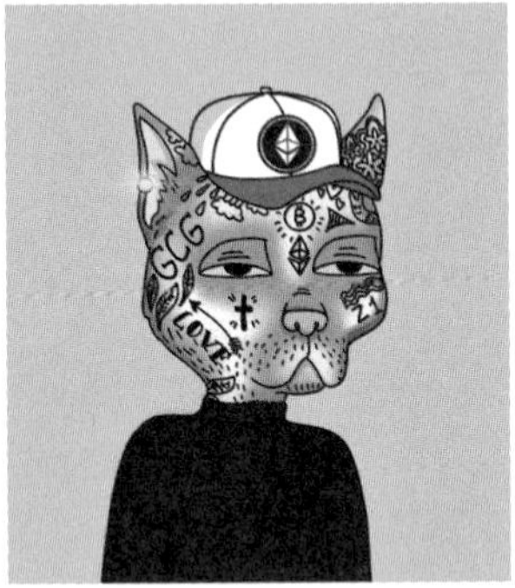

Crypto-investor Cooper Turley, aka Coopahtroopa, related on an episode of the WAGMI podcast how a CryptoPunk NFT he bought for $300 is now worth half a million dollars. He also noted that the "social capital thatcomes from owning the punk is so much higher than any amount of money. You're going to get lifetime benefits from having it. You get entry into a very exclusive club of collectors and holders. I think that the cachet of just holding something like that is something that's never going to go away."

Why it's interesting

Whether NFT characters have long-term staying power is so far unclear, but perhaps more interesting is the wider trend toward virtual status signifiers. Wunderman Thompson Intelligence's "Into the Metaverse" report identified a strong consumer appetite for virtual ownership. Virtual possessions seem to have the same symbolic value and convey status in the same way as real-world luxury cars or watches do. As we head to the metaverse, it seems unequivocal that our avatars will be the focus of significant investment.

Left: Gutter Cat Gang Dog avatar
Right: Gutter Cat Gang Cat avatar

WUNDERMAN THOMPSON

SpottieWiFi avatar

74

Long recovery spas

These revitalizing resorts mean it when they invite guests to "stay a while."

Spas and wellness resorts are promoting new treatments for long COVID, extending the stay of their guests to allow full recovery.

At RAKxa medical spa outside Bangkok, a new COVID-19 health rejuvenation program is growing in popularity. The group offers a three-day holistic operation to restore lung capacity using hyperbaric chambers of concentrated oxygen, blood ozone infusions and chest-muscle strengthening exercises in an Olympic-grade gym. Services are tailored to each guest's needs.

The SHA Wellness Clinic on the coast of Spain started offering a seven-day post-COVID program in May 2021. Guests are tested upon arrival and then given a course of treatments based on the results. The assessment includes a stress test, carotid ultrasound and bloodwork, the results of which could lead to treatments ranging from reflexology to Watsu therapy to "brain photobiomodulation" that stimulates and regenerates brain cells.

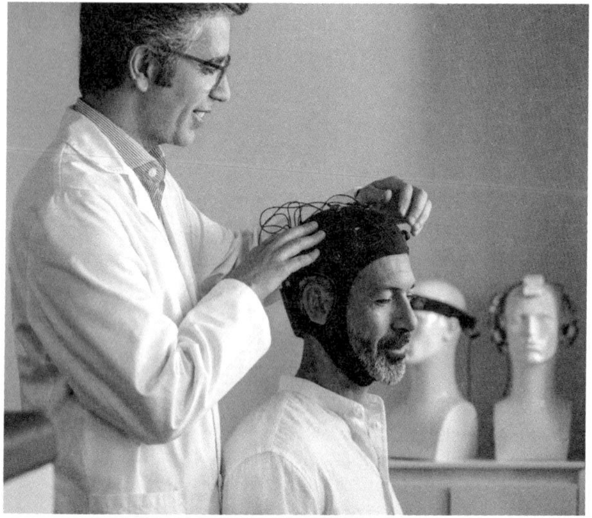

The Lanserhof resort in the Austrian Alps offers a two-week retreat claiming to cure the effects of long COVID. Traditionally an upscale, expensive destination for detoxifying body treatments, it has devised this new offering to include personalized energy cuisine, a chewing trainer, healing massage, breathing therapy, urinalysis to identify infections or kidney problems, and personal training sessions, depending on the patient's symptoms.

Why it's interesting

After a period of pause in travel and hospitality, resorts are reframing their offerings to a new wave of consumer wellness needs. Extended stays for medical wellness and rejuvenation are breaking the mold in hospitality.

Left: The SHA Wellness Clinic offers a seven-day post-COVID program
Right: RAKxa wellness and medical retreat

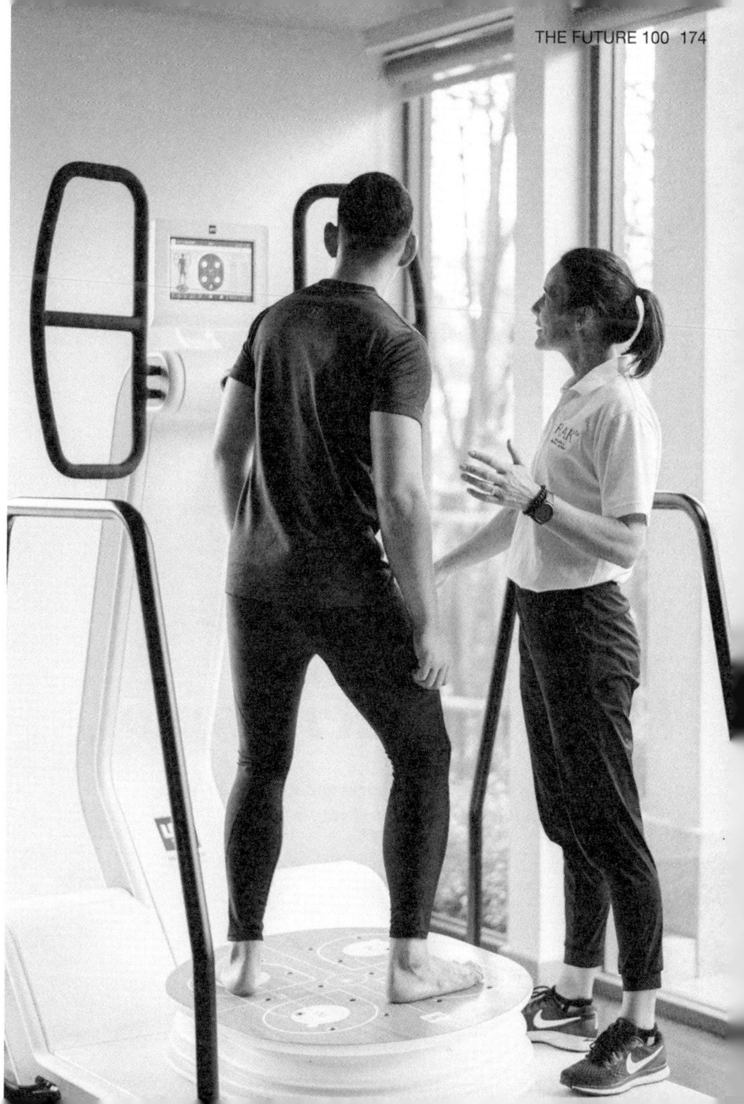

The Lanserhof Resort in the Austrian Alps. Photography by Alexander Haiden

75

Suburban luxe

Are the suburbs the new luxury shopping destination?

As luxury shoppers decamp to sprawling second homes and vacation destinations, designer brands and high-end retailers are following their path from city centers to suburban outposts.

Gucci opened a store in Oak Brook, Illinois in fall 2021, as well as its first permanent store in the Hamptons in the summer of 2021. Dior has a new shop in Scottsdale, Arizona, and Louis Vuitton opened up in Plano, Texas, while Hermès opened a store in Detroit, Michigan—its first in the state—in June 2021.

Demand for vacation and suburban shopping historically hasn't been high or consistent enough to warrant permanent stores, but that's starting to change. "It used to be that our market was too small, but now everyone wants to be here permanently," Angi Wang, a commercial broker in Aspen who works for the real estate firm Setterfield & Bright, told the *Washington Post*. "They're clamoring to get in, to the point where we honestly don't have any space left."

Why it's interesting

Luxury brands are shifting their focus away from urban hotspots. "The pandemic has decentralized luxury retail," Milton Pedraza, chief executive of market research firm the Luxury Institute, told the *Washington Post*. "It seems like everyone has moved to the suburbs or to their vacation homes—so that's where the stores are going, too."

> **"The pandemic has decentralized luxury retail."**

Top: Hermès store in the greater Detroit area
Bottom: Louis Vuitton store in Plano, Texas

76

Upending fakes

Counterfeit goods could soon be consigned to the past.

Artificial intelligence (AI) and blockchain technology are being used to catch and ultimately upend luxury fakes circulating in the secondhand market.

In April 2021, three luxury giants, LVMH, Prada Group and Richemont, joined forces with a united vision to protect the authenticity and trustworthiness of the industry. The pact formed the Aura Consortium—a new global system using blockchain technology to authenticate luxury goods, from sourcing to the sale transaction and even through to the resale market. In October 2021, Group OTB, which owns a mix of high street and luxury brands including Diesel and Marni, joined the Aura Consortium as a founding member.

AI-powered luxury authenticator Entrupy bills itself as the "first and only on-demand authentication solution for high-value goods," and has a reported accuracy rate of 99.1%. The New York-based company, launched in 2016, employs deep learning to compare images to determine a genuine luxury item versus a fake.

Trade in counterfeit products was valued at $464 billion in 2019, reports the Organisation for Economic Co-operation and Development, and according to a study by Certilogo the online counterfeit market hit an all-time-high during the pandemic, growing 5% between May 2020 to April 2021. This coincides with the rising popularity of the secondhand market, which is forecast to reach $77 billion by 2025 according to ThredUp.

Why it's interesting

Luxury resales will remain popular, particularly among the growing cohort of conscious consumers. Leaders in luxury and tech are creating faster solutions to identify fakes and protect the authenticity of luxury brands.

77

Prescribing happiness

A booster shot of happiness? Now, that's luxury!

Dior Spa Cheval Blanc Paris's Happiness Shots offer 30- to 45-minute concentrated "bursts of pleasure."

Luxury brands are launching modern vehicles for emotional wellness, presenting consumers with original, indulgent offerings for physical and emotional uplift.

Dior Spa Cheval Blanc Paris, which opened in September 2021, is offering Happiness Shots to guests. These concentrated treatments are 30- to 45-minute "bursts of pleasure," indulgence or efficacy that can be combined with other treatments so that guests can personalize their experience to the fullest. The shots can be added to massages, micropeeling, microabrasion services and more.

Estée Lauder launched a new luxury fragrance range developed to evoke a range of positive feelings. Catering to consumers from different locations around the world, the eight variations were crafted using neurosensory studies on the emotional effects of each fragrance, which were found to evoke feelings such as "positivity and joy" or "calm and happiness," according to the brand.

Why it's interesting

Whether in a spa or at a bricks-and-mortar shop, luxury brands are meeting consumers at every corner with more than their usual product or expected service. Focusing on positive emotions and physical wellness, luxury brands are determined to ensure their consumers leave feeling objectively better than when they arrived.

Estée Lauder's luxury fragrance collection. Image courtesy of Facebook

78

Extended stays

Long-term getaways are turning into luxurious escapes for extended family and friends.

Antsy travelers are discovering unique destinations that provide a new kind of getaway: long-term stays for large groups. Resorts are offering extended stays, introducing a lifestyle reset rather than a quick trip.

The island of Ithaafushi offers luxurious stays for guests and 24 of their closest friends. For $85,000 a night, travelers can take over the entire island for a completely private, long-term getaway. Part of the Waldorf Astoria Maldives, the private island has beachfront views, bungalows, a spa, gym, water sports, a personal chef—the works—not to mention a personal concierge available 24 hours a day.

Travelers seeking a fairytale experience can now rent the entire Castello di Reschio in the Umbrian hills of Italy. For €290,000, guests can bring their friends and family to stay in a minimum of 11 rooms (there are 36 rooms in all). The all-inclusive price covers meals, drinks and musical entertainment alongside the sloping olive groves, vistas and vineyards. With anything up to the entire hotel at their disposal, guests can enjoy the spa, cooking and art classes, horseback riding and more during their stay.

Why it's interesting

Travelers searching for exciting new venues want to bring their loved ones along, so resorts are repurposing their expansive premises into luxurious hideouts where guests can congregate with extended family and friends. Travelers are now taking advantage of getaways that everyone can enjoy, and relocating for long-term relaxation.

The private island of Ithaafushi, part of the Waldorf Astoria Maldives, offers luxurious stays for guests and 24 of their closest friends

79

Sonic luxification

Luxury brands from fashion to auto are investing in audio hardware, luxifying the listening experience.

WUNDERMAN THOMPSON

The Louis Vuitton portable Horizon Light Up speaker, modeled after the brand's Toupie handbag

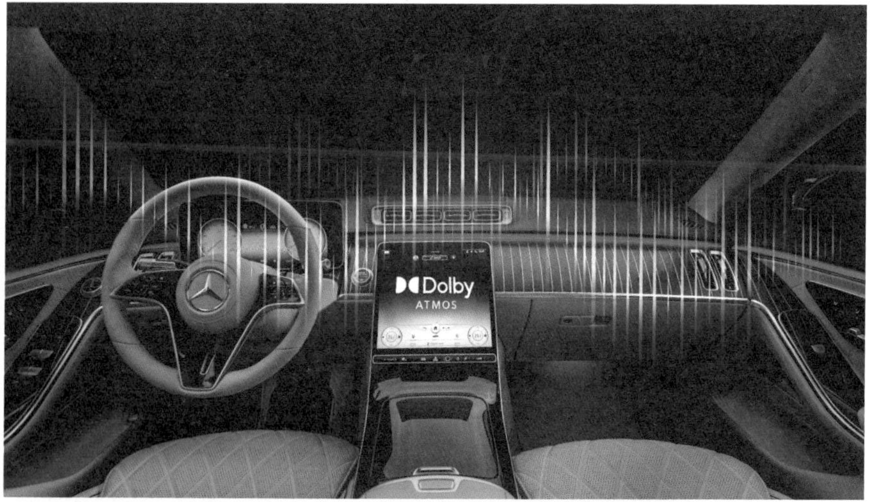

Mercedes-Benz will add Dolby Atmos speakers to its models from summer 2022

“Audio will be a key channel for luxury brands moving forward.

Louis Vuitton is dipping a toe into audio tech. The designer clothing and accessories brand released a portable speaker in July 2021. The Horizon Light Up speaker, which rings in at nearly $3,000, is loosely modeled after the brand's Toupie handbag—complete with the signature LV pattern.

Mercedes-Benz is the latest luxury automaker to partner with a high-end audio company. The car company announced that it will add Dolby Atmos speakers to its top-of-the-line models from summer 2022.

The evolution of Apple's listening devices over the past five years offers a perfect case study: where Apple once included free corded headphones with every new iPhone, it is now nudging iPhone users to purchase increasingly high-end headphones. Since releasing the first generation of AirPods in 2016, starting at $159, Apple has progressively stepped up both function and price—peaking with AirPods Max, which were released in December 2020 and sell for $549. At the end of 2020, Apple stopped including free headphones with iPhone purchases altogether.

Why it's interesting

The premiumization of audio is underway. Audio will be a key channel for luxury brands moving forward—and a crucial element to consider when crafting luxury experiences.

80

Superyachts of the skies

Airship travel is back, reincarnated as a low-emission luxury alternative.

With air travel predicted to soon return to pre-pandemic levels, the industry must reduce carbon emissions. Incremental changes are no longer enough and new solutions are needed.

Could airships reclaim the skies? Airships are positioning themselves as sustainable upscale alternatives to passenger flights and sky cruises, and some experts say they could revolutionize air travel in the coming decade.

Airships present a distinctive luxury travel experience. Their large and comfortable cabins, lounges, fine dining areas and panoramic windows offer immediate advantage.

Luxury travel company Ocean Sky Cruises is already planning airship expeditions to the North Pole for 2024. With tickets marketed toward “true pioneers of the world,” the company will make history by being the first to land an airship on the North Pole. The 38-hour journey will include wildlife spotting opportunities, views of the aurora borealis, and onboard cocktail experiences.

Also tapping into the luxury market is Israel-based aviation company Atlas LTA. Its luxury aircraft give passengers an elevated sightseeing experience from bird’s-eye view observation decks.

British manufacturer Hybrid Air Vehicles is behind Airlander, the world’s first hybrid aircraft. Its latest iteration, fitted with hydrogen fuel cell-powered electric motors, can be

WUNDERMAN THOMPSON

Top: OceanSky Cruises
Bottom: Airlander, the world's first hybrid aircraft, by Hybrid Air Vehicles
Right: Flying Whales

configured with luxurious seating, and offers floor-to-ceiling windows for an uninterrupted view.

Airships offer wider eco-potential too. Airlander's owner aims for it to perform short-haul intercity flights by 2025 and is also positioning the craft as a freight solution. Similarly, French company Flying Whales is developing a fleet of airships as an eco-solution for air cargo transportation. The fleet will reach isolated, difficult-to-access locations around the world while maintaining a small environmental footprint.

Why it's interesting

A new class of airships offers sustainable voyages that don't compromise on luxury. These high-end, low-impact experiences could herald a new golden era in luxury aviation.

The Pressed Roots hair salon in Dallas, Texas

81
Health
90

81

Prescription gaming

The newest way to administer medication? Via a screen.

An emerging class of techceuticals is pressing play on the future of health management. Doctors are prescribing video games and virtual reality (VR) to treat conditions such as brain fog, attention deficit hyperactivity disorder (ADHD), depression, and post-traumatic stress disorder.

In November 2021, the Food and Drug Administration (FDA) approved the VR therapy EaseVRx as a prescription treatment for chronic back pain. In October 2021, the FDA also approved a VR-based treatment for children with the visual impairment amblyopia, also known as lazy eye.

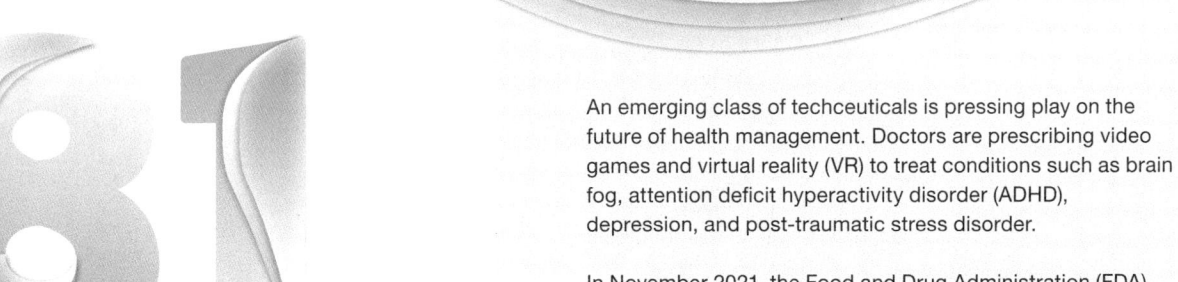

In April 2021, digital therapeutic company Akili Interactive partnered with Weill Cornell Medicine, NewYork-Presbyterian Hospital, and Vanderbilt University Medical Center to evaluate the EndeavorRx video game as a treatment for COVID-19 patients experiencing brain fog. Originally created to treat ADHD in children, EndeavorRx made history in June 2020 as the first ever prescription-strength video game approved by the FDA. Akili Interactive states that after following the recommended dosage of 25 minutes of play per day, five days per week for one month, one in three kids "no longer had a

measurable attention deficit on at least one measure of objective attention." In May 2021, the company secured $160 million in funding to expand its prescription gaming portfolio.

Why it's interesting

Does the future of medicine lie in gamified technology? Michael Phillips Moskowitz, digital nutritionist and founder and CEO of AeBeZe Labs, thinks so. Digital content has "tremendous curative potential," he tells Wunderman Thompson Intelligence. "Digital therapeutics are going to be the next emerging vertical in pharmaceuticals." Expect to see more prescription content and digitally administered medication.

Left: AppliedVR's EaseVRx prescription treatment
Right: EndeavorRX by Akili Interactive

82

Male fertility startups

Biotech startups are now targeting fertility solutions at men.

For a long time, women have been the focus of failing fertility. Now biotech startups are starting to target men, offering sperm analysis and freezing—services designed for those delaying having children for career reasons, as well as those who simply want to freeze their sperm as insurance against injury or waning fertility.

Boston-based startup Legacy sells home kits for sperm analysis, and partners with sperm-freezing centers. It has raised $20 million in funding from backers such as Y Combinator and Bain Capital Ventures. Founder Khaled Kteily said he got the idea after he spilled hot tea on his lap in a car, suffering second-degree burns and causing him to fear for his future fertility. Kteily envisions a wide range of candidates for sperm freezing, including soldiers about to be deployed; same-sex couples who plan to use a surrogate; and transgender people who want to preserve their fertility before they transition. "We see this as something that every man might do as they go off to college, and investors see that big picture," Kteily told *TechCrunch*.

Dadi, launched in 2019 in Brooklyn, boasts a temperature-controlled kit to transport sperm from home to lab and has raised $10 million in venture capital. Others, such as Los Angeles-based Yo and London-based ExSeed Health, use devices attached to smartphones to analyze sperm at home.

Why it's interesting

Employers who have been covering egg freezing for female employees might similarly start looking at sperm freezing as a health benefit. Low male fertility is also considered a canary in the coal mine, and early sperm analysis may also offer clues about overall health.

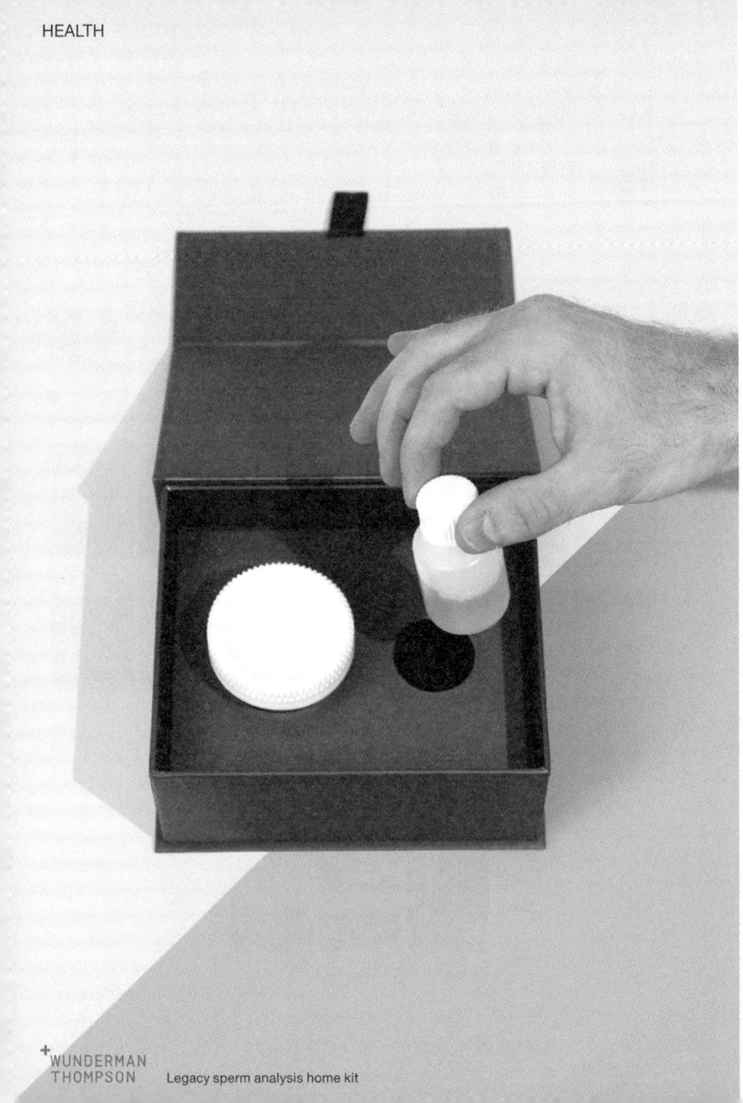

Legacy sperm analysis home kit

> Biotech startups are starting to target men, offering sperm analysis and freezing.

83

TikTok therapy

Gen Z are turning to TikTok for mental health advice.

Images courtesy of TikTok

Mental health professionals are taking to TikTok to offer guidance to an anxious generation. Therapists use quippy videos with pop music and dances to answer questions about stress, trauma and therapy, and offer lists of ways to express emotions healthily—attracting millions of followers and views.

Licensed doctoral therapist Courtney Tracy's TikTok account, @the.truth.doctor, where she addresses everything from intergenerational trauma to healthy ways to express rage, had 1.7 million followers as of December 2021. Licensed trauma therapist Micheline Maalouf offers tips in the form of self-soothing tools and signs of unresolved trauma to her 1.1 million followers.

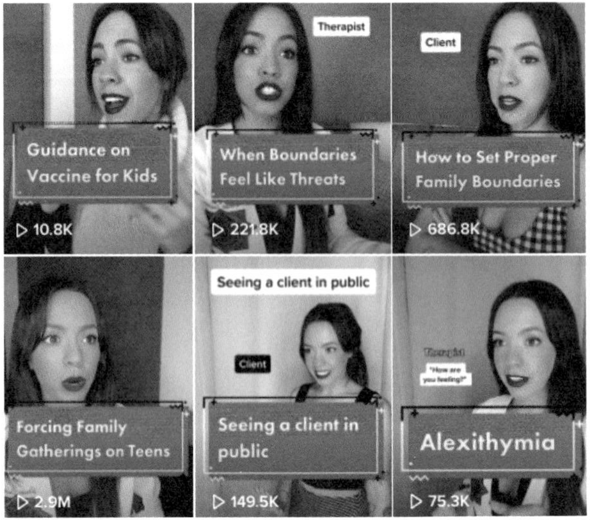

In early December 2021, the TikTok hashtag #mentalhealth had 21.6 billion views, #therapy had 5.3 billion views, #therapytiktok had 447.5 million views, and #therapistsoftiktok had 357.6 million views.

Why it's interesting

TikTok is gen Z's preferred app, with usage beating out Instagram and Snapchat. For a generation markedly open about mental health, gen Z are legitimizing the app as a source of bite-sized insight, education and professional counsel.

@the.truth.doctor. Images courtesy of TikTok

84

Metabolic brands

Metabolic health is the latest metric for health-conscious consumers to monitor and boost.

Slow metabolism is not the cause of middle-age weight gain, according to a study published in August 2021 by *Science*, which revealed that the rate of metabolism remains stable between ages 20 to 60 years old. The findings cast new light on the link between gut health, energy levels and digestion. Now wellness startups are helping consumers to optimize, promote, and even hack their metabolism with healthy boosts that are easy to digest.

UK-based soft drink brand OhMG launched a range of magnesium-enriched waters in May 2021. Magnesium can help to reduce anxiety, aid relaxation, and regulate the nervous system, as well as contributing to energy-yielding metabolism. Prebiotic soda startup Mayawell launched in 2020 and uses organic, hand-harvested active agave, shown to boost metabolism, strengthen the immune system and improve digestion.

Influential figures in the wellness industry are also lauding metabolic health. Gwyneth Paltrow swears by Dr Will Cole's intuitive fasting program, which aims to recharge metabolism and reset gut health. Paltrow's wellness company Goop also sells Metabolism-Boosting Superpowder.

Metabolism monitoring is becoming the new health metric, as trackers in this space increasingly gain attention. Lumen, launched in May 2020 after raising over $17 million in funding, promises to "hack your metabolism." New York-based Levels created a biowearable that monitors and maximizes metabolic fitness for users to live a "longer, fuller, healthier life." Helsinki-based Veri is another biowearable startup, founded in 2020. Its wearable device tracks blood-sugar levels and pairs with Veri's app, which acts as a "metabolic compass."

Why it's interesting

Research has shown that only 12% of Americans are considered metabolically healthy, according to a 2018 study by the University of North Carolina at Chapel Hill's Gillings School of Global Public Health. As health becomes a prominent focus for everyone, metabolic brands are launching into the market to monitor overall wellness needs for health-conscious consumers.

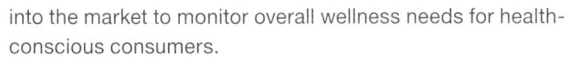

Left: OhMG offers a range of magnesium-enriched waters
Right: Levels created a biowearable that monitors metabolic fitness

85

Mental health pharmacies

Customers can now find band aids, medication and therapy sessions all in one place.

Top: CVS Health connects customers with licensed therapists
Bottom: Image courtesy of Aetna

> *Convenience models are revolutionizing access to mental health treatment.*

In the United States, 65% of people aged 18 to 34 have had mental health concerns for themselves or for friends and family members since the outbreak of COVID-19, according to Aetna's 2021 "Mental Health Pulse Survey". This reflects a steep increase in symptoms of anxiety or depression in 2020 and 2021. To meet the need for help, convenience giants including CVS, Walgreens, Rite Aid and Walmart are offering mental health services to their customers via virtual, app, and in-person appointments.

CVS Health began connecting licensed therapists to customers aged 18 and over in January 2021 via its CVS MinuteClinic providers. Customers can seek assessments, referrals, and even private consultations and counseling at select CVS pharmacies. Originally available in Texas, Pennsylvania and Florida, services have now expanded to New Jersey. CVS plans to expand its in-person and telehealth counseling services to cover 34 locations.

The Walgreens Find Care program began in March 2021, offering virtual therapy sessions with licensed therapists, and currently also helps to coordinate appointments for customers seeking therapy. Thanks to the brand's partnership with Mental Health America, customers can also schedule online mental health screenings with teletherapy companies BetterHelp and Sanvello.

Walmart, which acquired MeMD in May 2021, offers virtual mental health care in addition to its counseling services with Walmart Health. In June 2021, Rite Aid also started offering teletherapy sessions in 10 states: Delaware, Idaho, Maryland, New Hampshire, New Jersey, Ohio, Pennsylvania, Texas, Virginia and Washington.

Why it's interesting

These convenience models are revolutionizing access to mental health treatment. Aligning counseling services with more traditional medical treatments and supplies will reshape the way consumers consider their mental health needs, closing the gap between physical and mental health care.

Walmart and MeMD

86

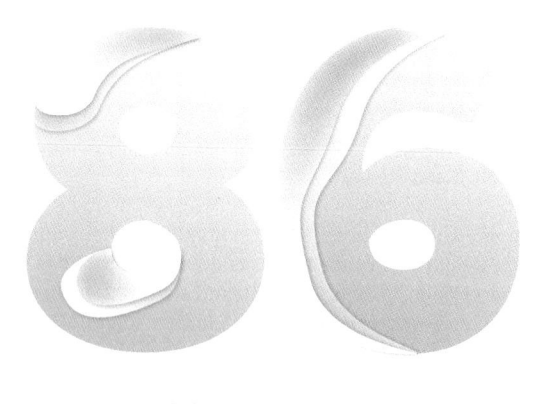

Audio healing

Wellness seekers are tuning into audio platforms and sound technology to achieve relaxation and mental restoration.

Autonomous sensory meridian response (ASMR) has become a well-known term across the music, wellness and relaxation industries. Consumers are now turning to ASMR, sound and audio for selfcare and physical wellness benefits.

Sona is a new music therapy app for anxiety that launched at CES 2022. “We're on a mission to validate music as medicine,” Sona founder Neal Sarin tells Wunderman Thompson Intelligence. All music is created in-house by curated composers and Grammy-winning engineers using a proprietary composition process that increases alpha brain waves to help listeners relax, Sarin explains.

In October 2021, audio-experience startup Spatial partnered with Catalyst by Wellstar and the nonprofit digital streaming platform HealthTunes to utilize the restorative power of sound for healthcare workers. Together, the platforms will design a sound sanctuary that employs scientifically based MusicMedicine, creating a space where frontline hospital workers can pause in their work days to reduce stress and anxiety. Spatial COO Darrell Rodriguez told *Fast Company* that “immersive sound has potential as a therapeutic tool” and that the company “wants to have a social impact.”

Audio app Dipsea uses audio that combines soothing, calming sounds and erotic stories to help guide its listeners to sleep. Dipsea's extensive Sleep library offers users a plethora of audio options for sleep aid, relaxation benefits, and even to improve libido. Sexual wellness apps such as Kama and wellness brands like Maude are also utilizing audio erotica as an additional platform benefit.

Why it's interesting

Heightened audio is more than just audio branding: it's a new space for healing. As audio's impact grows in spaces for selfcare, healing and wellness, brands are incorporating sound offerings to satisfy consumer wants and needs.

Dipsea combines soothing sounds with erotic stories to guide listeners to sleep

87

Antibody health

COVID-19 patients are counting their antibodies like calories, and research is under way for antibody treatments.

As COVID-19 variants continue to infect people around the world, medical institutions are scrambling to determine whether antibodies are the key to a universal vaccine or treatment.

Medical concierge services are measuring COVID-19 antibodies as an added perk for patients. Those with access to high-end medical offices around the world are seeking reassurance by counting antibodies "like calories," according to the *New York Times*. Locations offering these services include My Concierge MD in Beverly Hills, Sollis Health in Manhattan, and Montecito Concierge Medicine, a private provider in Montecito, California.

Breakthrough research published in November 2021 by the University of North Carolina and Duke University showed potential for the treatment of COVID-19 and its variants using isolated antibodies. The study suggested that an antibody identified as DH1047 can both prevent and fight the infection after a person is diagnosed. The research is a path to the design of a universal vaccine that could work against a wide variety of variants.

AstraZeneca announced the inauguration of a separate division for vaccines and antibody therapies in the same month. The new division will focus closely on the company's COVID-19 treatments, combining the research, development and manufacturing of antibody treatments, and addressing future variants of COVID-19. Positive results from the antibody treatment trials show potential and more research is under way.

Why it's interesting

As research on antibody treatment shows promise, medical services may continue to home in on the benefits of measuring, monitoring and maintaining COVID-19 antibody levels for their patients.

88

Next gen mental wellbeing

A mental health emergency among children is sparking reformed platform restrictions and limitations for apps and online games.

An increase in mental health referrals for children has led to online platforms and social apps having to recognize their impact on young users and redirect efforts and platform abilities to offer adequate protection.

In the United Kingdom, mental health referrals for children almost doubled to 200,000 during the pandemic, according to the Royal College of Psychiatrists. Urgent referrals in particular rose sharply from 5,219 between April and June in 2019 to 8,552 in 2021.

In the United States, experts from the American Academy of Pediatrics, the Children's Hospital Association, and the

#kidsoftiktok. Image courtesy of TikTok

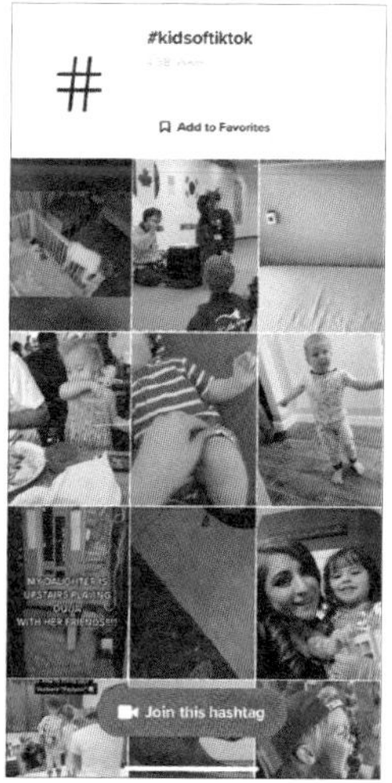

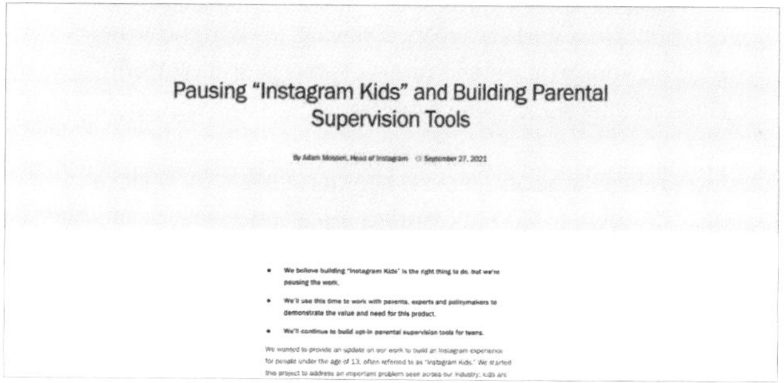

American Academy of Child and Adolescent Psychiatry deemed the mental health crisis among kids a national emergency "inextricably tied to the stress brought on by COVID-19 and the ongoing struggle for racial justice." Their data indicates that emergency department visits for mental health rose by 24% from 2019 to 2020 for children between the ages of five and 11, and by 31% for those aged 12 to 17.

Some platforms are reconsidering their strategy. In September 2021, work on Instagram Kids was paused to allow a refocus on input from parents, policymakers and experts before building out the reformed platform. Meta, which owns Instagram, anticipates building this separate, adless platform for kids aged 10 to 12 with only age-appropriate content, allowing full parental supervision and requiring parental permission to join.

Also in September 2021, ByteDance introduced a youth mode to TikTok for kids in China, limiting those under 14 years old to 40 minutes a day on the app, and falling into line with the Chinese government's video game restrictions for children under 14. The previous month, the Chinese National Press and Publication Administration had announced new rules restricting gaming for children under 18 to Fridays, weekends, and holidays between 8pm and 9pm.

Why it's interesting

The substantial impact of social media and gaming on young children is evident, and governments and parents are demanding protection for kids online. Tech companies are responding with refocused strategies to protect the mental wellbeing of younger generations.

Top: Images courtesy of TikTok
Bottom: Instagram announces work on Instagram Kids has been paused

89

5G healthcare

As China rolls out its 5G infrastructure faster than the rest of the world, healthcare is one of the first sectors to benefit.

Telemedicine in China and other Asian markets has gone from basic video consultation to providing comprehensive medical services akin to physical ones. While the previous 4G network could lead to latency and unstable connection, restricting the locations where patients could use telemedicine, the application of 5G has improved the quality of video consultation, remote patient monitoring, and, ultimately, even remote and robotic surgery assistance.

As early as January 2020, China's ZTE and China Telecom providers deployed China's first 5G remote diagnosis of COVID-19. The technology connected doctors at West China Hospital, part of Sichuan University, as the central node to remotely diagnose and treat COVID-19 patients at two dozen other hospitals, Shenzhen-based ZTE said.

In Guangzhou, a city located in a region dubbed China's Greater Bay Area because of its similarity to Silicon Valley, the Guangdong Second Provincial General Hospital is using 5G to collect, transmit and monitor patient data. Chen Xiaofang, a nurse at the hospital, appeared in an Associated Press (AP) video report in November 2021 demonstrating how she uses a smartwatch to monitor procedures such as intravenous infusions, saying "we are now able to save a lot of time." According to the AP report, some 10,000 devices and sensors at the hospital are 5G-connected and collect health data such as electrocardiograms in real time, for hospital staff to monitor.

In June 2021, CUHK Medical Centre, in partnership with Commercial Group HKT, announced it was the first private hospital in Hong Kong to deploy 5G, allowing medical images such as those from endoscopies, ultrasounds, CT scans, and other high-resolution images to be transferred in real time for remote consultation.

Why it's interesting

Chinese patients can already book appointments, receive lab reports and scans, and get basic advice from doctors on smartphone apps such as Ping An Good Doctor and Tencent's WeDoctor. The advent of 5G means they will soon be able to do much more. "The end point is that we can do everything virtually online … and then doctors can practice anywhere in the world, the patient can access the doctors anywhere in the world," Kenneth Chung, CEO of clinic operations for IHH East China, a private hospital chain, told CNBC.

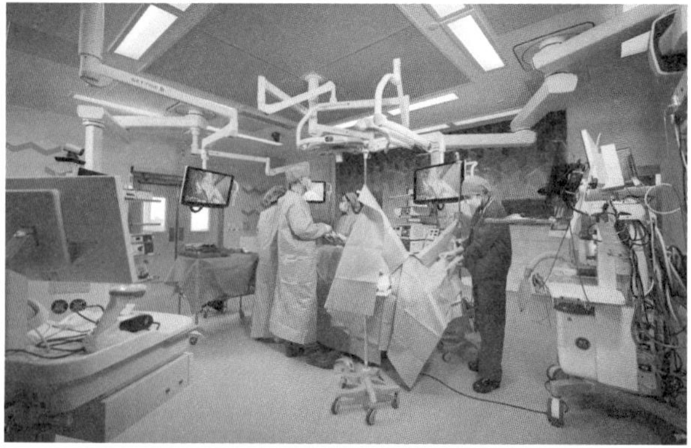

WUNDERMAN THOMPSON HKT has partnered with CUHK Medical Centre to bring 5G technology to the hospital, enabling live remote consultation with participants at different locations

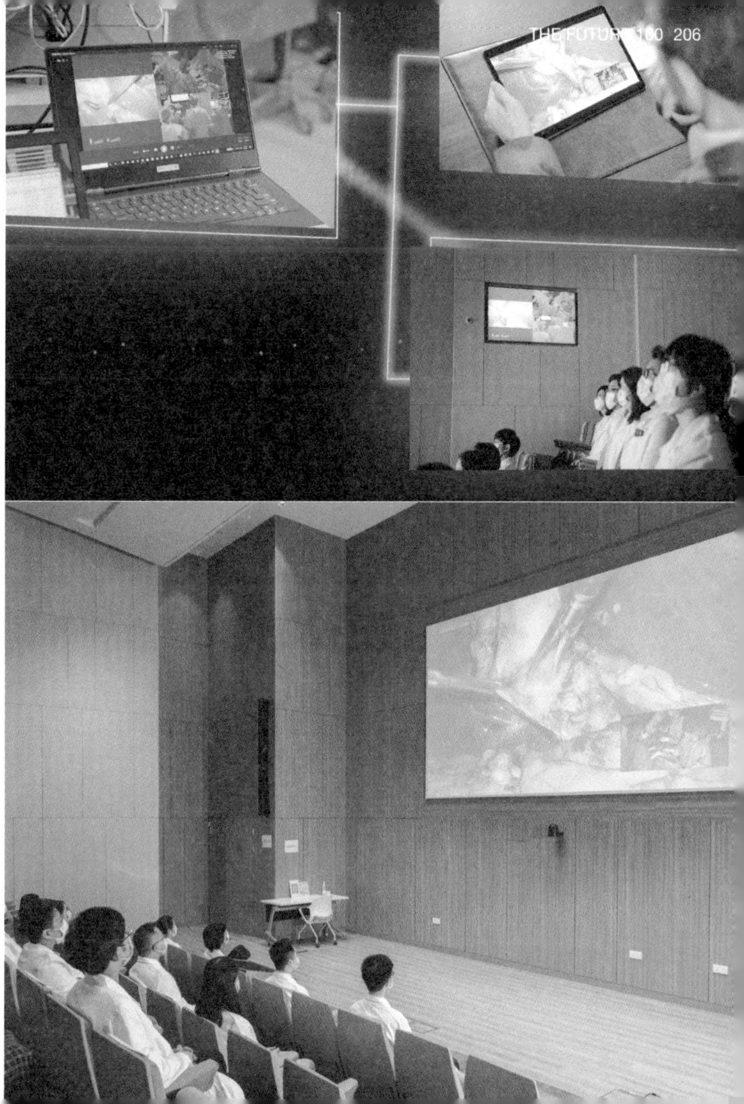

90

Emotional health

Recharge zones for emotions are emerging in public spaces around the world.

WUNDERMAN THOMPSON

Dwight White. Image by Jaylen Prater, courtesy of Pinterest Havens

Public spaces for mental health and emotional wellbeing are popping up as the stigma around addressing mental health begins to dissolve.

A public art space in Madrid allows visitors to address and visualize the status of their mental health. La Lloreria (the Crying Room) seeks to banish taboos around mental health issues, reserving space for the deliberation, acknowledgement, and artistic visualization of emotional wellbeing. In October 2021, Spanish prime minister Pedro Sanchez announced a €100 million ($116 million) mental healthcare drive, indicating a greater public focus on mental health in the country.

The Rubin Museum of Art's Mandala Lab. Image by Rafael Gamo

Social media brand Pinterest launched Pinterest Havens in October 2021, aiming to create "an online and offline space for community-driven inspiration." The company also commissioned Havens: Invest in Rest, a physical installation in Chicago featuring a mural by local artist Dwight White, physical Pins of relaxing imagery, immersive art, and community programming to combat burnout and encourage viewers to focus on their emotional wellbeing.

In October 2021, the Rubin Museum of Art in New York City opened the Mandala Lab, a cultural healing space designed to encourage emotional wellness and inspire connection through Buddhist principles. Visitors can explore the complexity of their emotions, address them and transform them. Executive director Jorrit Britschgi said the space was designed to "empower us to face today's challenges: to widen our imagination, understand and manage our emotions, enrich our capacity for empathy, and connect with others."

Why it's interesting

Are these emotionally charged spaces the playgrounds of the future? Room set aside to connect, rest and meditate is being molded into public areas grounded in community.

The Rubin Museum of Art's Mandala Lab. Image by Rafael Gamo

91
Work
100

91

Metawork

Teleportation, holograms and roaming avatars—the future of work has arrived.

Virtual offices are taking over as the shift to remote and hybrid work is likely here to stay. Microsoft is set to launch Mesh for Microsoft Teams in 2022, enabling mixed reality for users, with the option to attend meetings as customized avatars and collaborate on projects through shared holographic experiences. Mesh for Microsoft Teams also gives companies the option to build immersive virtual environments and Microsoft describes the feature as “a gateway to the metaverse.”

“As a company whose focus is on productivity, on knowledge workers, it’s something that customers are really asking us for, and it’s coupled with the vision of mixed reality that we’ve been working on for 12 years,” explains Microsoft technical fellow Alex Kipman. “It’s all coming together.”

Meta introduced Horizon Workrooms in August 2021. By connecting through virtual reality (VR), coworkers can collaborate and create together in the same virtual workspace. “Meet teammates across the table, even if you’re

Mesh for Microsoft Teams. Image courtesy of Microsoft

across the world—and transform your home office into your favorite remote meeting room," Horizon Workrooms promises.

Building branded virtual workspaces are gaining popularity. Wunderman Thompson launched a virtual conference hub at CES 2022. Breakroom by Sinespace, a "new social hub for remote teams," launched in April 2020. The company can also set up a branded office within 24 hours. Gather launched the following month, and aims to make "virtual interactions more human." Kumospace and gen-Z startup Branch operate in similar ways to Gather, focusing on heightening organic interactions using virtual rooms that mimic physical environments, where users' avatars can move around and interact.

Why it's interesting

The way we connect, live and work is transforming thanks to the metaverse. The future of work will foster a hybrid setup for many, leading with virtual workspaces that generate new forms of creativity, collaboration and immersion.

> "The way we connect, live and work is transforming thanks to the metaverse.

WUNDERMAN THOMPSON The Wunderman Thompson Metaverse in collaboration with Odyssey

92

Chief impact officers

A new C-suite position is rising in popularity: the chief impact officer.

Taco Bell named Lil Nas X as the chain's first CIO

Corporate C-suites are adding chief impact officers (CIOs) to their boardrooms, with the role designed to showcase a brand's community and societal impact.

A former Taco Bell employee himself, Lil Nas X was appointed as the fast-food chain's first CIO in August 2021. The honorary position coincided with the artist's "Montero" record release and supports Taco Bell's scholarship program for young creatives. Lil Nas X has appeared in ad campaigns for Taco Bell's breakfast menu and is "leveraging his deep-rooted history to create an impactful experience for all Taco Bell team members," the brand states.

The Duke of Sussex started a new position in March 2021 as the CIO of Silicon Valley startup BetterUp. The coaching and mental health platform says that its missions to "unlock the potential in people everywhere necessitates innovation, impact and integrity." The role includes strategizing product decisions and charitable contributions, and the duke advocates publicly for mental health.

Why it's interesting

Consumers have demanded more from brands in recent years, enforcing executive engagement and integrity. CIOs serve as a company's public-facing leader, embracing charitable causes and ensuring brands are impacting communities and consumers in positive ways.

Taco Bell named Lil Nas X as the chain's first CIO

93

Rewilding the office

Garden plots, beehives and bird watching—the latest office perks are upleveling biophilic design.

Employees at Nuveen, an investment company headquartered in midtown Manhattan, can help harvest honey on their lunch breaks on a terrace surrounded by high-rises. The company installed two beehives as part of a $120 million renovation concluding in 2021, hiring a beekeeper to care for the bees and give employees lessons in honey harvesting.

Springdale Green, a new development in Austin, Texas, is reimagining the office with bird blinds and hammocks, and surrounded by native plants and woodland. The office is "more outside than inside," Philip Mahoney, executive vice chairman at commercial real estate company Newmark, told the *New York Times*.

Employees who work at the Victor Building in Washington—recently renovated by Brookfield Properties—can pick herbs such as parsley and basil from rooftop vegetable gardens before heading home to cook dinner.

Uber's new headquarters in San Francisco, opened in March 2021, features a major design element to provide fresh air: 180 14-foot-tall glass panes open and shut throughout the day, counteracting stale recirculated air and bringing some of the outdoors in.

Why it's interesting

"The overarching trend of the past five years has been the hotelification of the office," Lenny Beaudoin, an executive managing director at CBRE, told the *New York Times*. Over the next five years, expect to see this shift to the "outdoor-ification" of the office as companies bet on nature as the future of office design.

WUNDERMAN THOMPSON

The Victor Building hosts a garden of herbs and vegetables that employees can harvest to cook with

94

Crypto artisans

The Web 3.0 economy is providing an alternative to corporate employment in the form of digital autonomous organizations.

CryptoTwitter is alight with excitement over digital autonomous organizations (DAOs). In simple terms, this is a digitally native community or organization that could potentially represent the future of work—your next employer could be a DAO.

Strictly speaking, a DAO is a community-led digital organization that runs on blockchain technology. It is managed not by a CEO or board of directors but by lines of code that define its operations, known as a smart contract. In practice, many DAOs are not yet fully autonomous and so the term is also used colloquially to refer to digital organizations in general. These are more like online collectives that have common interests and goals, and are often centered around a Reddit group or Discord server.

Crucially, DAOs also have built-in treasuries linked to cryptocurrency, which means members can earn tokens in return for their contributions. A new breed of crypto worker is already being drawn to DAOs as an alternative to the corporate nine-to-five.

In September 2021, community builder and consultant Rafa Fernandez posted a long-form piece on the Web 3.0 publishing platform Mirror about his decision to quit his dream job at a tech startup to work for a DAO. Fernandez is not the only one and participation in the DAO economy is growing fast. According to DeepDAO, a platform that tracks the industry, there were 1.6 million members and token owners in December 2021, a number that had swelled by 356,000 from the previous month alone. In another signal of

this explosive growth, a budding DAO service economy is emerging, with companies such as Opolis offering DAO workers access to healthcare plans, payroll, and other shared services.

From an employee's point of view, DAOs have a lot to offer. They are digital so there are no physical headquarters or geographic boundaries—both already outdated notions for many gen Zers. DAOs have little to no hierarchy so there are no bosses either. Instead, they offer members the ability to collectively influence decisions and share in profits. Above all they offer a readymade community of likeminded, passionate, and highly invested people all pursuing the same goal.

"At the core of it, it's just a group of people that really care about something, and they want to work on it together," Anne Connelly, who teaches blockchain and social impact at Boston University, explained to the WBUR radio station. This raises the question: could traditional companies morph into DAOs? The answer is that it's already happening. ShapeShift, a crypto-trading platform established in 2014, plans to dissolve its corporate structure and transition to a DAO model in 2022.

DAOs have their challenges. Community insiders acknowledge there's much to figure out, from gaining clarity on legal status to resolving conflicts. Nevertheless, the combined lure of community, flexibility and shared purpose are so far proving strong.

Why it's interesting

While not every company will want to copy the DAO model, nor will it be universally appropriate, there are interesting lessons to learn from this new model in terms of community, culture building and worker empowerment. In an era of employee activism, many want to shape the place they work to fit their values, as Julia Rosenberg, cofounder and CEO at Orca Protocol, recently explained at the Mainnet conference: "If you disagree, you have the opportunity to effect change, which is not something that exists in centralized organizations."

Left: ShapeShift
Right: Mirror. Image courtesy of Twitter

95

Micropreneurs 2.0

Americans are reassessing their work lives, driving an unprecedented wave of resignations and career pivots.

Toward the end of 2021, a record number of Americans had left their jobs. In April that year, the number of workers who quit their jobs in a single month broke an all-time US record and the figure has climbed steadily since, with more than 4.4 million American workers quitting in September alone. According to Microsoft's global Work Trend Index, published in March 2021, 41% of people around the world were likely to consider leaving their jobs within the next year, rising to 54% of gen Z. The *Washington Post* dubbed the shift the "great reassessment of work."

So where are workers going? Many are leaving for higher-paying jobs, whether that's retail and service workers taking entry-level positions or mid-career professionals switching jobs. As of December 2020, resignations among managers were 12% higher than the previous year, according to workforce analytics company Visier.

Others are pursuing passions or side hustles full-time. Microsoft's research revealed that 46% of people were planning to make a major career pivot or transition. And British workers are going freelance in droves. April 2021 data from freelancer platform PeoplePerHour found that almost one in five freelancers had become self-employed as a side hustle alongside an employee position, and nearly two-fifths of those began freelancing in the past 12 months.

Jake Kenyon decided to turn Kenyarn, his Providence, RI-based hand-dyed-yarn side hustle, into a full-time career in January 2021, after quitting his job as a speech pathologist.

The pattern follows a nascent trend that first grew legs in the initial months of the pandemic in 2020, with workers quitting their desk jobs to pursue passion projects full-time. Now the trend has snowballed into a nationwide reassessment of work that is precipitating the next era of employment.

Why it's interesting

If 2020 had consumers reassessing their lives and values, 2022 and beyond will see them taking action to bring their work more in line with these values. Employees are scrutinizing what they want from a career and a workplace, potentially bringing about the "end of the workplace as we know it," according to *Business Insider*.

Jake Kenyon's Kenyarn side hustle turned into a full-time career

96

The shecovery

To combat the shecession, global workplaces are stepping up initiatives that optimize the workplace for women.

The shecession saw women worldwide drop out of the workforce in significant numbers; a loss which has not yet been reversed. Now a host of industries, from financial services to hospitality, are also facing an unprecedented battle for talent. Workplaces that optimize for women will build relevance, not to mention significant competitive advantage. So, one year on, what are workplaces doing to build the shecovery?

The biggest transition, of course, is the shift to flexible working, adopted by businesses from Spotify to Facebook to American Express. Flexible options are appealing for women juggling work and home life, though some commentators, including Bank of England economist Catherine Mann, have warned of work-from-home stigma that could ultimately end up costing women if men don't take up remote work in equal numbers.

Looking ahead, normalizing flexible work options in company culture will be imperative to mitigate inequity. To that end, British construction firm Multiplex introduced a new formal flexible working policy in October 2021 aimed at making its workplace more attractive for women.

> Workplaces that optimize for women will build relevance, not to mention significant competitive advantage.

The Multiplex Flex initiative offers a range of options including four-day weeks, remote working, and time off in lieu of overtime pay. PwC is also committed to ensuring remote workers don't lose out. The Big Four accounting firm announced in fall 2021 that not only is it embracing permanent remote work, it also pledges to monitor raises, pay and bonuses for remote staff compared to their office-based counterparts, and act wherever it sees a lag.

Women who remained in the workforce throughout the pandemic have faced a different challenge. The "Women in the Workplace 2021" report from McKinsey & Co and LeanIn.org found the gap between women and men who report feeling burned out has doubled since 2020. The survey of 65,000 workers in North America also reports that one in three women has thought about downsizing her career or leaving work altogether, compared to one in four earlier in the pandemic.

The report also notes that female leaders spend more time on employee wellbeing, but such efforts are often overlooked. Further, while women are statistically more likely to devote time to diversity, equality and inclusion initiatives than their male equivalents, less than a quarter of companies surveyed formally recognize this work. Bucking that trend is LinkedIn, which has pledged to pay the chairs of its employee resource groups $10,000 annually, as well as developing a non-financial rewards system to recognize contributions. This follows a similar commitment by Twitter in 2020.

Why it's interesting

The shecession is likely to affect businesses for years to come, highlighting the urgent need for employers to act now. Those companies that choose to adopt policies that value the work of women and caregivers as well as employee wellbeing will be best placed to weather the storm.

 Images courtesy of Multiplex

97

Gen Z workforce

Brands refocus their recruitment strategies to attract gen Z employees for the long term.

Fashion brands are turning their recruitment efforts to younger pools of applicants, looking to diversify their talent pipeline and maintain entry-level applicants for long-term employment.

In September 2021, French luxury brand LVMH announced its plan to recruit 25,000 employees under 30 by the end of 2022. The brand's gen Z hiring binge indicates a focus on young, global talent and a desire to broaden and diversify recruitment across the company. LVMH also emphasized a desire to recruit for the long term, and from a wider pool of applicants, not only those from prestigious universities or affluent families.

Clothing brand Hollister announced the appointment of its first chief gaming scout in October 2021. Kyle "Bugha" Giersdorf, 18, the *Fortnite* world champion with an impressive 4.9 million Twitch followers as of November 2021, is designing gamer-inspired clothing, catapulting the surf and beach brand into a new space. Bugha will also lead Team Hollister, a new division aimed at developing up-and-coming streamers, placing the brand in the center of the gaming universe and attracting a new wave of teens to its products.

Why it's interesting

Gen Z's youthful market insight is in demand. Hiring young recruits for long-term positions benefits brand recruitment efforts while also satisfying gen Z and millennial desire for adequate training and career advancement. A focus on long-term success from brands is attracting high-caliber applicants early in their careers.

WUNDERMAN THOMPSON

Hollister appointed Fortnite World Cup champion Kyle "Bugha" Giersdorf as its first chief gaming scout

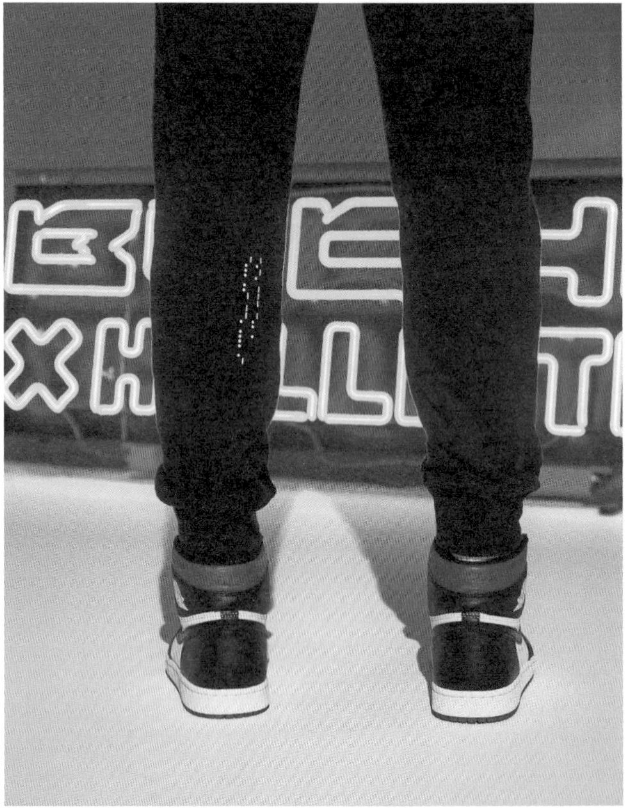

98

The great reskill

Reinvention is the name of the game for the next generation of employees.

Business is changing—and required employee skillsets are changing with it. As the digital revolution races on, brands are realizing that the fastest and most effective way to keep pace is to upskill their existing workforce. Where specialized college or graduate degrees may once have been a prerequisite, companies are now encouraging employees to learn as they go.

Rachel Carlson, cofounder and CEO of Guild Education, predicts that this will give rise to a new formula for education—one that may even supplant a college degree. Carlson told the *Masters of Scale* podcast that the "four and 40," which previously saw the majority of employees go to school for four years, then work for 40, is "dead" and supplanted by a new model. "What's now is the every four," said Carlson. "You're going to have to learn some sort of new skill every four years."

Levi Strauss & Co announced a new company-wide digital upskilling initiative for its employees in May 2021. The keystone of the initiative is the Machine Learning Bootcamp, an eight-week, full-time, paid program that offers employees training in digital skills such as coding and machine learning. Graduates of the bootcamp will either return to their current job with new skills or will join the company's strategy and AI team.

Verizon invested over $200 million in employee learning and development programs in 2020, offering training in topics like data science, 5G technology and artificial intelligence. By the end of 2021, Verizon had equipped 100,000 employees with digital skills "to ensure team members are ready to keep pace with ever-changing demands of building the future."

Walmart employees can earn a high school or college degree for $365 (or $1 per day for a year), through a partnership with Guild Education. From April 2020 to April 2021, Walmart said the program saw a 93% spike in both high school and college graduates.

Why it's interesting

Traditional career trajectories are being reinvented, replacing specialized degrees with practical education and on-site reskilling.

Images courtesy of Guild Education

The nomad economy

As the world awakens to the possibilities of working remotely, a new economy is springing up to cater to digital nomads.

The days when work was done solely at the office already seem like history. Pandemic-induced lockdowns forced companies around the world into arrangements that broke traditional working habits. With this came a surge of remote workers, some of whom became digital nomads for the first time, choosing to work in new cities, states, or even new countries.

Unfortunately for these digital nomads, social safety nets such as health insurance have historically only been available within their home countries and are therefore off limits to those working across borders and in different jurisdictions.

Now, in response to their growing numbers, a new economy is emerging that caters to these administrative, financial and logistical needs.

Insurer SafetyWing offers cover for remote workers regardless of location. Having fortuitously launched in early 2020, the company's Nomad Insurance covers remote workers in the event of unforeseen health problems or travel complications. After raising $8 million in 2021, SafetyWing is looking to launch additional products that offer access to remote doctors and remote pensions.

Also looking to provide peace of mind to global citizens, Insured Nomads is a US-based insurtech company that provides coverage for everything from medications to cybersecurity to telehealth appointments. Having launched just before the pandemic, the company has added new offerings that address the ever-changing needs of global workers. In April 2021, the

> A new economy is emerging that caters to digital nomads' administrative, financial and logistical needs.

brand launched new mental health counseling services alongside other benefits such as 24/7 emergency evacuation assistance.

Self-storage solutions for nomadic workers are also on the rise. Launched at the end of 2020, Stuf is a startup that transforms unused basements and similar spaces into self-storage locations. Unlike traditional warehouse storage facilities that tend to be located on the outskirts of cities, the company identifies smaller inner-city footprint spaces that are more convenient for those with transient lifestyles who want to access their items more frequently. The startup currently has four locations across Los Angeles, the Bay Area, Washington DC and New York, with a further 4,000 locations in the works for 2022.

Why it's interesting

The future of work is borderless. As ingenious companies step up to iron out the complications that accompany a transient lifestyle, digital nomads will continue to grow in numbers and financial clout.

Insurer SafetyWing offers coverage for remote workers

100

Metaverse recruits

From virtual material designers to creatives across the board, companies are hiring for a metaverse workforce.

The metaverse virtually recreates pretty much all aspects of life, and recruitment is no different. “In the coming years, companies of all kinds are increasingly going to be re-orienting towards a hybrid model of virtual and physical work, production, commerce and communications,” Grant Paterson, head of gaming and esports at Wunderman Thompson, explains. “The dual forces of converging technologies and emerging consumer behaviors in virtual places makes the cultivation of a ‘virtual pillar’ critical for many, if not all, businesses.”

Nike filed seven trademark applications in October 2021; they include use of “downloadable virtual goods” and “retail store services featuring virtual goods.” In the same month, the company started recruiting virtual material designers to sit within its digital product creation team. The job spec describes the role as helping to “build the future of Nike Footwear materials” and ignite “the digital and virtual revolution at Nike.”

In November 2021, British television broadcaster ITV posted a position for a metaverse creative within its new Metavision initiative, which “looks to combine the worlds of gaming, entertainment and advertising.” The role involves creating metaverse brand activations from concept stage to execution.

"Is it time to hire a chief metaverse officer?" *Vogue Business* mused in an October 2021 article that noted the rise in augmented retail, virtual venues and digital possessions. Partnering with external tech and games companies has been the trend of the past year; now brands are seeking out talent of their own to accelerate the technological offerings of the metaversee.

Why it's interesting

Remember when social media became mainstream and companies scrambled to hire social media leads? Recruiting talent to help build offerings around the metaverse will be reminiscent of that hurry to hire, and maybe even more urgent.

Nikeland on Roblox is the company's first step into the metaverse

ABOUT WUNDERMAN THOMPSON INTELLIGENCE

Wunderman Thompson Intelligence is Wunderman Thompson's futurism, research and innovation unit. It charts emerging and future global trends, consumer change, and innovation patterns—translating these into insight for brands. It offers a suite of consultancy services, including bespoke research, presentations, co-branded reports and workshops. It is also active in innovation, partnering with brands to activate future trends within their framework and execute new products and concepts. The division is led by Emma Chiu and Marie Stafford, Global Directors of Wunderman Thompson Intelligence.

For more information visit:
wundermanthompson.com/expertise/intelligence

About The Future 100

Wunderman Thompson Intelligence's annual forecast presents a snapshot of the year ahead and identifies the most compelling trends to keep on the radar. The report charts 100 trends across 10 sectors, spanning culture, tech and innovation, travel and hospitality, brands and marketing, food and drink, beauty, retail and commerce, luxury, health and work.

WUNDERMAN THOMPSON

CONTACT
Emma Chiu
Global Director of Wunderman Thompson Intelligence
emma.chiu@wundermanthompson.com

EDITOR-IN-CHIEF
Emma Chiu

EDITOR
Emily Safian-Demers

WRITERS
Marie Stafford, Chen May Yee, Elizabeth Cherian, Sarah Tilley, Carla Calandra, Jamie Shackleton, Safa Arshadullah

SUB EDITORS
Hester Lacey, Katie Myers

CREATIVE DIRECTOR
Shazia Chaudhry

COVER
Raspberry Dream Labs

FONTS USED
Lust Didone; Helvetica Neue (TT)